The Victoria Crosses That Saved The Empire

The Story of the VCs of the Indian Mutiny

The Victoria Crosses
That Saved The Empire

The Story of the VCs of the Indian Mutiny

Brian Best

Frontline Books

THE VICTORIA CROSSES THAT SAVED THE EMPIRE
The Story of the VCs of the Indian Mutiny

This edition published in 2016 by Frontline Books,
an imprint of Pen & Sword Books Ltd,
47 Church Street, Barnsley, S. Yorkshire, S70 2AS.

ISBN: 978-1-47384-476-6

CIP data records for this title are available from the British Library

Printed and bound by Gutenberg Press
Typeset in 10/13 point Palatino

For more information on our books, please email: info@frontline-books.com,
write to us at the above address, or visit:
www.frontline-books.com

Contents

Author's Note   vi

Introduction   vii

Chapter 1   The Siege of Delhi, May to September 1857   1

Chapter 2   The Capture of Delhi and Pursuit of the Rebels,
            August to September 1857   25

Chapter 3   The Other Outbreaks, June to November 1857   46

Chapter 4   Delhi's Flying Columns, September to October 1857   68

Chapter 5   Against the Odds: Havelock's March, June to September 1857

                                                                           78

Chapter 6   The Defence of Lucknow, June to November 1857   105

Chapter 7   The Second Relief of Lucknow, October to November 1857   128

Chapter 8   The Tide Turns, October to November 1857   158

Chapter 9   Lucknow Taken, November 1857 to June 1858   177

Chapter 10 Campbell's Oudh Campaign, January to June 1858   186

Chapter 11 Mopping Up, January to April 1859   203

Postscript   219

References and Notes   221

Bibliography   228

Index   231

Author's Note

The Victoria Cross actions are grouped together by campaign with an introductory description of each stage of the Mutiny as events unfolded. Although the descriptions are broadly chronological, there are inevitable crossovers where actions in different parts of India took place at similar times.

Readers should note that some place names may be spelt differently today than they were in nineteenth century India. To maintain the authenticity of the quoted passages the contemporaneous spellings have been retained. This also applies to the grammar which at times is at variance with conventional or modern English.

Introduction

On the morning of Friday, 26 June 1857, Britain's largest military parade took place at the eastern end of Hyde Park. It was a perfect midsummer's day with soaring temperatures as 9,000 troops and 100,000 spectators assembled to watch the first investiture of a new gallantry award named for, and presented by, Queen Victoria. Although the first eighty-five recipients had their citations published in *The London Gazette* on 24 February 1857, only sixty-two were present to receive their Victoria Crosses from the sovereign. It was her express wish to present her new gallantry award but not until later in the season, hence the long gap between announcement and presentation. At 9.30 a.m., the Queen, dressed in a specially-designed quasi-military riding habit, mounted her pony, Sunset. Accompanied by her husband Albert, dubbed that day as Prince Consort, along with her future son-in-law, Prince Frederick William of Prussia, and members of the Royal family and household, she rode up Constitution Hill and entered the Park through the gate at Hyde Park Corner. This moment was probably the high-water mark of Victoria's reign with the Queen at her happiest and the country at ease with itself. For even as the Queen made the first presentations of the Victoria Cross to her Crimean heroes, dark shadows were appearing in a far off eastern country where many of the twenty-two absentees[1] were about to become involved in one of the most traumatic events of the Victorian period: the Indian Mutiny[2].

For the British, the Mutiny is a difficult period to contemplate, an odd mix of pride and shame, pity and anger. The pride derives from the courage and endurance of men who were faced with a harsh climate and a numerically superior enemy. The shame is engendered by the indiscriminate savagery meted out to not only the guilty, but the many innocent who could not possibly have been involved. The number of women and children who were slaughtered, bereaved or who endured starvation and disease warrants pity. The complacency, insensitivity and arrogance of the British administrators and officers who allowed the simmering discontent to boil over causes anger.

In fact, there had been mounting evidence of the Indian population's increasing discontent with the Honourable East India Company (HEIC). Originally a British joint-stock company formed to trade with the East Indies, it ended up trading mostly with the Indian subcontinent. The HEIC was one of the greatest commercial enterprises ever seen and, as it grew, it was allowed to have its own armies. Over a period of a century, three quite distinct armies came into being at different times and places. In chronological order these were the armies of the Presidencies of Bombay, Madras and Bengal, formed to protect the HEIC's growing expansion throughout India's interior.

As the decades passed, so the quality of British administrators and officers declined. Although 'John Company's' profits slumped, there was still money to be made through corruption and nepotism. Lassitude and a growing contempt for the locals by second-rate white employers increasingly opened a void between the rulers and the ruled.

In December 1855, Lord Charles Canning, the new Governor-General of India, was prescient when he declared the following at a farewell dinner in London before he departed to take up his post: 'In the sky of India a small cloud may rise, at first no bigger than a man's hand but which may at last threaten to overwhelm us with ruin.'

There had already been incidents of rebellion amongst some of the native regiments in the Bengal Army. It was an accumulation of grievances rather than a single event that triggered the outbreak in May 1857. The Bengal Army drew its recruits from higher castes as opposed to those in Bombay and Madras, who enlisted more localised and caste-neutral sepoys, as Indian soldiers were called. The domination of higher castes in the Bengal Army was one of the factors that led to the rebellion. There was a growing irritation that the Bengal Army was receiving special treatment as it was the only part of the Company's forces that refused to serve overseas.[3] The General Service Enlistment Act of 1856 was passed to take soldiers out of India to places such as Persia, Burma and China. In the Bengal Army, only new recruits had to accept this commitment. The serving high-caste sepoys, however, saw this as the thin end of the wedge and added it to their list of grievances.

The Bengal Army further divided itself, with the infantry being *Brahmins* (high-caste Hindus) and Rajputs, while the cavalry, who lived apart, were, for the most part, Muslims. Promotion was extremely slow and based purely on time-served rather than talent. Another perceived threat was the increasing presence of British missionaries and chaplains, which led to fears of mass conversions to Christianity.

With all this resentment, it only took a rumour to spark the powder keg.

The Revolt of 1857 broke out over the new Enfield rifle and its ammunition: greased cartridges. Before loading the new percussion rifle, the sepoys had to bite off the end of the paper cartridge and ram it down the barrel. A rumour spread that the new paper cartridge was greased with cow and pig fat – an anathema to both Hindus and Muslims. Too late, the cartridge was withdrawn and concessions were made, including allowing the sepoys to grease the cartridges themselves. But to no avail – the British were still seen as attempting to defile the sepoys' religions.

On 26 February 1857, the 19th Bengal Native Infantry (BNI) refused to take the cartridge. At Barrackpore, on 31 March, the 19th BNI was disbanded for 'open and defiant mutiny'.[4]

Two days before, a sepoy of the 34th BNI, Mungal Pande, had run amok while high on drugs, firing at a British officer and NCO before being arrested and hanged.[5] The 34th was disbanded on 6 May but by that time it was apparent that the Bengal Army was on the verge of a major outbreak of rebellion. On Sunday, 10 May, at the military cantonment of Meerut, the dam finally burst.

With soldiers of the Queen's army spread around the world, it took some months before sufficient numbers could reach India to help turn the tide. There were a few regiments in India, Persia and Burma which were rushed to the scenes of mutiny and, together with the loyal HEIC soldiers, they managed to contain the Mutiny to the provinces of Oudh and Rohilkund.

For the next nineteen months there were atrocities committed by both sides. During the first months, many civilians took refuge in isolated towns defended by outnumbered British soldiers and a surprising number of loyal sepoys. As reinforcements began to arrive, so these pockets of resistance were relieved. Then followed the pursuit of the rebels, who still outnumbered the British and who fought with desperation, for surrender meant certain death.

The Indian Mutiny was one of the last conflicts in which hand-to-hand fighting was the norm. Officers engaged in sword versus *tulwar* (also spelt *talwar*; a type of curved sword or sabre) contests, often outnumbered, inflicting and receiving horrific wounds. The other ranks, on firing a volley, would charge amongst the enemy, giving thanks for all the hours of bayonet drill. Even the artillery exchanges were at close range, with the British-trained Indian gunners proving to be tenacious and expert. The fighting was brutal with no quarter given, and it is of little surprise that so many VCs were awarded.

This sprawling and cruel conflict, coming on the heels of the Crimean War, presented the establishment with many new controversies and anomalies resulting in adjustments to the Victoria Cross Warrants. In a conflict that lasted about the same time as the Crimean War, which had produced 111 Victoria Cross recipients, the Mutiny saw 182 Crosses awarded, the highest number until the First World War.

Those soldiers who fought in the Crimean War had no spur of a Victoria Cross to urge them to perform heroic actions as the award was instituted after the conflict was over. With another war following so closely, the prospect of winning the coveted Cross became the target for many young officers anxious to stand out amongst their peers. Frederick Roberts, for example, wrote to his mother declaring that the VC was vital in securing his advancement, while Lieutenants Robert Blair and Alfred Jones of the 9th Lancers together resolved that they would win the Victoria Cross in India. In the event all three were awarded the VC.

It must be acknowledged that many sepoys did not mutiny and fought alongside the British performing many acts of bravery. Indian troops were not eligible for the Victoria Cross as they could already receive the Indian Order of Merit which had been instituted in 1837 – the oldest British gallantry award – and claim increased pay and pension allowances. The soldiers mostly involved were the martial races of Sikhs and Gurkhas. They were both former enemies of the British, who had impressed the military authorities with their skill and courage and were quickly recruited into the Indian Army.

The rules governing awards of the Victoria Cross were added to and amended during the conflict and Queen Victoria signed three Royal Warrants in 1857-58. On 29 October 1857, the Warrant extended eligibility to soldiers of the Honourable East India Company. For the first time since its inception, the VC was awarded to soldiers not under the direct control of the Crown and was bestowed rather grudgingly in the case of Lieutenant William Alexander Kerr of the 24th Bombay Native Infantry.

The case of the fire onboard the SS *Sarah Sands* in November 1857, in which members of the India-bound 54th Regiment fought to extinguish the blaze and save the ship and passengers, resulted in a new Warrant signed on 10 August 1858 covering bravery but not before the enemy. Queen Victoria signed a final Warrant on 13 December 1858, which extended eligibility to civilians or, as the Warrant states, 'Non-Military persons Bearing Arms as Volunteers'. A proviso was placed in the Warrant stating that this acceptance of civilians only applied to those taking part in the Indian Mutiny and it was never used again.[6]

The Indian Mutiny produced a number of 'firsts', including the most VCs won on a single day, twenty-four at the Second Relief of Lucknow on 16 November 1857; the VC brothers, Charles and Hugh Gough; the oldest VC, 63-year-old William Raynor; one of the two youngest VCs, Thomas Flinn, at the age of 15 years 3 months; use of the ballot for the first time – of the forty-six awarded in this way, twenty-nine relate to the Mutiny; and for the first time there was a recommendation for a second VC Bar.

The Indian Mutiny was a truly fluid campaign fought out in brutal heat, monsoon weather and rough terrain covering hundreds of miles against a determined foe.

Chapter 1

The Siege of Delhi
May to September 1857

The 3rd Bengal Light Cavalry (BLC) triggered the mutiny that broke out on 10 May 1857 at the widespread cantonment of Meerut. In April, ordered by their insensitive commanding officer, Colonel George Carmichael-Smyth, to use the new Enfield cartridge, the regiment's ninety skirmishers refused. Word had spread amongst the native troops that the paper cartridge was impregnated with animal fat, which offended both Muslim and Hindu. During the firing parade, all but five of the skirmishers refused to accept the cartridge. Instead of quietly dealing with the problem, Carmichael-Smyth ordered their arrest. The subsequent sentences were extremely harsh and on 9 May, the prisoners were shackled before a humiliating special parade.

On that evening, an Indian officer visited Lieutenant Hugh Gough at his bungalow and warned him that the Indian garrison would mutiny the following day.[1] Gough immediately informed Carmichael-Smyth, who rejected the warning, reproving Gough for listening to such idle words. Gough then repeated the warning to the station commander, Brigadier Archdale Wilson, who was equally dismissive.

As predicted, the mutiny broke out the following day and the prisoners were released. It seemed that this was the extent of the *sowars'* (mounted soldiers) and sepoys' aim for there were only pockets of frenzied attacks on Europeans, while elsewhere in the cantonment life went on normally. But by the time British troops of the 60th (King's Royal Rifle Corps) Rifles and the mounted 6th (Carabineers) Dragoon Guards reacted, it was too late. Travelling by night, the mutineers made their unmolested way to the walled city of Delhi, some forty miles distant.

Some of their cavalry arrived early on the morning of 11 May and secured the bridge of boats over the Jumna river. This enabled the Meerut

1

mutineers to cross and infiltrate the city, where they spread their message. Soon there were crowds seeking out and killing the few Europeans who lived in the city. Two British signalmen managed to send off a brief warning to the post at Umballa before their station was overrun. Umballa quickly relayed the electrifying news to other stations in northern India, thus spreading the first news of the uprising.

The sepoys of the three native regiments that made up the Delhi garrison were soon in revolt. By a stipulation with the Mogul King of Delhi, no European troops were stationed there, despite locating a large magazine within its walls.

George Forrest, William Raynor and John Buckley

The first Mutiny VCs were awarded for an action that occurred the day after the initial outbreak at Meerut on 10 May 1857. For a VC action to take part so early in a conflict is almost unprecedented in the annals of the Victoria Cross. Also, the action was carried out by men who were elderly and non-combatant.

The local magistrate, Sir Theophilus Metcalfe, called at the house of Lieutenant George Willoughby, Bengal Artillery, to warn him that mutineers were crossing the Jumna and to prepare for the defence of the magazine.[2] Willoughby, a short, fat and unprepossessing man, was Commissary of Ordnance in charge of the Delhi Magazine. He went to the magazine and ordered the gates to be barricaded and covered by guns with the intention of holding out until evening, when it was expected that the European troops from Meerut would arrive.

His tiny garrison consisted of two elderly officers, 57-year-old Lieutenant George Forrest and 61-year-old Lieutenant William Raynor, both of the Bengal Veteran Establishment. Six members of the Ordnance Department made up the rest of the Europeans. They were Conductors John Buckley, William Shaw, John Scully, Sub-Conductor William Crow, Sergeants Bryan Edwards and Peter Stewart.

The magazine comprised several stone buildings surrounded by a high wall. Inside the gate were placed two 6-pounder guns doubly charged with grapeshot. Sergeants Edwards and Stewart stood by with lighted matches to fire simultaneously should the gate be forced. The second line of defence was the gate to the magazine itself, which was covered by two more guns with four others trained to give cross-fire. If all else failed, trails of powder were laid into the magazine ready to be lit on a given signal.

There was also a native contingent employed in the arsenal and they were issued with arms to help in its defence. However, it became very clear early

2

on that no help could be expected from them as they refused to obey orders. Meanwhile, the three native regiments stationed at Delhi joined the Meerut mutineers. Their numbers were quickly swollen by the population of the city, who swept though the streets killing any Europeans they could find.

The magazine was a priority target and expected to be taken easily. As the mob hammered at the outer gate, one of the native employees relayed to them the details of its defences. Then scaling ladders arrived, supplied from the nearby King's Palace. As soon as they were placed against the walls, the whole of the magazine's native establishment deserted by climbing up the sloped roofs and descending the ladders.

As the enemy swept over the walls, the nine Europeans coolly poured round after round of grapeshot at the multitude, who kept up heavy musket fire. John Buckley was hit above the elbow and George Forrest twice struck in the left hand. After four hours of resistance, and on the point of being overwhelmed, Willoughby shouted to Buckley, 'Now's the time!'. Buckley raised his cap, signalling to Scully to fire the powder trails.

The defenders ran for whatever cover they could find as the attackers swarmed into the courtyard in front of the magazine. Within seconds, there was a tremendous explosion that destroyed the buildings and demolished the wall, crushing to death over 400 of the mob. Thousands of rounds of ammunition were ignited and many onlookers in the surrounding streets were hit.

Not one of the defenders expected to survive, but miraculously, four of the nine did. Willoughby and Forrest managed to reach the Kashmir Gate, where a number of surviving Europeans had managed to assemble before attempting the hazardous journey to Meerut. During this journey, Willoughby, obviously disorientated and suffering from severe concussion, began behaving strangely and became separated from the main party. He and six other men, including a wounded Lieutenant Osborn of the 54th BNI, were fed and sheltered at the first village they came to. Leaving Osborn in the care of the villagers, they continued to the next village, where they were met by a crowd led by a Brahmin. In the confrontation that followed, Willoughby shot and killed the Brahmin, upon which the enraged villagers closed in and hacked Willoughby and the others to death. Ironically, Osborn was the only survivor and was eventually carried to Meerut. This illustrates the differing attitudes of villages and districts towards the British at this stage of the outbreak; one village would treat the refugees with kindness, while a neighbouring village would wreak revenge on the defenceless Europeans.

Buckley and Raynor, singed and dazed, managed to escape and set out separately for the comparative safety of Meerut. Buckley's trauma was increased when he learned that his wife and three children had been murdered that day. When he was captured by rebel sepoys, probably at Delhi, he was so grief-stricken that he was indifferent to his fate. He was identified as being one of the defenders of the magazine and, because of his bravery, his life was spared. Sometime within the following fortnight he escaped, for Lieutenant Forrest wrote a report from Meerut dated 27 May in which he states, 'Lieut.Raynor and Condr.Buckley have escaped to this station'.

All three survivors were recommended and received the Victoria Cross for their gallant defence of the Delhi Magazine and for preparing to die rather than let it fall into the hands of the enemy. They also received promotions backdated to 11 May. George Forrest and William Raynor became captains, while John Buckley was appointed Assistant Commissary of Ordnance.

Both Forrest and Raynor were awarded their Crosses the following year in India but did not survive for much longer. George Forrest fell ill, went on sick leave in November and died on 3 November 1859 at Dehra Dun.

William Raynor, who had been born in July 1795 in Plumtree, Nottingham, died on 13 December 1860 at Ferozepore. His service record must stand as the longest of any VC recipient. He had enlisted in the 1st Bengal European Regiment on 11 June 1812, the year of Napoleon's retreat from Moscow, and served in the Nepal War of 1814-16. At the time of his VC exploit he was 61 years 10 months, the oldest ever recipient.

John Buckley had been born on 24 May 1813 at Stalybridge near Manchester, and worked in the local textile mill. When he was 18, he enlisted in the Bengal Artillery and rose to the rank of Corporal before transferring to the Ordnance Department. The tragedies that befell his family life, in particular the slaughter of his last family at Delhi, made him indifferent to danger. He volunteered for active duty and repeatedly put himself at risk. He also sought revenge on the race that had robbed him of his family and relished the overseeing of 150 rebels strapped to the muzzles of cannon and blown apart.

Taken ill during early 1858, Buckley returned to an England he had not seen for twenty-six years. On 2 August 1858, he received his VC from Queen Victoria in an investiture at Portsmouth. Buckley stayed in his hometown of Stalybridge before returning to India with the retired rank of Major. His last years were spent back in East London, where he died at his home on 14 June 1876.

Because the VC was not awarded posthumously at that time, George Willoughby, who had led the gallant defence of the Magazine, has largely

4

been forgotten. His name, together with those of the other defenders, however, was recorded on a tablet erected by the Government of India over the gateway to the Delhi Magazine Memorial after the Mutiny.

BUDLI-KI-SERAI

With the recapture of Delhi now a priority, a hastily raised combined force of 2,500 men from Meerut and Umballa marched on the city under the command of General Sir Henry Barnard. On 8 June, six miles west of the city, they were confronted by about 3,500 mutineers at the walled village of Budli-ki-Serai. Although they were superior in numbers and had more artillery, the mutineers appeared leaderless and their flanks were vulnerable to turning. They opened up a ferocious cannonade upon the advancing regiment which marched across the open plain, during the process sustaining severe casualties. Despite their proficient gunnery, the rebels were driven back.

Henry Hartigan

Born in Ulster, Henry Hartigan was about 31 years old and a sergeant in the 9th Lancers. As the British closed in on the village, the 9th Lancers became involved in a mêlée with the rebel cavalry. Hartigan saw that Sergeant Henry Helstone had been unhorsed and wounded. Despite being surrounded by the enemy, Hartigan dismounted, lifted Helstone onto his horse and carried him to safety.

As with many Mutiny VC citations, more than one act of bravery appeared was listed in it. On 10 October at Agra, Hartigan was again responsible for saving a comrade's life when he ran to the assistance of Sergeant Crews who was being attacked by four rebels. Grabbing a *tulwar* from one of them with his right hand, he punched the *sowar* with his left. Armed with a *tulwar*, he turned on the other three, killing one and wounding two. In this action, Hartigan was dangerously wounded and was subsequently hospitalised at Agra for several months.

By the end of the year, there was a need for more mounted troops and Hartigan, now recovered, was offered an NCO position with a newly-raised irregular cavalry unit called Meade's Horse.[3] One hundred Sikhs and Punjabi Mohammadans formed the nucleus of the regiment, to which were added different religious groups and loyal members of disbanded native regiments. By the end of January 1858, Meade was able to split his multi-faith force into six separate troops. It was Hartigan's task to teach these recruits to ride, care for their mounts, as well as handle weapons on horseback. By March, when they were proficient enough, they joined Brigadier M.W. Smith's Brigade, Rajputana Field Force as they campaigned throughout 1858 in Central India.

At the conclusion of the Mutiny, Hartigan was gazetted on 19 June 1860 and received his Victoria Cross from Lady Hersey at Fort William, Calcutta on 24 December 1860. He was subsequently commissioned as a lieutenant in the 16th Lancers, which was stationed at Bangalore. In 1877 he wrote a book snappily entitled *Stray Leaves from a Military Man's Note Book – Containing Descriptions of Men and Things Regimental at Home and Abroad.* It was written in a humorous vein and broadly autobiographical.

Henry Hartigan died in Calcutta on 29 October 1886 at the age of 60.

Arthur Stowell Jones

Also taking part in the Budli-ki-Serai affair was Lieutenant Arthur Stowell Jones, born in Liverpool on 24 January 1832. He had purchased his commission in the 9th Lancers in 1852, living the leisurely life of a peacetime cavalry officer; pig-sticking, hunting, horse racing, eating and drinking heavily. Now for the first time Jones was to see some proper action.

As the enemy was driven out of the village, the retreating gunners were spotted by cavalry scouts. Colonel Yule led the 9th Lancers in pursuit. Lieutenant Jones was leading the right troop of the 4th Squadron as they galloped towards the distant cloud of dust identified as the retreating guns. Through the swirling dust Jones spotted six enemy gunners hauling away a 9-pound cannon. Without calling upon support, Jones dashed off after the gun and soon overhauled the enemy team. Drawing alongside the lead horse, Jones slashed the driver across the shoulder, causing him to fall beneath the wheels of the limber. Then, controlling his mount with his knees, he leant over the lead horse, grabbed the traces and brought the galloping team to a juddering halt. The other five drivers could not keep control of their rearing horses and they fell beneath the stamping hooves. Jones was joined by Sergeant Major Thonger, who had seen Jones charge off towards the gun and followed him with three troopers, who made short work of the injured sepoys.

Jones then set about spiking the gun with one of the two spikes carried by the officers. Before he could complete this, Colonel Yule arrived and ordered the spike removed so they could load and fire at the enemy. The captured gun was found to have belonged to the Bengal Field Artillery, which had mutinied at Delhi, and it had been actively used against the British. Lieutenant Jones was permitted to seize the gun as a prize and later return it to the Artillery.

Having put the mutineers to flight, the column moved on to occupy the Delhi Ridge, a thin spur of high ground to the north of the city. The Bengal Native Infantry barracks was to the west of it and, in a gesture of contempt and defiance, it was set on fire. This proved to be a senseless act as it condemned the British to live in tents during the heat of the summer and the monsoon season. What has been described as a siege was in reality a holding exercise until enough forces could be brought in to assail Delhi.

It was on this bare, dusty ridge that Jones found his vocation.[4] He had read a book by Doctor Edmund Alexander Parkes entitled *Military Hygiene* which had greatly impressed him. The Ridge soon became a pestilential area, with unburied animals attracting bloated flies, mosquitoes and vermin of all kinds. Dysentry and cholera soon took hold and men died for the want of simple hygiene.[5] On a limited scale, Jones oversaw the digging of latrines and the burying of dead animals.

Jones's gallantry later came to the attention of Colonel James Hope Grant, Commander of the Cavalry Division. Grant duly recommended Jones for the Victoria Cross for two separate actions; the first for his capture of the gun at Budli-ki-Serai and the other for a fight where Jones was fortunate to survive.

After the fall of Delhi, two mobile columns were formed to comb the country for bands of mutineers. The 9th Lancers was attached to General Edward Harris Greathed's column, which set out for Mutra, eighty miles to the south, having heard that a large force of the enemy had regrouped. On the march, Greathed learned that civilians had retreated to the fort at Agra and were besieged by the rebels. With some reluctance, Greathed diverted his column and, in a forced-march of forty-four miles in twenty-eight hours, they arrived at Agra only to find that the fort was safe and the mutineers had moved on. Greathed was greatly put out, as were his men, and he ordered them to make camp on the parade ground. Soon the tension melted and both soldiers and civilians relaxed and, with no piquets posted, the troops enjoyed a peaceful night. Unbeknown to them, a large rebel force was camped just nine miles away and was already making its way back to Agra.

On the morning of 10 October, while breakfast was being prepared, the rebels opened fire with cannon and then charged in on the unsuspecting camp. Hope Grant wrote in his diary:

'The troops fell in as best [they] could, many of them in shirt-sleeves. The 9th Lancers were soon in the saddle, with the gallant Drysdale at their head. Poor French was shot through the body at the head of his squadron and died before he could be carried to the town. Jones was struck down from his horse by a shot and when on the ground was fearfully hacked about by some rebel sowers [*sic*] with their tulwars; he had twenty-two wounds about him. The squadron these two officers belonged to met a strong force of enemy cavalry, charged, drove them away, and retook one of our guns which had been captured by one of the rebels.'

Barely alive, Jones had been shot in the arm, cut with twenty-two sword wounds and his left eye ripped from its socket. Incredibly, he survived his wounds in the rudimentary hospital facilities at Agra, and, when he was well enough, returned to Britain for more medical treatment. He was fitted with an eye patch and, despite this handicap, was sent to Leeds Cavalry Barracks.

Jones did not see the citation that appeared in *The London Gazette* on 18 June 1858 nor hear about it from anyone else. It was not until two days before the investiture that he learned that he was receive the Victoria Cross from the Queen at Southsea. After a mad dash south, he only just arrived in time for the parade. He recalled: 'A young horse I was riding in the School at Leeds a few days before had thrown up his head and bruised my blind eye-brow, so my appearance was shocking, and made the Queen so nervous that she pricked me in pinning the Cross through my tunic.'[6]

Jones entered Staff College and graduated in 1860. He served as Deputy Assistant Quartermaster General (DAQG) and was able to put into practice the tenets of Dr Parkes and his *Military Hygiene*. To Jones the loss of men through lack of hygiene was an avoidable evil and he did all he could to educate and put in place remedies for a more healthy environment. In 1863, he married Emily Back and together they produced five sons and a daughter. He retired as a Lieutenant-Colonel in 1872, retrained and became a Member of the Institute of Civil Engineers. He operated a sewage farm in Wales and became a regular writer of papers and articles on the treatment of sewage. The rather thoughtless young cavalry officer had become one of those pioneering Victorian engineers who improved the lot of his fellow man. In 1895, the Army called on his expertise and for the next twelve years he managed the Sewage Works of the 1st Army Corps at Aldershot.

He and his wife lived in the Berkshire village of Finchampstead and his immediate neighbour was his old comrade-in-arms, General Sir John Watson VC. The two families were brought closer together when Watson's son, Arthur, married the Jones's daughter, Marguerita.

Arthur Stowell Jones final years were ones of sadness. Four of his five sons had died through sickness, accident or been killed in the Great War. He died on 29 May 1920 and is buried in the churchyard of St James's, Finchampstead.[7]

Cornelius Coughlan

Another Irish soldier was Colour-Sergeant Cornelius Coughlan, born in Galway in June 1828. He joined the 75th (Stirlingshire) Regiment and took part in the attack on Budli-ki-Serai. Under heavy fire and accompanied by three comrades, he braved the bullets and rescued Private Corbett, who lay severely wounded amongst a number of mutilated men. In the process, Coughlan was wounded in the left knee.

When the force reached the Delhi Ridge, their cantonment for four wretched months, they attempted to clear the rebels from the immediate area. On 18 July in one of these sorties, Coughlan led by example and charged down a lane in the outlying suburb of Subzi Mandi. Raked by gunfire from both sides he led his men and cleared the enemy from the buildings. He then made his way back under fire to collect *dhoolies* (litters) to carry off the wounded.

Coughlan again displayed his leadership qualities during the assault on Delhi on 14 September. The 75th was in No.1 Column, led by Brigadier John Nicholson. When Nicholson was mortally wounded, Coughlan encouraged the wavering troops to return to the attack on the Kabul Gate, where another British column was poised to enter once it was captured by Nicholson's men. Kabul Gate was taken; the achievement was so noteworthy that a memorial tablet and monument were erected over the Gate and inscribed on the tablet was the name of Sergeant-Major Coughlan.

Queen Victoria wrote a personal letter complimenting him on his bravery and expressing regret that she was unable to pin the Victoria Cross on his breast herself. His citation did not appear in *The London Gazette* until 11 November 1862, five years after the event, even though, at the beginning of 1862, the Duke of Cambridge had expressed a wish that a line should be drawn at some point. A few more recommendations still filtered through, including Coughlan's. There was some disagreement between Edward Pennington, the Clerk at the War Office, and his chief, Sir Edward Lugard. In the event, Lugard won the argument presuming the 75th's commanding officer had been under great pressure at the time. On his return from India, Coughlan received his Cross, not from the Queen, but from Major-General Sir William Hutchinson, in a ceremony at Devonport. He served for a further twenty-one years back in Ireland with the 3rd Battalion Connaught Rangers.

Sergeant-Major Cornelius Coughlan VC died on 14 February 1915 at his home in Westport, County Mayo. He was buried with full military honours in a funeral that was the largest and most impressive to have passed through the town. A firing party from the Royal Field Artillery and a fife and drum band from the Hampshire Regiment accompanied the hearse, whilst hundreds lined the route.

Coughlan's body was interred and awaited a headstone that was never installed. The Rising of 1916, which led to civil war and ultimately the independent state of Ireland, caused much bitterness and antipathy towards Britain. It became unpopular to admit that an Irishman had served in the British Army and the veterans of the 10th and 16th Divisions, made up of the famous now-disbanded Irish regiments, arrived home after the First World War, not to cheering crowds and stirring speeches, but to suspicion and danger. It was in this climate that the grave of Cornelius Coughlan remained unmarked and forgotten for eighty-nine years.

On 7 August 2004, at the Aughavale Cemetery, Westport, there was performed a ceremony of great significance. For the first time an Irish politician formally recognised on Irish soil the sacrifices made by Irishmen in the British Army by dedicating a grave to a VC hero. The fact that an Irish Minister was involved in such a magnanimous ceremony speaks volumes for changing attitudes.

Thomas Cadell
Born 5 September 1835 in Cockenzie, East Lothian, Thomas Cadell was a cadet at the HEIC military academy at Addiscombe near Croydon. In 1854, he was commissioned into the 2nd European Bengal Fusiliers and promoted to lieutenant in 1856.

On 13 May the 2nd Bengal European Fusiliers, who had been stationed at Subathu in the hills near Simla, proceeded by two forced marches to Umballa, reaching there on 17 May. From there they joined the 1st Bengal European Fusiliers, other East India Company and British Army regiments, and on 7 June marched on Delhi.

Between the 8th and 16th of that month, there were several severe skirmishes before Delhi. The Flagstaff Tower on the Delhi Ridge was often a point of attack by the mutineers when they attempted a sortie in their efforts to raise the siege. On 12 June, a large body of the mutineer infantry launched a vigorous attack and the picquets of the Bengal European Fusiliers and the 75th Regiment were forced to retire by overwhelming numbers.

Lieutenant Cadell, seeing a bugler of his own regiment fall severely wounded, went to his assistance, and, carrying him from among the enemy under heavy fire, saved him from certain death. Again, on the same evening, when his regiment was ordered to retire to Sir Theophilus

10

Metcalfe's house, on hearing that a wounded man of the 75th was left behind, he immediately went back towards the advancing mutineers, taking with him three men, and brought him to safety. This act of devotion to duty by Cadell and his men was accomplished under a ferocious fire of cannon and musketry.

It was for these two acts of bravery that he was awarded the Victoria Cross. *The London Gazette*, 29 April 1862 states the following: 'Thomas Cadell, Lieutenant, late 2nd Bengal European Fusiliers, Date of act of bravery, June 12th 1857. For having, on 12 June 1857, at the flagstaff picquet at Delhi, when the whole of the picquet of Her Majesty's 75th Regiment, and 2nd Bengal European Fusiliers were driven in by a large body of the enemy, brought in from amongst the enemy a wounded bugler of his own regiment, under a most severe fire who would otherwise have been cut up by the rebels. Also, on the same day, when the Fusiliers were retiring, by order, on Metcalfe's house, on its being reported that there was a wounded man being left behind, Lieutenant Cadell went back of his own accord towards the enemy, accompanied by three men, and brought in a man of the 75th Regiment, who was severely wounded, under a most heavy fire from the advancing enemy.'

Thomas Cadell gave an account of his actions on 12 June in a letter home to his father dated 29 June. He made no big deal of his own bravery: 'The most severe fire I have been under was on the 12th. I went up with a party of my Regiment to relieve a picquet of the 75th. We had broken off our men when I went to the front of the Flag Staff Tower to see what was going on. I went to the brow of the hill with Knox of the 75th (he was knocked over five minutes afterwards) and no sooner had we got there than about thirty bullets whizzed by our heads. I asked the senior officer present to take out my company. He allowed me to take out only a sub-division. I had just got there in skirmishing order in line with the tower when about a thousand Pandies (rebel sepoys) jumped over the brow of the steep hill like so many spectres. We kept them back for about ten minutes when we were forced to retire. Eleven out of the twenty men who were with me were killed or wounded, so you see it was rather sharp work. We soon rallied again and of course drove them back.'

When the attack on the walls of Delhi began on 14 September, Cadell's regiment was with Brigadier Jones's 2nd Column. They advanced towards the breach in the Water Bastion and took it. The fighting was extremely violent with no quarter given. 'Lots of blackguards are hanged every morning,' Thomas Cadell wrote to his sister. 'The more the merrier'. In an earlier letter to his father he describes the close shaves he experienced: 'I myself was hit once with a spent bullet out of a shrapnel shell: another time a musket ball hit the barrel of my pistol in my belt leaving a great blue mark on my thigh: another bullet hit the hilt of my sword and another went right into the little pouch in which I carried cartridges, and which was fastened to my belt.' Cadell bemoaned the fact that many acts of bravery went unremarked: 'I have always been well to the front, and still have never been mentioned.' In another letter he complained: 'The Delhi army has been most unlucky in not having any good men, like Brigr. Inglis, to write dispatches and many a deed has been done which in the Crimea would have rewarded with the greatest of all honour to a soldier, the Victoria Cross.'

Thomas Cadell was one of those soldiers whose VC recommendation was not received until 1862, beyond the cut-off date. Like Cornelius Coughlan, he was accepted by Sir Edward Lugard and received his Cross from Brigadier-General James Travers VC at Bhopal. Ironically, Travers experienced a similar investigation for a late recommendation and had only just received his own VC.

Cadell left his regiment in November 1858 and joined the 4th Bengal Irregular Cavalry. After the Mutiny, he joined the Bengal Staff Corps. In December 1879 a major change took place in his life: he was appointed Chief Commissioner and Superintendent of the Andaman and Nicobar Islands, serving there from 1879 until 1892. Despite his contempt for the mutineers in India, he turned out to be a humane and considerate administrator for the convicts and the native Andamanese.

Cadell retired as a colonel and died on 6 April 1919. At the time of his death, he was the oldest holder of the Victoria Cross.

Thomas Hancock

Two more members of the 9th Lancers became involved in another VC action. The British were in a poor state, unable to do more than fend off the attacks made by the rebels. On 19 June, a major coordinated attack was mounted from three directions which very nearly forced the British to retreat. In one of these attacks, in which the cavalry fought, an attempt was made to carry away guns from Major Scott's battery during which Colonel James Hope Grant was unhorsed and surrounded by mutineers. In a letter, used in the citations of Hancock and Purcell, he wrote: 'The guns I am happy to say were saved, but a wagon of Major Scott's battery was blown up. I must not fail to mention the excellent conduct of a sowar of the 4th Irregular Cavalry and two men of the 9th Lancers, Privates Thomas Hancock and John Purcell, who, when my horse was shot down, remained with me throughout. One of these men and the sowar offered me their horses, and I was dragged out by the sowar's horse. Private Hancock was severely wounded and Private Purcell's horse was killed under him. The sowar's name was Roopur Khan.'

Hancock had been badly wounded and had his arm amputated. When he was able to return to the UK, he was honourably discharged from the army, so ending seventeen years of service. Born in 1822 in Ealing, Thomas Hancock had joined the 3rd Light Dragoons in 1840. A year later, he transferred to the 9th Lancers and was sent to India. He took part in campaigns at Gwalior in 1843, the First Sikh War 1845-46 and the Second Sikh War (Punjab) 1848-49 and attained the rank of Corporal. It would appear that his disciplinary record was not good for he served in the Mutiny as a Private.

Now unemployed, Hancock applied to Captain Sir Edward Walter, a retired cavalry officer, who had recently set up the Corps of Commissionaires as a way to provide employment for ex-servicemen.[8] Hancock joined the Corps on 12 March 1859, just after his citation appeared in *The London Gazette*. Now in the uniform of the Corps of Commissionaires, Hancock attended Buckingham Palace on 8 June 1859 to be presented with his VC by the Queen.

There is some confusion as to where he worked. Some accounts have him employed by Messrs Hunt and Roskill, silversmiths and jewellers to Queen Victoria. Others have him serving as lodge keeper in the Home Park at Windsor from 1859 to 1865. Queen Victoria, who met him, reportedly described him as a 'fine looking man, covered in medals'.

He was discharged from the Corps on 14 November 1865 and little is known of his remaining years. He died at the age of 48 in the Earls Court Kensington Workhouse on 12 March 1871 and was buried in an unmarked grave at Brompton Cemetery.[9]

John Purcell

Thomas Hancock's comrade in saving Hope Grant was James Purcell, who was born in 1814 in Galway. His action has been described alongside that of Hancock. In a letter of 10 January 1858 from the grateful Brigadier-General Hope Grant to Major H.W. Norman, Assistant Adjutant-General of the Army, the former wrote: 'I had the sincere gratification of naming two privates of the 9th Lancers, who displayed signal gallantry in the fight – Privates Thomas Hancock, who lost an arm on the occasion, and John Purcell who had his horse shot under him, and was, I regret to say, afterwards killed at the assault of Delhi. Sir Henry Barnard was pleased to recommend that the Victoria Cross should be conferred on both.

The following day, Colonel Hope Grant recounted: 'I took the cavalry back to camp and then visited all the wounded men in hospital. Among them was poor Purcell, who as my orderly had behaved so gallantly on the 19 June when in the darkness of the night I was almost alone and riderless in the midst of the rebels. He had been shot through the chest and could scarcely speak, but was full of hope. He died a few days later on 19 September 1857.'

John Purcell was buried by Father Bertrand, a Franciscan RC Chaplain, the following day. The two VCs for Purcell and Hancock were sent to General Sir Colin Campbell from the War Office. Although Purcell died on 19 September, Sir Henry Barnard had approved the recommendation for a Victoria Cross before he, too, had died on 5 July of the same year, thus enabling Purcell to be awarded the Cross. This was presented to his brother, James, who was also serving in the 9th Lancers.

Samuel Turner

Samuel Turner was born in Witnesham, Suffolk in February 1826. A private in the 1st Battalion 60th Rifles he had been stationed at Meerut when the Mutiny broke out. A series of desperate struggles took place on the Ridge, including one on the night of 19 June. In his VC citation of 20 January 1860, Private Turner was described thus: 'For having, at Delhi, on the night of 19 June, 1857, during a severe conflict with the enemy, who attacked the rear of the camp, carried off on his shoulders, under heavy fire, a mortally wounded officer Lieutenant Humphreys of the Indian Service. During this service Private Turner was wounded by a sabre-cut in the right forearm. His gallant conduct saved the above-named officer from the fate of the others, whose mangled remains were not recovered until the following day. Lieutenant M.A. Humphrys [correct spelling] was attached to the 60th Rifles after his Regiment, the 20th BNI, mutinied at Meerut.'

Turner had left the 60th in March 1860 and received his Victoria Cross that December at Simla. He took his pension, returned to Meerut and set himself up as a farrier and hotel keeper. He died on 13 June 1868 and was buried at St John's Cemetery, Meerut.

Stephen Garvin

Stephen Garvin was born in Tipperary in 1826 and enlisted in the British Army at the age of 16. He joined the 1st Battalion 60th Rifles in 1842 and was sent to India in 1845. He took part in the Second Sikh War in 1848-49 and in a punitive expedition on the North-West Frontier in 1849-50. By the time of the Mutiny, he had been promoted to Colour-Sergeant. Stationed at

14

Meerut, he had witnessed the outbreak and taken part in the assault on Budli-ki-Serai.

The mutineers sensed they could push the British from the Ridge and kept up the pressure with almost daily attacks. The 23 June was a significant date for it was exactly 100 years earlier that the British had won a decisive victory at the Battle of Plassey and the mutineers were determined to exact revenge. The attack went in at 5 a.m. and raged until sunset, when the rebels withdrew to the security of the Delhi walls.

One of the aims of the attack was to take a temple, the Swansi, a name the British corrupted to 'Sammy House', which stood on the southern tip of the Ridge. The mutineers managed to occupy the temple and to bring up some artillery pieces. The British artillery, being sited above the Sammy House, could not sufficiently depress their guns and called upon the exhausted infantry to clear out the rebels. Lieutenant Hare of the 60th called for volunteers.

Sergeant Garvin answered the call and, with a small party of men, charged down on the enemy-held temple. In the face of heavy fire, the 60th entered the temple and in desperate hand-to-hand fighting managed to dislodge the enemy. Sergeant Garvin was singled out and was gazetted on 20 January 1860, receiving his Cross from the Queen at Windsor Castle on 9 November 1860.

In another action on 3 September, Garvin was shot in the left side of his groin, therefore missing the assault on Delhi. He was later awarded the Distinguished Conduct Medal.[10] On his return to Britain he transferred to the 64th (North Staffordshire) Regiment before taking his discharge in 1865. In 1870, he was appointed a Yeoman of the Guard and four years later he died at Chesterton in Cambridgeshire.

John McGovern

Born on 16 May 1825 in Co. Cavan, John McGovern enlisted in the Bengal Army during the height of Ireland's Potato Famine of the 1840s. The HEIC set up recruiting centres in Ireland and at that period her armies and those of the British consisted mainly of Irish soldiers. McGovern joined the 1st Bengal European Fusiliers and sailed for India in 1845.

McGovern first saw action in the Burma War of 1852-53. He was regarded as 'bad soldier', always in the defaulters' book. His life, however, took a different turn during the Indian Mutiny. During the determined attack on the Ridge on 23 June, he performed his VC action. When his citation, noted for its brevity, was announced in *The London Gazette* of 18 June, it read: 'For gallant conduct during the operations before Delhi, but more especially on

23rd of June, when he carried into camp a wounded comrade under a very heavy fire from the enemy's battery, at the risk of his own life.'

He could have won the VC twice over for an even more daring exploit he performed at the Battle of Narkoul on 16 December 1857. Three sepoys took refuge in a small fortified tower and were proving difficult to dislodge. The Fusilier's sergeant-major was ordered by his officer to make a determined effort to clear the tower. McGovern was standing nearby and volunteered to go. As he started up the staircase, he heard the sergeant-major say to the officer, 'Never mind, sir; he'll be no loss'.

This made McGovern determined to carry out the attack on his own. Climbing the narrow staircase, he reached the roof, where the sepoys were waiting for him. They all opened fire but McGovern managed to dodge back down the stairs. Before they could reload, he rushed in, shooting the leading sepoy and bayoneting the other two.

Afterwards, McGovern was a changed man, giving up both heavy drinking and fighting in camp. After the Mutiny, he elected to remain in India but later he emigrated to Canada where died in November 1888.

James Hills

The hard-pressed defenders on the Delhi Ridge were heartened when John Nicholson's 4,200-strong Movable Column reached them. Under the command of Captain Henry Daly, they set out on 12 May on a forced march of 580 miles which they accomplished in twenty-six days, mostly at night to avoid the worst of this, the hottest season of the year.

There was still, however, a 'them and us' manner with which Her Majesty's officers viewed those of the HEIC. Daly recalled: 'Only those who remember the too frequently attitudes of superiority adopted by the officers of the Queen's service towards those in that of "John Company" will realise how great the tribute to a dominating personality was the fact that [these same officers] should have been willing to serve under this regimental Captain in the Company's service, the General by the grace of God, who had ridden into camp like a king.'

In the event, it was fortunate that John Nicholson reached the Ridge as it was his energy and determination that overcame the indecision of his querulous superiors in planning and leading the attack on Delhi in September. In the meantime, two more HEIC officers distinguished themselves in the defence of the Ridge.

James Hills was half Scottish, half Italian by blood, Indian by birth and finally a Welshman by adoption. His association with the sub-continent went back to his birth in Bengal on 20 August 1833, the son of James Hills, a Scottish indigo planter, and Charlotte, the daughter of Angelo Savi of Bengal. Educated in Edinburgh, he was commissioned into the Bengal Artillery in 1853, via the East India Army College at Addiscombe, Surrey.

On 9 July, Second Lieutenant Hills was in command of two field guns at the Mound, an outpost on the right rear flank of the British camp, overlooking the suburb of Subzi Mandi. At about 11 a.m. rumours began to spread that rebel cavalry were approaching. Hills moved the cavalry picquet guarding his men into the pre-arranged position ready to repel any attack when, without warning, a large body of sepoys from the rebel army charged the unprepared field guns. He later recorded:

'You must have seen accounts of their [the mutineers] rush into our Camp on the 9th; it was a bold thing to do, so much so, that when they were in they were quite aback at their audacity. My guns were ridden over before I could get them into action, and I was very nearly polished off — Tombs saving my life by potting a Pandy [sepoy] who was in the act of splitting my skull. I was down on the ground, regularly done up, without a single thing to defend myself with. I have got great "kudos" for my conduct. This is it. The alarm went, and off I started with my two guns to a position laid down for them, when, to my astonishment, through the opening to my right, only fifty yards off, dashed a body of enemy cavalry.'

The mounted picquet of the Carabiniers, made up of largely untrained young troopers, immediately fled, leaving Hills alone to protect the gunners. Desperate situations called for desperate action.

'Now I tried to get my guns into action; but only got one unlimbered when they were upon me. I thought that by charging them I might make a commotion and give the guns time to load, so in I went at the front rank, cut down the first fellow, slashed the next across the face as hard as I could, then two sowars charged me. Both their horses crashed into mine at the same moment, and, of course, both horse and myself were sent flying. We went down at such a pace that I escaped the cuts made at me, one of them giving my jacket an awful slice just below the left arm — it only, however, cut the jacket.

'Well, I lay quite snug until all had passed over me, and then got up and looked about for my sword. I found it a full ten yards off. I had hardly got hold of it when these fellows returned, two on horseback. The first I wounded using a pistol, and dropped him from his horse. The second charged at me with his lance. I put it aside and caught him an awful gash on the head and face. I thought I had killed him. Apparently he must have clung to his horse, for he disappeared. The wounded man [whom Hills had shot] then came up, but got his skull split. Then came on the third man ... I found myself getting

17

very weak from want of breath, the fall from my horse having pumped me considerably, and my cloak, somehow or other, had got tightly fixed round my throat, and was actually choking me. I went, however, at the fellow and cut him on the shoulder, but some 'kupra' [cloth] on it apparently turned the blow. He managed to seize the hilt of my sword and twisted it out of my hand, and then we had a hand-to-hand fight, I punching his head with my fists, and he trying to cut me, but I was too close to him. Somehow or other I fell, and then was the time, fortunately for me, that Tombs came up and shot the fellow. I was so choked by my cloak, that move I could not until I got it loosened. By-the-bye, I forgot to say I fired at this chap twice, but the pistol snapped, and I was so enraged I drove it at the fellow's head, missing him, however. Then, when I got up, Tombs was so eager to get up to a mound near us, that I only picked up my sword and followed him.

'After being there some time, we came down again to look after the unlimbered gun which was left behind. When we got down, I saw the very man Tombs had saved me from, moving off with my pistol (the brute had only been wounded, and shammed dead). I told Tombs, and we went at him. After a little slashing and guarding on both sides, I rushed at him and thrust; he cleverly jumped aside and cut me on the head, knocking me down, not, however, stunning me, for I warded his next cut when down. Tombs, following him up, made him a pass, and up I jumped and had a slash at him, cutting him on the left wrist, nearly severing it. This made him turn round, and then Tombs ran him through. He very nearly knocked over Tombs, for he cut through his cap and puggrie, but fortunately did not even cut the skin. I fancy I am indebted again to Tombs for my life, for, although I might have got up again and fought, still I was bleeding like a pig, and, of course, would have had a bad chance.

'One thing, however, if Tombs had not been there the second time I should have fought more carefully. It was the wish to polish off the fellow before Tombs could get up to him that made me rush at him in the way I did. I wanted awfully to pick up the swords of the men I had killed as trophies, but I was getting very faint, and had to come to my tent as fast as I could; but before I got the wound bound up, the swords had been looted off. I lost an awful lot of blood, as two veins were cut through; but I fancy it did me good, keeping off inflammation. The wound was a beautiful one, just as if it had been done with a razor. It was four inches long, and down to the skull, a line being left on it; so I had a narrow escape.

'However, if I live to see the end of these mutinies, I shall have good reason to thank the 'sowars' for their courage — Tombs' name and mine having been sent up to the governor-general by the commander-in-chief, the latter recommending us 'worthy of the highest honour for distinguished bravery and gallantry'.

For this action in defending the guns Hills was mentioned in the despatch of Lieutenant–Colonel Mackenzie, GOC 1st Brigade Horse Artillery, 10 July 1857 and subsequently awarded the VC by Sir Colin Campbell, the C-in-C of India. His saviour, Major Tombs, received the same award.

James Hills went on to a long and distinguished career and retired as Lieutenant-General Sir James Hills-Johnes, having added his wife's surname to his. He was not the only VC in the family. His sister Isabella's husband, William Cubitt, was awarded the Victoria Cross for gallantry at Chinhat while serving with the 13th Bengal Native Infantry in June 1857. His nephew, Brigadier Lewis Pugh Evans, of the Black Watch gained the Victoria Cross at Zonnebeke, Belgium in October 1917.

In September 1915, aged 82, Hills-Johnes visited the Western Front in Belgium, travelling as far as the front line and coming under direct artillery fire. This grand old soldier died at his home on 3 January 1919, one of the millions of victims of the influenza pandemic.

Henry Tombs
The son of a major-general, Henry Tombs was the seventh son of 2nd Bengal Cavalry commander John Tombs. Born in Calcutta on 10 November 1825, Henry was educated at Haileybury, and commissioned from Addiscombe College into the Bengal Artillery. He served in the Gwalior War of 1843, the Sutlej Campaign of 1845-46 and the 1848-49 Punjab Campaign. By the outbreak of the Mutiny, he was a Major commanding the 2nd Troop of the 1st Brigade Bengal Horse Artillery at Meerut. On the way to join forces with Sir Henry Barnard's column on the advance to Delhi, he fought in a stiff fight at Ghazi-ud-din-Nagar on the left bank of the river Hindun. On the afternoon of 30 May, under a scorching hot sun, Tombs led his troop across the iron bridge and put the rebels to flight. In the process, he had his horse shot under him. This was to be the first of five horses killed while carrying him into action during the following four months.

Lord Frederick Roberts wrote about Henry Tombs in his autobiography, *Forty One Years in India*:

'Henry Tombs was an unusually handsome man and a thorough soldier … On 17 June, 1857, we were attacked from almost every direction – a manoeuvre intended to prevent our observing a battery which was being constructed close to the Igdah (mosque) situated on a hill to our right, from which to enfilade our position on the ridge. As it was very important to prevent the completion of this battery, Barnard ordered it to be attacked by two small columns, one commanded by Tombs of the Bengal Horse Artillery, the other by Reid. Tombs with 400 of 60th Rifles and 1st Bengal Fusiliers, 30 of the Guides Cavalry, 20 Sappers and miners, and our own troop of Horse Artillery, moved towards the enemy's left ... Tombs drove the rebels through a succession of gardens, till they reached the Idgah, where they made an obstinate but unavailing resistance. The gates of the mosque were blown open and thirty-nine defenders killed. Tombs himself was slightly wounded ... His gallantry in the attack in the Idgah was the talk of the camp ... He grasped the situation in a moment and issued orders without hesitation, inspiring all ranks with confidence in his power and capacity. He was something of a martinet and was more feared than liked by his men until they realise what a grand leader he was.'

As described by James Hills, Tombs arrived in the nick of time to twice rescue his subaltern and was recommended for the Victoria Cross.

He was also prominent at the battle of Najagarh on 25 August when the rebels attempted to intercept the siege-train from Firozpur but were driven off by the artillery commanded by Henry Tombs. For this he was Mentioned in Despatches by Brigadier John Nicholson. In fact he received four MiDs published in *The London Gazette* from October 1857 to January 1858. Although there is no record of when and where Tombs received his VC, it is probable that he invested at the same time as James Hills, by Sir Colin Campbell in December.

After the attack on Delhi, Henry Tombs was active in many actions throughout 1857 and 1858. He was promoted to brevet lieutenant-colonel in July 1858 and received a eulogy by Lord Panmure, the Secretary of State for War, in the House of Commons. Following the Mutiny, Tombs was promoted and commanded the right column of the Bhutan Field Force in 1865. Afterwards he was appointed ADC to Queen Victoria and was awarded the KCB in 1868. In 1869, he married Georgina Janet Stirling, whose mother was the cousin of Ross Mangles, another Mutiny VC. It is quite a coincidence that both Tombs and Hills should become related through marriage to fellow Mutiny VCs.

In 1874, Sir Henry Tombs became so ill with what was probably cancer that he travelled to Paris for an operation. The prognosis was not good and on reaching England he was told it was incurable. He moved to the Isle of Wight and died there on 2 August 1874 at the early age of 49.

James Thompson

Rifleman James Thompson was born in 1829 at Hadley, near Yoxall in Staffordshire. He worked as a farm labourer before enlisting in the 1st/60th

Rifles on 30 January 1852. Present at the uprising in Meerut, he fought at Budli-ki-Serai and the defence of Delhi Ridge. On 9 July, Captain F.R. Wilton led his Company into the Subzee-Mandi and was surprised by a party of mutineers which appeared from a courtyard and surrounded him. The day was wet and his pistol misfired leaving him defenceless. James Thompson spotted the danger and rushed forward, bayoneting two of the assailants and chasing off the rest.

At some point in the assault of 14 September, Thompson was wounded in the left arm. This was amputated and he was invalided out of the Army. Thompson was elected for the Victoria Cross by his fellow riflemen in a ballot. His citation was published in *The London Gazette* on 6 January 1860 and he received his Cross from the Queen at Windsor Castle on 9 November 1860. Meanwhile, his old captain had not forgotten his bravery and gave him a job as a gamekeeper on the Wilton family estate in Scotland. In 1865, he returned to the West Midlands and worked as a colliery watchman. By 1890, poverty and infirmity forced him to sell his VC and the following year, he died in Walsall at the age of 61.

Richard Wadeson

Richard Wadeson was one of that rare breed who rose from private to commanding officer of his regiment. Born in Gaythorse near Lancaster on 31 July 1826, Wadeson enlisted at Plymouth with the 75th (Stirlingshire) Regiment on 17 November 1843. For such a young soldier, promotion came quickly; first to corporal in 1846, then sergeant in 1848. The following year, the 75th embarked for India and in early 1854, he was appointed sergeant-major.

The 75th made forced marches from their base at Kussauli in the Himalayas to join Barnard's column at Umballa. During June and July, they were constantly in action, repelling the frequent attacks by the rebels. On 2 June, Wadeson was commissioned without purchase to ensign and advanced to lieutenant on 19 September. This rapid rise may have had more to do with the high casualty list caused by fighting and sickness than Wadeson's outstanding officer qualifications. Nonetheless, he performed his VC action on 18 July at the nearby cluster of buildings called Sabzi Mandi. In an attack to push out the rebels, he saved Private Farrell from being cut down by a *sowar* by bayoneting the rebel. Later he rescued Private Barry when he, too, lay helpless under attack by an enemy cavalryman. For these acts, Wadeson was recommended for the Victoria Cross, which was gazetted on 24 December 1858. Unfortunately, there is no record of any presentation, which could mean that he was one of those disappointed recipients to receive their VCs through the post.

Lieutenant Wadeson took part in the assault on Delhi and was wounded on the first day. On 11 March 1859, he was appointed adjutant until he was promoted Captain in late 1864. He was in Canada during the Fenian disturbances of 1866-67 and served in Gibraltar, Singapore, Hong Kong, Mauritius and the Cape. In 1873, the 75th returned home and on 18 December 1875, Richard Wadeson was promoted to lieutenant-colonel of his regiment.[11] As a reward for his outstanding achievement, he was given the appointment of Major and Lieutenant-Governor of the Royal Hospital at Chelsea, which is where he died on 24 January 1885.

John Divane

Galway-born Rifleman John Divane (probably a misspelling of Duane), enlisted in the 60th Rifles in April 1854 and, from the start of his military service, he was a problem soldier. Periods of detention and forfeiture of pay lasted up to 1857, when he seems to have disciplined himself. He was born in November 1823, so he was an older than usual recruit. As the 60th had been in India since 1845, he was immediately sent to join them. Divane was awarded the VC for an action on 10 September as the Delhi Field Force made its moves prior to the assault on the city. In the briefest of citations, it reads: 'For distinguished gallantry in heading a successful charge made by the Beeloochee (Baluchi) and Sikh troops on one of the enemy's trenches before Delhi, on 10th September 1857. He leaped out of our trenches, closely followed by the Native Troops, and was shot down from the top of the enemy's breastworks.'

He was elected by his peers for the Victoria Cross, which was announced in *The London Gazette* on 20 January 1860. Divane was later badly wounded, probably in the assault on Delhi and had his leg amputated. The result was that he was invalided out of the Army in January 1858. He returned to England and received his Cross from the Queen at Windsor Castle on 9 November 1860. He spent his last impoverished years as a fish hawker on the streets of Penzance where he died on 1 December 1888.

Patrick Green

Another Galway-born VC recipient was Patrick Green, born in 1824. Little is known of his service record other than that he enlisted in the 75th Regiment and arrived in India with his regiment in 1849. On 11 September, he was on picquet duty at Qudsia Bagh, a garden complex sited north of the walls of Delhi. In what was part of the build-up to the assault, the British had moved men closer to the city and the overgrown Qudsia Bagh was an area heavily fought over. A large body of rebels entered the gardens and

22

attacked Green's picquet and, as he fell back, he saw one of the skirmishers lying wounded; going forward, he managed to carry his comrade to safety. For this he was awarded the Victoria Cross. On 28 July 1858, Green was invested with his Cross by Sir Colin Campbell at Allalabad. He later reached the rank of Colour-Sergeant before leaving the army. He died on 19 July 1889 in Cork.

William Sutton

William Sutton was born in the village of Ightham, Kent in 1830.[12] It would seem that he and his siblings were orphaned when he was about 11 and he was brought up by his older brothers. Rather than follow them as an agricultural labourer, he enlisted in the 60th Rifles as a bugler. Along with his fellow riflemen, he was active in the defence of the Ridge. Ensign Alfred Heathcote referred to Sutton in a letter he wrote on 6 August:

'At 10.30 pm (1 August) when it was pitch dark, an order was sent me to take my section to the breastwork in front of our right heavy batteries. We had to cross over very rocky ground, and in crossing the ridge we came in for their grape, shrapnel and musketry ... The air was every minute lighted with the fuses of the enemy's shells whizzing over our heads, then flashed right in front from their muskets, and the sharp ping of their bullets with the bursting of the shrapnel close among us and in our rear.

'At last we got safely down to the breastwork which the enemy was attacking. Volley after volley was poured in by the enemy ... Then they would shout and charge, when up would jump our men and give them a volley that would fairly stagger "John Sepoy". This went on all night, their heavy guns and ours playing over our heads. The enemy occupied a breastwork about forty yards in front of us, and they were in there in such numbers that we dare not charge them with our few. It was then a young bugler of ours, named Sutton, without any order from me, got upon the parapet of the breastwork and sounded our "Regimental Call", the "Retire" and the "Double". I was fearfully angry, and told him that I had a good mind to cut him down, and why did he do it, for, as he knew, the Rifles never retreat. His answer was, "Never mind, sir, you'll see what will come of it." Sure enough on they came out of their breastwork with their bayonets fixed, thinking we were on the go, when I gave the order to fire and the guns opened on them with canister and grape. Seeing that it was a dodge of ours to draw them on, they hastily retreated with heavy loss ... and then with a cheer we charged them and drove them from their position.'

Sutton received his VC recommendation for taking part in the night-time reconnaissance of 13 September of one of the breaches made in the city's walls by the British artillery. This was a highly risky task as the patrol had to slip through the advanced enemy trenches and climb down into the dry moat in front of the city walls. It would appear that William Sutton's task was to climb up to the wall and check on the breach. The artillery kept up a constant barrage which kept the rebels occupied and it was with some relief that the patrol returned safely.

Sutton was elected by ballot by his comrades for the Victoria Cross. His citation was published on 20 January 1860 and he went to Windsor Castle to be presented with his Cross by the Queen on 9 November 1860. William Sutton was one of seventeen VCs invested that day at a parade in the Home Park in front of Windsor Castle. This would be the last time the Queen presented the VC for fourteen years, leaving it to the General Officers Commanding to perform this function. This abrupt break is explained by the death of her husband, Prince Albert, on 14 December 1861, after which the Queen went into a prolonged period of mourning, shunning her public duties.

Little is known of Sutton's subsequent career but he appears to have been with the Antrim Militia in 1872, where he received a replacement Cross for the original that he had lost. He returned to Ightham and, rather typically of worn-out veterans, he ended his days in the Union workhouse, dying on 16 February 1888.

Chapter 2

The Capture of Delhi and Pursuit of the Rebels
August to September 1857

The hastily raised British force of 4,000 men had successfully occupied the Delhi Ridge but was far too weak to attempt to retake the city itself. Faced by over 30,000 mutineers they were hard-pressed to keep hold of this tenuous foothold so close to the city.[1] As reinforcements gradually arrived from the Punjab, including a siege train of thirty-two guns and 2,000 men under the command of Brigadier-General John Nicholson, it was now thought possible that Delhi could be taken, despite the barely improved disparity in numbers. It was the presence of Nicholson, a charismatic and authoritarian figure, which gave backbone to the rather indecisive command of newly-promoted Major General Archdale Wilson.

At the relatively young age of 34, Nicholson had the energy and drive to change the direction of the siege. He also possessed something that many of the HEIC officers lacked, namely a devotion from his fiercely loyal men bordering on fanaticism. As Lord Roberts later wrote: 'Nicholson was a born leader, and this was felt by every officer and man in the column before he had been amongst them many days.'

ROHTAK

Having arrived at the Delhi Ridge, Nicholson became concerned about keeping open communications with the Punjab. He had brought as his cavalry commander one Captain William Hodson, who had organised a new regiment named the Guides Cavalry, into which he took officers whose own regiments had mutinied. Two of these were the brothers Charles and Hugh Gough, formerly of the Bengal Light Cavalry. Freshly attired in khaki tunics and red turbans, the new regiment was manned with wild frontier tribesmen from the north-west.

25

On the night of 14-15 August, a cavalry force consisting of 103 Guides Cavalry, 233 Hodson's Irregular Horse and twenty-five Jind Horse left the British lines. They had received intelligence that a party of the enemy had left the city with the intention of threatening the British lines of communication, particularly the important Grand Trunk Road.

By noon on the 15th, they reached the village of Khurkowdeh, where they learned that several of the enemy were resting. Hodson surrounded the village and took the mutineers by surprise. A large party, however, took refuge in the upper story of a house and defended themselves desperately. After a fierce fight, in which Hugh Gough was wounded, the rebels were overpowered. Those who survived were summarily executed.

On hearing that the main body of the enemy was heading towards Medinha, Hodson led his men to Rohtak to intercept them. On the 17th they found armed men ranged in front of the old fort and, in a brief skirmish, beat them off leaving thirteen dead. At 7am the next day, a large body of horsemen suddenly appeared from the town followed by 1,000 sepoys. Hodson's men quickly mounted up and the first twenty or so made a charge to stall the attackers. The rest formed themselves into three lines and made the appearance that they were retiring. The rain had been heavy the previous day and Hodson wanted to draw the enemy into the open and a comparatively dry area. The ruse worked and the enemy charged after them. Hodson ordered his men to turn and they rushed at their attackers. The enemy was taken by surprise and fled back to Rohtak. In the pursuit, the rebels lost fifty killed and many wounded before they scattered. The three days of fighting had caused only six of Hodson's force to be wounded. Overall, the foray had been a success and both Gough brothers were singled out for praise.

Charles Gough

In the fierce fight at Khurkowdeh, Charles and Hugh found themselves fighting side by side within the confines of the building. When Hugh was wounded, Charles came to his rescue, killing two sepoys who were at the point of killing his fallen brother. By the end of the Mutiny, Charles Gough had performed many more acts of gallantry, which were reflected in his citation published on 21 October 1859:

'Charles John Stanley Gough, Major, 5th Bengal European Cavalry. Dates of Acts of Bravery: 15 Aug.1857; 18 Aug.1857; 27 Jan.1858; 23 Feb.1858.

'First, for gallantry in an affair at Khurkowdah, nears Rohtuck, on 15th Aug.1857, in which he saved his brother, who was wounded, and killed two of the enemy.

'Secondly, for gallantry on the 18th Aug., when he led a troop of the Guides Cavalry in a charge and cut down two of the enemy's sowars, with one of whom he had a desperate hand-to-hand combat.

'Thirdly, for gallantry on the 27th Jan.1858, at Shumshahbad, where, in a charge, he attacked one of the enemy's leaders, and pierced him with his sword, which was carried out of his hand in the mêlée. He defended himself with his revolver, and shot two of the enemy.

'Fourthly, for gallantry on 23rd Feb., at Meangunge, where he came to the assistance of Brevet Major O.H. St.George Anson, and killed his opponent, immediately afterwards cutting down another of the enemy in the same manner.'

Charles Gough was born in Chittagong, Bengal on 28 January 1832, and was commissioned in the Bengal Cavalry at the age of sixteen. He was immediately involved in the 2nd Sikh War in the army commanded by his uncle, Field Marshal Hugh, First Viscount Gough. His first taste of battle was the ignominious defeat at Ramnuggar on 22 November 1848. He took part in the battles of Sandulpar, Chillianwala and Gujarat, and was Mentioned in Despatches. On 1 September 1849, he was appointed to the 8th Bengal Light Cavalry and promoted to Lieutenant.

He took sick leave on 8 February 1859 and returned to England which enabled him to receive his Cross from the Queen at Windsor Castle on 4 January 1860. Like his brother Hugh, Charles was transferred into the newly-formed 19th (Princess of Wales's Own) Hussars, before joining his old resurrected regiment, now named 5th Bengal Cavalry on 26 May 1864.

In 1869, he married and his second son, Johnny, was awarded the Victoria Cross for gallantry in Somaliland in 1903. He retired as Major General Sir Charles Gough and lived in the family home in Tipperary, Ireland, where he died in 1912.[2]

THE DELHI ASSAULT

With the arrival of the decisive John Nicholson, the lacklustre and inexperienced Major General Wilson gradually passed the reins of command to his number two.[3] Nicholson proposed assaulting Delhi in about four weeks, confiding in his staff officer, Lieutenant (later Field Marshal) Frederick Roberts: 'Delhi must be taken and it is absolutely essential that this should be done at once; and if Wilson hesitates any longer, I intend to propose at today's meeting that he should be superseded.' It was a statement that shocked Roberts with its mutinous intention of removing the commanding officer. Fortunately, Wilson agreed to

27

Nicholson's plans and a coup was avoided.

To prepare for the attack, the mutineers had to be pushed back from their positions between the city and the Ridge. Comparatively few in numbers, the British attack was focused on the north face of the Delhi defences between the Water Bastion, by the River Jumna, and the Moree (Mori) Bastion a mile away to the west, with the Kashmir Gate in between as the prime target.

For just over a week, the sappers worked under heavy fire from the city to build emplacements for the fifty-four guns and mortars. The most distant battery was 700 yards away, with the closest only 140 yards. As they were completed, the artillerymen brought up their cannons and mortars and began bombarding the twelve-feet-thick walls. Concentrating their fire, the artillery made two substantial breaches between the Water Bastion and Kashmir Gate. The reconnaissance on the night of 13 September persuaded Wilson and Nicholson that the attack should proceed the following morning.

John Nicholson was in overall command of the assault which was to be made by five columns. He would lead the 1st Column storming the breach near the Kashmir Gate. It was made up of 1,000 men of 75th Regiment, 1st Bengal Fusiliers and 2nd Punjab Infantry. The 2nd Column, under the command of Brigadier H.R. Jones, would attack the breach near the Water Bastion and comprised 850 men from 8th (The King's) Regiment, 2nd Bengal Fusiliers and 4th Sikhs, after which No.1 and No.2 Columns would link up, turn right and make for the Kabul Gate. The 3rd Column of 950 men, commanded by Colonel George Campbell of 52nd (Oxfordshire & Buckinghamshire) Regiment, was made up of 52nd Regiment, Kumaon Battalion and 1st Punjab Infantry. Their objective was to storm the Kashmir Gate once it had been blown up, advance into the heart of the city and ultimately link up with the other columns. No.4 Column under Major Reid would be waiting to pour through the captured Kabul Gate and join the 1st and 2nd columns. The 5th Column commanded by Brigadier Longfield was kept in reserve to act as reinforcement where needed. The plan was audacious, for disease, fatigue and fighting had considerably reduced their numbers but there was general belief in the camp that Delhi would be taken.

The Kashmir Gate
Probably the VC feat most associated with the assault on Delhi was the blowing up of the huge double doors that blocked the entrance to the Kashmir Gate. The whole operation was reliant on this near-suicidal attempt, which was accurately termed a 'forlorn hope'. lieutenant-colonel

Richard Baird Smith, commander of the Bengal Sappers and Miners, selected Lieutenant Duncan Home to lead the 'explosion party' made up of three other men carrying canvas bags containing 25lbs of black powder. The bags would be laid against the doors with fuses exposed ready for firing. Following right behind was the 'firing party' of six men led by Lieutenant Philip Salkeld. They carried a slow match and small sacks of sand to hold the explosive bags firmly against the doors.

At first light on the morning of 14 September, Wilson and Baird Smith had taken positions where they could view the attack.[4] In particular they would watch out for 'the forlorn hope' party as they faced almost certain death. Led by Home and Salkeld, the two parties made their way from the ruined Ludlow Castle, about half a mile north of the Kashmir Gate, taking advantage of any remaining cover until their reached the open ground leading to the gate. Moving as fast as their 25-pound loads would allow, they reached the deserted outer gate and were joined by skirmishers from the 60th Rifles. Now they had to negotiate the timber bridge crossing the ditch, which had been made more hazardous as much of the cross planking had been removed.

Braving a hail of fire, Home was first across the bridge, dumping his canvas powder bag hard against the right leaf of the door and jumping for cover in the ditch. Although Lieutenant Home wrote a report, it was Sergeant Smith's account that has the authentic feel for the danger and noise of the action:

'I went on, and only Lieut Salkeld and Sergt Burgess were there; Lieut Home and the bugler had jumped into the ditch, and Sergeant Carmichael was killed as he went up with his powder on his shoulder, evidently having been shot from the wicket while crossing the broken part of the bridge along one of the beams. I placed my bag, and then, at great risk, reached Carmichael's bag from in front of the wicket, placed it, arranged the fuse for the explosion and reported all ready for Lieut Salkeld, who held the slow match.[5] In stooping down to light the quick match, he put out his foot, and was shot through the thigh from the wicket, and in falling had the presence of mind to hold out the slow match, and told me to fire the charge. Burgess was next to him and took it. I told him to fire the charge and keep cool. He turned round and said, 'It won't go off, sir; it has gone out, sir.' I gave him a box of lucifers, and as he took them, he let them fall into my hand, he being shot through the body at the wicket also, and fell over after Lieut Salkeld. I was then left alone, and keeping close to the charge, seeing where the others were shot, I struck a light, when the port-fire in my fuse went off in my face, the light not having gone out as we thought.

'I took my gun and jumped into the ditch, but before I had reached the ground the charge went off, and filled the ditch with smoke so I saw no one. I turned while in the act of jumping, so that my back would come to the wall to save me from falling. I stuck close to the wall, and by that I escaped being smashed to pieces, only getting a severe bruise on the leg, the leather helmet saving my head.'

As soon as the door was blown off, Home ordered Bugler Robert Hawthorne of the 52nd Regiment to sound the 'advance' for Colonel Campbell's column to come on and take the Gate. Despite the dust, Hawthorne stood in the centre of the ditch, moistened his lips and sounded the agreed signal. About fifty yards to the rear, Campbell strained to hear the bugle call above the tumult of battle. Sending his orderly bugler forward to listen, he received a wave of acknowledgement, and drawing his sword, led his column forward.

Colonel Baird Smith was unstinting in his praise for this operation while Major General Archdale Wilson went even further. As he was General Officer Commanding, he felt empowered to recommend the Victoria Cross to Home, Salkeld, Smith and Hawthorne.[6] Salkeld, who was mortally wounded, evidently learned of this before he died on 10 October.

Strictly speaking, Home, Salkeld and Smith were not eligible to receive the VC as they were not members of Her Majesty's Army. This problem was rectified by a new Warrant dated 29 October 1857, which included members of the HEIC. It did not get around the fact that Home and Salkeld both died before the Queen had approved of their awards and the original VC Warrant made no provision for posthumous awards. It is one of the anomalies of the Victoria Cross that Home and Salkeld were regarded as special cases and their Crosses awarded and sent to their families.[7] Carmichael and Burgess would probably also have been decorated, but they had the misfortune to die before Archdale Wilson could confer the award. All the Indian sappers received the Indian Order of Merit, promotion and grants of land.

Duncan Home

Born in Jubbulpore, Central Provinces on 10 June 1828, Duncan Charles Home was the son of Major General Richard Home of the Bengal Army. As with many sons of serving Indian officers, he was sent to England at the early age of eight for his education. As planned, he progressed to the HEIC Seminary at Addiscombe and passed out head of his class in July 1846. After further instruction with the Royal Engineers at Chatham, he returned to India as a subaltern in the 3rd Company, Bengal Engineers. He arrived in time to take part in the final battle at Gujurat in the Punjab Campaign (Second Sikh War) in 1849.

Home spent five years working more as a civil engineer than a military man, supervising the construction of canals in the Punjab. In 1854, he was promoted to Lieutenant. When news of the outbreak of mutiny reached the Punjab, Lieutenant Home was delegated to select 160 of his best men, now named the Punjab Sappers, and take them to the British Camp at Delhi. They arrived on 20 August and Home and his canal diggers were immediately assigned to prepare gun emplacements for the forthcoming assault.

Duncan Home had been with one of the reconnaissance parties that crept forward to examine the breaches in the walls. When he returned at midnight, he learned that he was to lead the 'explosion party'. Once the door had been blown, Home remained in the ditch while Campbell's No.3 column dashed across the bridge and through the Gate. Pausing to make sure the wounded were taken care of, he climbed out of the ditch and followed Campbell's men into the city. He caught up with them locked in a savage hand-to-hand battle amongst the narrow streets. Unable to join in the fighting, he found a sheltered corner and fell asleep, having been awake for over thirty-six hours.

When he awoke, he rejoined the advance and was slightly wounded. For the next few days, Home was with the troops as they closed in on the Royal Palace. Repeating his feat at the Kashmir Gate, Home dashed forward, placed an explosive charge and blew in the doors. By 20 September, the city was in British hands and the surviving mutineers streamed away to the south and east.

Home now joined one of the columns that went in pursuit of mutineers. He was appointed Chief Field Engineer in Colonel Greathed's column which left Delhi on 24 September. On 28th, they caught up with a strong force of rebels at Bolandshahr and, after a sharp fight, captured the town. From there, cavalry patrols were sent out to scour the surrounding countryside and one reported that a small, deserted fort at Malagarh had been used as an arsenal. They also reported that it was in a dangerous condition with large quantities of munitions scattered all about.

Duncan Home was given the task of blowing up the fortifications and making the area safe. For the next three days he worked with his sappers and some men of the 9th Lancers sorting through what could be safely saved and what should be destroyed. On the third day, with his work nearly completed, he was killed. In a letter to Home's brother, fellow-Bengal Engineer Lieutenant Arthur Lang described what happened:

'I saw him run up to the slow-match with his port-fire in his hand. Heaven only knows how, but instantaneously the mine sprung, to our horror! We rushed down and called all men to dig, but after a moment I looked round to see if I could see him anywhere near, and in a hollow some fifteen yards off I found your poor brother's body. He must have been killed instantly … Fancy escaping from the blowing of the Cashmere [sic] Gate, where he and Salkeld earned the Victoria Cross to meet his end in exploding mines before a deserted fort. It is not now half and hour since the accident occurred.'

Duncan Home's VC was sent to his parents. Sometime in the 1920s it was lost when the son of the owner took the VC outside the house to play soldiers with it in a field. Despite intensive searches then and later, it has never been found.

Philip Salkeld

Born on 13 October 1830 to a Dorset parson, Philip Salkeld was the fourth son of thirteen children. Despite financial constraints due to the size of the family, a sponsor was found and Philip was sent to Addiscombe, emerging with a commission into the Bengal Engineers. Like Duncan Home, he was employed in India in various canal and road construction projects. In 1853, he was stationed at Meerut and worked on a stretch of the Grand Trunk Road. In 1856, he moved to Delhi as Executive Engineer with the Public Works. This meant that he was in Delhi when the Mutiny broke out and the rebels ran amok, killing all Europeans they could find. He narrowly escaped death in the early rioting and found himself with other survivors near the Kashmir Gate. With the enemy closing in, he led a group to the top of the bastion and helped form an escape rope from sword-belts. Under heavy fire, he managed to escape through the shanties and scrub north of the walls. He teamed up with a small party of four officers, one of whom was Lieutenant George Forrest from the Delhi Magazine, who had been shot in the hand and was in a state of shock. Also in the party was his wife, who had been shot through the shoulder and his three daughters, the youngest being nine. Together they suffered a torrid journey in which they had to wade across the Ganges Canal, the River Jumna and were robbed by bandits. Salkeld made the journey barefoot, having given his shoes to one of the girls. After considerable help from friendly villagers, they were eventually rescued by Lieutenant Hugh Gough with about forty loyal sowars of the 3rd Cavalry.[8]

Recovering from his ordeal, Salkeld returned to the Delhi Ridge with Wilson's Meerut Column. When the Ridge was occupied, Salkeld's sappers constructed artillery batteries by the Hindoo Rao's House, a focus of heavy fighting during the siege. On 22 June, he took a party of sappers and blew up an important bridge carrying the Grand Trunk Road over the Nujufgurth Jheel drain. In the early hours of 14 September, he was awoken and told to report to Lieutenant Home, who explained to him of the planned attack on the Kashmir Gate and that he would be second-in-command.

As he lay wounded in the ditch, covered with dust and debris from the explosion, Salkeld was comforted by Home and helped by Sergeant John Smith. He was taken to the field hospital, where his left arm was amputated. The insanitary conditions and shock of an amputation without anaesthetic contributed to Salkeld's death on 10 October. He learned that he had been rewarded with the Victoria Cross and one of General Wilson's aides pinned a length of crimson ribbon to the barely conscious Salkeld's bed-shirt. The joint citation for the deceased Engineers appeared in *The London Gazette* on 18 June 1858:

'Duncan Charles Home, Lieutenant; Philip Salkeld, Lieutenant, Bengal Engineers. Date of act of bravery: 14 Sept 1857. (Upon whom the Victoria Cross was provisionally conferred by Major General Sir Archdale Wilson, Bart, KCB). For their conspicuous bravery in the performance of the desperate duty of blowing in the Cashmere Gate of the Fortress of Delhi, in broad daylight, under heavy fire of musketry, on the morning of 14 Sept 1857, preparatory to the assault. Would have been recommended to Her Majesty for confirmation in that distinction had they survived.'

Both fathers of Home and Salkeld received their sons VCs by post on 7 July 1858.

Philip Salkeld had saved £1,000, a considerable amount, which he intended to send home to help his brothers' education at the Addiscombe Seminary. When the rioters looted and destroyed the London and Delhi Bank, the money was lost. A fund was raised, which was generously oversubscribed. Salkeld's brothers received their education and the balance went to erect a handsome memorial in the churchyard of his father's church at Fontmell Magna, Dorset.

John Smith

John Smith proved to be the typical tough and reliable NCO, as depicted in many British war films. He was born in Ticknall, Derbyshire, in February 1814, the sixth of eight children. He followed his father's and uncle's profession as a cordwainer (maker of boots and shoes). At the age of 22, driven by boredom, unemployment or a family dispute, he accepted a Recruiting Sergeant's drink and a shilling and he was on his way to the HEIC depot at Chatham to start his eighteen-month engineering training.

In 1839, he endured the six month sea-voyage to India and joined the 3rd Company, Bengal Sapper and Miners. Soon he was promoted to sergeant and took part in the First Afghan War in 1841 and the Sutlej campaign of 1845-6. It was at the Battle of Gujarat where he would have met Lieutenant Duncan Home for the first time. He remained in the Punjab for a number of years working on a variety of civil projects.

He was serving at Roorkee, a town on the banks of the Ganges Canal, when news of the outbreak at Meerut reached the cantonment. Colonel Baird Smith quickly organised boats to carry several hundred loyal sappers and infantrymen under the command of Captain Fraser, and sailed the seventy miles down the Canal to reach Meerut on 13 May. The reaction to the appearance of Fraser's force was hostile and the officers at the Meerut garrison insisted on disarming these native troops that had come to help them. Bewildered and dismayed at this reaction, some of the native troops killed Fraser and fled, many to join the mutineers at Delhi.

All that remained at Meerut were John Smith with forty-five NCOs and privates, and 124 Indian sappers. Two weeks later, Smith's party joined Archdale Wilson's column on its way to join the Delhi Field Force.

As Sergeant Smith recalled when the 'forlorn hope' party approached the Kashmir Gate, it was, 'my duty to bring up the rear, and see that none of them remained behind. Lieut Salkeld had passed through the temporary (outer) gate with Sergts Carmichael and Burgess, but four of the natives had stopped behind the above gate and refused to go on. I had to put down my bag and take my gun, and threaten to shoot them, when Lieut Salkeld came running back and said, "Why the hell don't you come on?" I told him that there were four men behind the gate, and that I was going to shoot them. He said, "Shoot them, damn their eyes, shoot them!" I said, "You hear the orders, and I will shoot you," raising my gun slowly to the 'present' to give fair time, when two men went on Lieut Salkeld said, "Don't shoot; with your bag it will be enough".'

After Smith landed in the ditch, narrowly escaping death from the premature explosion, he set about checking the other survivors. Burgess was beyond help but Salkeld was still alive. Smith bound up the wounded officer's thigh and arm and made him as comfortable as possible. He then fetched a stretcher, now in short supply due to the numbers of casualties, and ordered Hawthorne to remain with Salkeld until he was safely brought to the field hospital.

Sergeant Smith then assisted in clearing the debris away from the Gate. The door that had been blown up was intact and was dragged and laid across the damaged bridge so that the British guns could be pulled into the city.

34

After the recapture of Delhi, Smith joined Brigadier George Barker's flying column, which was on the march for the next eighteen months.

He was gazetted with his VC on 27 April 1858, two months before the announcements of Home and Salkeld. This would indicate that there was still some hesitation about awarding the VC posthumously. There is no information when Smith received his Cross. When he died from dysentery on 26 June 1864, at the age of 50, he left his medals to his wife; their whereabouts is unknown.[9] A memorial to John Smith was unveiled on 18 May 2014, at Ticknall.

Robert Hawthorne

Born into poverty in 1812, Irishman Robert Hawthorne was already working as a labourer at the age of 10. At the age of 14, he enlisted as a boy soldier in the 52nd Regiment and saw service in the West Indies, Canada and Ireland. In 1853, the regiment was sent to India and took part in the operations on Delhi Ridge.

Once the city had been taken, the 52nd was relegated to guarding the empty city while flying columns were sent off in pursuit. Hawthorne's citation appeared in *The London Gazette* dated 27 April 1858:

'Bugler Hawthorne, who accompanied the explosion party, not only performed the dangerous duty on which he was employed, but previously attached himself to Lieutenant Salkeld, of the Engineers, when dangerously wounded, bound up his wounds under heavy musketry fire, and had him removed without further injury.'

This is somewhat at variance with Sergeant Smith's version but no doubt they both tended to Salkeld. Hawthorne's moment of glory had gone and he elected to leave the army on his return to England on 20 June 1861. Like John Smith, there does not appear to have been any investiture ceremony.

Hawthorne retired to Manchester and was employed as a porter at the bank of Cunliffe, Brooks and Co. He married and had five children. When he died on 2 February 1879, his old regiment learned of his passing and arranged for a funeral with full military honours. His VC medal group was purchased by the officers of the 52nd and is on display at the Rifles Museum, Winchester. Sadly, his headstone was removed in 1950s when the cemetery was levelled.

Henry Smith

A fellow member of the 52nd to be awarded the VC was Lance Corporal Henry Smith, who received an immediate recommendation by Colonel

Campbell for saving the life of a wounded comrade under heavy fire. As part of No.3 column, Smith had charged through the smoke and rubble of the Kashmir Gate and fought his way to the Chandni Chouk (Silver Bazaar), where it was planned to link up with the other columns. It met with such fierce resistance that Campbell's men fell back and regrouped at the Bagam Bagh for eighty minutes. Pressure again forced the column to retire to St James's Church, which they were able to hold. It was during this retirement that Henry Smith performed his lifesaving action and was mentioned in Campbell's despatch of 16 September. In General Wilson's General Orders of 21 September it was declared that Smith had been awarded the Victoria Cross. He was gazetted on 24 April, 1858, the same date as John Smith and Robert Hawthorne but, like them, there appears to have no formal presentation of the VC.

Smith was born in Thames Ditton in 1825 but little is known of his subsequent life, other than that he attained the rank of sergeant and chose to remain in India. He died at the age of 36 during an epidemic of cholera at Gwalior on 18 August 1862 and was buried in a mass unmarked grave the same day.

George Waller

George Waller was born at West Horsley, Surrey, on 1 June 1827 and enlisted as a boy soldier with the 39th (Dorset) Regiment in 1843. He transferred the following year to the 60th Rifles and sailed for India in 1845. He took part in the Second Sikh War and fought at the battles of Mooltan and Gujarat. He also served on the North-West Frontier in 1849-50 during the sporadic fighting against the Afghan tribes.

During the defence of the Delhi Ridge he was wounded during the desperate fighting on the night of 19 June, but recovered sufficiently to take part in the attack on 14 September. His citation, published in *The London Gazette* dated 20 January 1860, reads: 'For conspicuous bravery on 14th of September 1857, in charging and capturing the enemy's guns near the Cabul Gate; and again, on 18th of September 1857, in the repulse of a sudden attack made by the enemy on a gun near the Chaundney Chouk [sic]. Elected by the Non-Commissioned Officers of the Regiment.'

George Waller returned to Britain after the Mutiny and received his VC from the Queen at Windsor Castle on 9 November 1860, along with Stephen Garvin, William Sutton, John Divane and James Thompson. Waller was discharged from the Army on 7 March 1865 and became a Permanent Staff Instructor with the 13th Sussex Rifle Volunteers until his death at Cuckfield in Sussex on 10 January 1877.

THE BALLOT

It was Prince Albert who suggested the Ballot, which was inserted as Clause 13 in the original Warrant. He probably had in mind the Charge of the Light Brigade; in a gallant act performed by a body of men, not all could be awarded the Victoria Cross. Instead it was accepted that the officers would choose one of their number, with one NCO and two privates from the other ranks. In fact the Light Brigade made their selections without recourse to Clause 13 and the VC ballot was not used in the Crimean War. Instead, the Indian Mutiny saw the first use of the VC ballot when the 60th Rifles became the first unit to use it for their part in the siege and assault at Delhi.[10]

Alfred Heathcote

The last of the quartet elected by the 60th Rifles was Alfred Spencer Heathcote. He was born in Winchester on 29 March 1832, the first of four children born to Henry Spencer Heathcote and his wife, Ann (née Currie). He was educated at the town's famous Winchester College. He was obviously a young man with a wanderlust and the money to indulge it, for when he left school, he sailed for Australia during the Gold Rush of 1851. Stopping at Christchurch, New Zealand, he decided to purchase 500 acres of land, but soon tired of farming and continued on to Australia. He staked a claim at Bendigo and purchased land in Melbourne, which was a major boomtown during the Gold Rush.

Heathcote either did not make his fortune or he wanted to explore more of the world, for he served on board an East Indiaman and sailed to the USA, Mexico, China and Singapore. After five years, he returned to the UK and, with parental influence and money, was commissioned into the prestigious 60th Rifles as an Ensign on 16 May 1856. His first posting in India was to Meerut, where he saw the outbreak first-hand. Heathcote was very prominent during the assault and Frederick Roberts wrote in his memoir of the Delhi attack:

'Home of the Engineers, hero of the Kashmir Gate exploit, first advanced with some sappers and blew in the outer gate [of the Palace]. At this, the last struggle for the capture of Delhi, I wished to be present, so attached myself for the occasion to a party of the 60th Rifles, under the command of Ensign Alfred Heathcote. As soon as the smoke of the explosion cleared away, the 60th, supported by the 4th Punjab Infantry, sprang through the gateway; but we did not get very far for there was a second door beyond, chained and barred, which was with difficulty forced open, and the whole part rushed in. The recesses in the long passage which led to the Palace buildings were crowded with wounded men, but there was very little opposition; only a few fanatics still held out. One of these – a Mahomedan sepoy in the uniform of a Grenadier of the 37th Native Infantry – stood quietly about thirty yards up the passage with his musket on his hip. As we approached he slowly raised his weapon and fired sending a bullet through McQueen's helmet. The brave fellow then advanced at the charge and was, of course, shot down.'

Heathcote continued to take part in many actions in Oudh and Rohilkund during the following year and was promoted to Lieutenant on 22 June 1859. Alfred Heathcote was elected by his fellow officers for the award of the Victoria Cross, which was gazetted on 30 January 1860. He received a glowing testimonial from Major F.R. Palmer, later lieutenant-colonel:

'No one ever better deserved the Victoria Cross; he obtained with not only one act, but for many acts during his active service, commencing with the march on Delhi. On one occasion an advanced post in Delhi was retained by his declaring to the officer in command, who wished to retire, that he could do so with his own men, but that he, Lieut. Heathcote, would endeavour to hold the post with six riflemen he had with him. On another occasion he made his way to the front with six men, supported by fourteen under my command. He and his party killed eight or ten of the enemy. This was the first forward step taken after the Army had been three days in the portion of Delhi first occupied by it.'

Preferring to remain campaigning, he transferred out of the 1/60th, which was returning to Britain, to the 2nd Battalion 60th, which was en-route to China, where the war with China had been put on hold until the Mutiny had been suppressed. Heathcote subsequently took part in the assault on the Taku Forts and the capture of Peking. Belatedly he received his Cross on 11 January 1861 from Lieutenant General Sir James Hope Grant.

Heathcote returned to England and retired from the Army in 1863. His health had been affected by the constant campaigning and he decided to return to Australia. Here he married Mary Harriet Thompson and served with the New South Wales Volunteers. The family fell on hard times and his old commander, General Sir Edward Hutton, found him in hospital almost totally blind; when a fund was raised, over £200 was sent to the old veteran. He died in Sydney on 21 February 1912, aged 79.

Everard Aloysius Lisle Phillipps

The case of Ensign Phillipps is a complicated one and must have caused some consternation for those responsible for awarding the Victoria Cross.

It was a case that had been dormant for fifty years until Lord Roberts's son, Freddy, was mortally wounded at Colenso in 1899. Despite his death, he was awarded the Victoria Cross and this finally cleared the way for posthumous awards.

Everard Lisle Phillipps was born on 28 May 1835 at Grace Dieu Manor, Coleorton, Leicestershire, the second son of Ambrose Lisle Phillipps de Lisle and Laura Mary (née Clifford).[11] He joined the HEIC Army and was commissioned in the 11th Bengal NI, arriving in Meerut on 4 May 1857 and had a grandstand view of the mutiny on 10 May.

When the grenadiers of the 20th BNI refused orders to disperse the mob, Phillipps accompanied his commanding officer, Colonel John Finnis, as he rode over from his regimental lines in an attempt to restore order. As Finnis harangued his men, he was shot in the back and fell from his horse, where he was hacked to pieces. This was a signal for the sepoys of the 11th Bengal NI to join the mutiny. Young Phillipps joined other officers in fleeing from the native lines and became one of the Company's officers, now without a regiment, who became attached to the Queen's Army. Phillipps joined the 60th Rifles as an orderly officer or galloper to Colonel John Jones. In a pleading letter to his father, he wrote: 'As soon as ever this row is over I shall retire from the Company's service … Try and get me a commission in the Queen's service … Now perhaps I may fulfil your idea about distinguishing myself!'

He followed this with another letter four days later, suggesting that being Colonel Jones's orderly may be a way to receive a commission without purchase, 'but I may need to purchase as I want you at once to get me in the [60th] Regiment. If I am not granted a commission without purchase, I want you to use what I shall get out of the legacy which is settled on the younger children.'

Phillipps was certainly driven to distinguish himself and took every opportunity to take part in all the fights he could, sustaining three wounds and having his horse shot under him. Leading the storming of the Water Bastion, Phillipps entered the breach and gathered a few Sikhs in a charge which scattered a large body of sepoys. As the street fighting continued during the next three days, Ensign Phillipps was in the vicinity of Bank House on the afternoon of 17 September helping to prepare a small breastwork, when he was shot in the head and died soon after.

Colonel Jones wrote a letter of condolence to Phillipps' father, in which he expressed a hope that his son would obtain a commission with the regiment without actually confirming he had done so. Nevertheless, the inscription on his gravestone at Delhi records that he was an 'Ensign in the

60th Rifles' and the Regiment backdated his commission to 5 June 1857. Sadly for Phillipps, he was unaware of this when he died. The announcement seems not to have been widely received for *The London Gazette* published on 21 October 1859: 'Ensign Everard Aloysius Lisle Phillipps of the 11th Regiment of Bengal Native Infantry would have been recommended to Her Majesty for the decoration of the Victoria Cross, had he survived, for many gallant deeds which he performed during the Siege of Delhi.'

In 1907, following the award of Freddy Roberts' VC, there was a spate of claims from relatives of men who would have been awarded the Cross had they survived. Particularly vociferous were the widow and father of Lieutenants Melvill and Coghill respectively, who would have been recommended for the Cross had they lived.[12]   Edwin de Lisle received his brother's Cross fifty years after the event and it is on loan to the Rifles Museum at Winchester.

In the 1870s, a private and probably singular unofficial presentation, was made by Queen Victoria to her friend, Laura Mary (née Clifford), Phillipps' mother. Presented in a beautiful domed velvet lined case, lay a privately commissioned authentic Victoria Cross made from the bronze of captured Russian cannon and correctly engraved on the reverse to Ensign Phillipps, 60th Rifles. This unique decoration can be viewed in the Lord Ashcroft Gallery at the Imperial War Museum.

James McGuire and Miles Ryan

Sergeant McGuire and Drummer Ryan of 1st Bengal Fusiliers were involved in the assault on the Kabul Gate on 14 September. Along with their comrades, they were awaiting final orders and refilling their ammunition pouches when three ammunition boxes caught fire, possibly from sparks from surrounding buildings. Within moments, two had exploded and the others began to burn. While others ran about in a panic or stood too frozen to react, McGuire and Ryan ran forward, dragged the burning ammunition boxes from the pile and began throwing them over the parapet into the water-filled ditch below. For their prompt action which saved the lives of their comrades, they were awarded the Victoria Cross which was gazetted on 24 December 1858.

Little is known of Miles Ryan except he was born in 1826 and came from Derry. He elected to remain in India and died in Bengal in January 1887.

More is know about James McGuire, who suffered the ignominy of having his hard-won Cross taken from him. Born in Enniskillen in 1827, at the age of 18 he enlisted in the Honourable East India Company's 1st

Bengal European Fusiliers and served in the Burma War of 1852-53. Promoted to sergeant, McGuire took part in the siege and attack on Delhi. On 4 January 1860, he was presented with his VC by the Queen at Windsor Castle.

McGuire had taken his discharge on 19 May 1859 and returned to Enniskillen. In what would appear to be a family dispute, McGuire was then accused of stealing a cow from his uncle. At his trial on 12 July 1862, he said it had been taken in lieu of an unpaid debt but the court found him guilty and sentenced him to nine months in Derry gaol. Like others who had fallen foul of the law, McGuire's VC was forfeited, and his name was struck off the list of recipients on 22 December 1862.[13] When he was released in March 1863, he petitioned to have his VC and annuity restored. These two petitions were supported by the magistrates involved in his case. Unfortunately, the judge who sentenced him, in order to justify his harsh sentence, did not support the petition. The Secretary of State at the War Office would not submit the case to the Queen and McGuire appears to have given up. Interestingly, the VC Pension book shows McGuire was not on a normal pension but received the £10 annual annuity, which indicated either that his annuity was restored – or that it was a clerical error.

Robert Shebbeare

Robert Haydon Shebbeare was born on 13 January 1827 in Clapham, London. He was educated at King's College School, London and was a fellow pupil of Philip Salkeld. After training at Addiscombe, he was commissioned on 29 February 1848 in the 60th BNI. He was with his regiment at Umballa when they learned of the Meerut mutiny and ordered to march to Rohtak, which was in danger. When they arrived on 9 June, the sepoys of the 60th Bengal NI, who had behaved well on the march, mutinied. The British officers saddled up and rode as a body to join the Delhi camp.

Now without a regiment, Shebbeare was appointed second in command of the Guides Infantry of Sikhs from the Punjab. He saw much action as his regiment defended Hindoo Rao's House, a particular target for the rebels. During the siege, Shebbeare was wounded no less than six times. In a letter to his mother he wrote: 'I was wounded by three bullets on 14th July and again by one on 14th September … In addition to these wounds, two musket balls went through my hat. The first slightly grazed my scalp; giving me a severe headache and making me feel very sick. The second cut through a very thick turban and knocked me down on my face, but without doing me any injury. On the same day and shortly afterwards a ball hit me on the right

41

jawbone but glanced off with no worse effect that making me bleed violently and giving me a very mumpish appearance for some days.' One wonders if this sort of detail was what a mother wanted to hear about her son.

When the assault on Delhi started on 14 September, Shebbeare's regiment was attached to No.4 column, tasked with taking the Lahore Gate. The column was in a perilous position from the start as they had to contend with the maze of Kissengunge suburb on the right flank before they could reach the Gate. The rebels had constructed a strong breastwork across the approach to the city and enfilade fire from Kissengunge held up any advance. Even when the breastwork was taken in a charge, the column was unable to follow through and was forced to pull back. It was at this phase of the fight that Lieutenant Shebbeare performed his act of gallantry as published in his citation dated 21 October 1859:

'For distinguished gallantry at the head of the Guides with the 4th column of assault at Delhi, on the 14th September 1857, when after twice charging beneath a wall of the loopholed serai, it was found impossible, owing to the murderous fire, to attain a breach. Captain (then Lieutenant) Shebbeare endeavoured to reorganise his men, but one-third of the Europeans having fallen, his efforts to do so failed. He then conducted the rear-guard of the retreat across the canal most successfully. He was most miraculously preserved through the affair, but yet left the field with one bullet through his cheek and a bad scalp wound along the back of his head from another.'

After all the action he had seen and the wounds he had suffered, he received his Victoria Cross by registered post. Curiously, it was engraved with his disbanded 60th Bengal NI regiment and not the Guides, as published in his citation.

He raised and commanded the 15th (Pioneer) Regiment of Punjab Infantry and in 1860, led them during the Second China War, but ill health forced him to leave in September. After sixteen years away from the UK, he sailed from China on SS *Emau* to be reunited with his family again. When the ship docked, his family were eagerly waiting on the quayside to welcome him home. It was only then that they learned the crushing news that he had died from malaria whilst en route, and been buried at sea.

Herbert Reade

Herbert Taylor Reade was born in Perth, Ontario on 20 September 1828. His father was Staff Surgeon George Hume Reade of the 3rd Regiment of Canadian Militia, who died at the hospital at Scutari during the Crimean War. Herbert Reade was educated in Canada and qualified as a surgeon in

Dublin before joining the 61st (Gloucestershire) Regiment in 1850 as Assistant Surgeon.

During the assault of 14 September, the 61st Regiment were part of the No.5 reserve column that followed in the wake of No.3 column through the Kashmir Gate. Soon Reade and his medical companions had their hands full with the large numbers of wounded. But it was not his medical expertise that was called upon for his act of outstanding gallantry. His Commanding Officer recommended Reade for the award, until he fell dangerously ill. There followed a frequent change of COs who overlooked the initial recommendation until, three years later, Reade's claim finally reached the board of inspecting officers at the War Office. After several late claims had been rejected on the grounds of the time-lapse since they were performed, Reade's claim seemed destined for the same fate. Fortunately, the reason for the claim's tardiness was accepted and Herbert Reade received his well-merited VC from the General Sir R. Douglas, the Governor of Jersey in July 1862. His citation, published on 5 February 1861, reads:

'Dates of Acts of Bravery: 14 and 16 Sep 1857. During the Siege of Delhi, and on the 14th Sep 1857, while Surgeon Reade was attending to the wounded at one end of one of the streets of the city, a party of rebels advanced from the direction of the Bank, and, having established themselves in the houses of the street, commenced firing from the roofs. The wounded were thus in very great danger, and would have fallen into the hands of the enemy, had not Surgeon Reade drawn his sword, and calling upon a few soldiers who were near to follow, succeeded, after a very heavy fire, in dislodging the rebels from this position. Surgeon Reade's party consisted of about ten in all, of whom two were killed and five or six wounded. Surgeon Reade also accompanied the regiment at the Assault on Delhi, and on the morning of the 16 Sep 1857, was one of the first up at the breach in the magazine, which was stormed by the 61st Regiment, and Belooch Battalion, on which occasion he, with the sergeant of the 61st Regt. spiked one of the enemy's guns.'

In 1864, Herbert Reade was appointed to the Staff and became Brigade Surgeon in 1879 and Deputy Surgeon General the following year. He was promoted to Surgeon General in 1886 and retired the following year. He was appointed an Honorary Surgeon to Queen Victoria in 1895 and died on 23 June 1897.

George Renny

George Alexander Renny was born on 12 May 1875 in Riga, in present day Latvia. His father, a merchant whose family had settled in Russia for more than a century, died shortly after his son was born and his widow took their children to Scotland, where young George was brought up. He attended Addiscombe and obtained a commission in the Bengal Horse Artillery, one of the smartest regiments in the Company's Army. He took part in the Sutlej Campaign in 1846 and by the time of the Mutiny, commanded the 5th Native Troop of the 1st Brigade.

He first saw action on 7 June 1857 at Jalandhar and was at the Delhi siege by 23 June.

When the assault was made, Renny commanded No.4 siege battery and when the infantry stormed the defences, he took some gunners of his troop with 12-pounder mortars to shell the houses and streets in front of the attack. During the taking of the Kashmir Bastion, he turned a captured gun on the enemy.

On 16 September, the British reached the Delhi magazine, which was taken, but the rebels immediately counter-attacked.[14] Covered by heavy fire from the surrounding tall buildings the rebels managed to set the thatch alight on some of the building near the wall. Despite the heavy fire, Renny climbed to the top of the magazine wall and pelted the enemy with live shells, which were handed up to him with their fuses lit. This had the desired effect for the rebels withdrew and Renny was then able to turn his mortars on the trouble spots. For this improvised act of bravery, Renny was awarded the Victoria Cross, gazetted on 12 April 1859. He was one of the 12 recipients who attended the investiture at Windsor Castle on 9 November 1860.

Renny continued to impress his superiors during the rest of the Mutiny campaign and was specially mentioned in a supplementary despatch and received a brevet majority.

He took part in the Hazara Campaign of 1868 when his mountain battery was carried on elephants. He retired with the rank of Major General on 31 December 1878 and died in Bath on 5 January 1887.

Edward Thackeray

Born in Broxbourne, Hertfordshire on 19 October 1836, Edward Talbot Thackeray was the son of the Reverend Francis Thackeray.[15] He was educated at Marlborough and then the HEIC College at Addiscombe. He was commissioned as Second Lieutenant in the Bengal Engineers in 1857 just weeks before the Mutiny and joined the Delhi column that fought the engagements at Hindun and Budli-ki-Serai.

On 16 September he was in the Delhi Magazine when the rebels attacked and started a fire in a shed filled with live shells; Thackeray remained there until he had extinguished the flames. In his own account he rather plays down his part in the action: 'In the afternoon they returned and attacked the magazine and set the roof on fire. We had got up on the roof with leather bags of water and put it out while they threw stones at us ... I think that day I had the narrowest escape of any. After putting out part of the fire, I was jumping down when three of them put their heads over the wall and took three deliberate shots at me, all of which missed. They could not have been above ten yards off. I fired my revolver at one, but don't remember whether I hit him or not. A Lieutenant of Artillery [Renny] then got on top of the Artillery Magazine with 10-inch shells in his hand. He lighted the fuse and dropped them on their heads.'

After Delhi, Thackeray was present at many actions during 1858-9 and thought little more of his part in the Delhi Magazine fight. A whole year had elapsed before the Bengal Engineers learned that Renny was to receive the VC – believing that their man Thackeray deserved the same, the former Chief Engineer, Colonel Baird Smith, petitioned the War Office, who despite the five year gap, finally agreed that Thackeray should also receive the Cross. This was presented to him at Dover in July 1862 by General A.A. Dalzell.

Edward Thackeray went on serve in the Afghan War of 1878-80 and made Commandant of the Bengal Sappers and Miners before retiring from the Army in 1888. He was an active member of the Red Cross and was Chief Commissioner of the Order of St. John of Jerusalem. He retired to Italy and during the First World War was Commissioner of the Bordighera branch of the British Red Cross, receiving Mentioned in Despatches with his British War and Victory medals – surely the only Indian Mutiny veteran to do so. He died in Bordighera on 3 September 1927, aged ninety-one.

Chapter 3

Other Outbreaks
June to November 1857

While the focus had been on Delhi, there were many other outbreaks in Oudh and beyond. News of the Meerut mutiny soon spread and reached the holy city of Benares situated on the left bank of the Ganges about midway between Calcutta and Delhi.

BENARES

The garrison at Benares consisted of three guns of No.12 Field Artillery, the 37th Bengal Native Infantry, the 13th Irregular Cavalry and Sikhs of the 15th Ludhiana Regiment. The cantonment was situated three miles from the city and under the new command of the elderly and ailing Brigadier George Ponsonby. When the news of the uprising reached Benares, it became clear that the sepoys of the 37th NI were affected and would likely mutiny. Equally, it was felt that the Sikhs would remain loyal.

The Europeans in the garrison were cheered by the arrival of about 150 men of the 10th (Lincolnshire) Regiment from Dinapur, followed on 4 June, by Colonel James Neill with some sixty men of the European Madras Fusiliers. News reached the garrison that the 17th Bengal NI at Azamgarh had mutinied and a council was called to discuss the prospect of disarming the 37th Bengal NI. Neill entered the discussion and forcefully urged Ponsonby that the 37th should be disarmed that afternoon.

The question was how the 250 European troops were to disarm a native regiment of nearly a thousand strong. A parade was ordered but not all the European troops assembled on time. As the men of the 37th formed up in front of their lines, the artillery and a few men of the 10th Regiment and Madras Fusiliers arrived to take up a position on their right with the Sikhs and cavalry positioned to their left. Colonel Arthur Spottiswood and the

European officers of the 37th then walked down the lines of the regiment and directed the men to lodge their muskets in the bell of arms attached to each company. Some quietly obeyed, but others called out that the Europeans were coming to shoot them down unarmed. Most responded and turned to face the group advancing from the right and opened fire. Eight men of the 10th were hit before the Europeans reacted. The artillery opened up with grapeshot and gaps appeared amongst the sepoys and some of the shells landed amongst the Sikhs, causing bewilderment and panic. The Sikhs began yelling and shooting indiscriminately, and the artillery assumed that the Sikhs had mutinied. Captain William Olipherts then ordered the guns turned on the Sikhs, who scattered, which added to the chaos.[1]

The disarming had been a disaster with most of the 37th escaping with their arms and going on the rampage. When the frenzy of firing stopped, it was found that many of the Irregular Cavalry had remained loyal and most of the Sikhs recovered from the wild firing and returned to duty. Colonel Neill then assumed command and embarked on ruthlessly weeding out the mutineers in the city and surrounding countryside. Soon the trees in the area were bearing new fruit – the hanged bodies of anyone suspected of being a rebel.

Out of the chaos, the slaughter and mismanagement of the Benares mutiny, three men performed acts of gallantry that were later recognised with the awarding of the Victoria Cross.

Attack on the Bungalow
After the confusing events of 4 June, the surrounding area around the cantonment was highly dangerous. As bands of mutineers and bazaar *badmashes* roamed the countryside, those Europeans who lived on the edge of the cantonment were in mortal danger. One such family was that of Captain Brown, the Pensions Paymaster, who lived in an isolated bungalow with his wife and daughter, which the rebels soon surrounded and set alight.

On learning this, Dublin-born Sergeant Major Peter Gill volunteered, along with Sergeant Major Matthew Rosamond, 37th BNI, to try and bring the family to safety. In this they succeeded and were awarded the Victoria Cross. Gill's citation, dated 23 August 1858 reads:

'This Non-Commissioned Officer conducted himself with gallantry at Benares on the night of the 4th June 1857. He volunteered, with Sergeant-Major Rosamond of the 37th Regiment of Bengal Native Infantry, to bring in Captain Brown, Pension Paymaster, and his family, from a detached Bungalow into the Barracks, and saved the life of the Quartermaster-Sergeant of the 25th Regiment of Bengal Native Infantry, in the early part of the evening, by cutting off the head of the Sepoy who had just bayoneted him. Sergeant Major Gill states that on the same night he faced a Guard of 27 men, with only a Sergeant's sword; and it is also represented that he twice saved the life of Major Barrett, 37th Regiment of the Bengal Native Infantry, when attacked by Sepoys of his own Regiment.'

This is quite a curious citation in that it tags onto the saving of the Brown family several brave acts that are glossed over.

Peter Gill

Peter Gill was born in Dublin in 1816 and trained as a tailor. Moving to London, he enlisted with the HEIC in 1842 and posted as a gunner with the Bengal Artillery. He took part in both wars against the Sikhs and transferred to the newly-formed Ludhiana Regiment of Sikhs as Sergeant Major in 1850.

As the senior NCO of the Sikhs, Gill would also have come under fire from his own side and would have been instrumental in persuading his men to return to duty. The Ludhiana Regiment remained at Benares for the duration of the Mutiny, but Peter Gill left on 16 April 1858 having been commissioned ensign of the newly formed Moradabad Infantry Levy. He remained with them for a year until the fighting in Oudh stopped.

Gill received his Victoria Cross in February 1859 but further details are unknown. He was promoted to lieutenant on 22 May 1863 and appointed Barrack Master at Lucknow for four years before taking up similar position at Meerut. While he was stationed at Morar, Gwalior, he died on 24 October 1868 aged 52 and was buried in the Artillery Lines Cemetery, Gwalior.[2]

Matthew Rosamond

Matthew Rosamond was born on 12 July 1823, either at Swallow Cliffe in Wiltshire or Eaton Socon, Bedfordshire; his early years were certainly spent at the latter. His parents were George, a former soldier, and Elizabeth. When Matthew enlisted he gave his employment as servant. Matthew's early army service mirrored that of Peter Gill. In London, he joined the HEIC Army on 8 May 1841 and served in both Sikh Wars in the 2nd Bengal (European) Regiment. Like Gill, he was promoted to Sergeant Major of the 37th Bengal Native Infantry.

When the sepoys of the 37th Bengal NI rebelled against being disarmed on the parade ground at Benares, Sergeant Major Rosamond joined his commanding officer, Colonel Spottiswoode, in trying to flush out the mutineers. His citations reads:

'This non-commissioned officer volunteered to accompany Lieutenant-Colonel Spottiswoode, commanding the 37th Regiment of Bengal Native

Infantry, to the right of the lines, in order to set them on fire, with the view to driving out the Sepoys, on the occasion of the outbreak at Benares on the evening of the 4 June 1857; and also volunteered, with Sergeant-Major Gill, of the Ludhiana Regiment, to bring off Captain Brown, pension paymaster, his wife and infant, and also some others, from a detached bungalow, into barracks. His conduct was highly meritorious and he has since been promoted.'

Rosamond and Gill were commissioned as ensigns in the newly-raised Moradabad Infantry Levy. They both received their VCs in February 1859. Rosamond returned to England and the census of 1861 shows him living in Eaton Socon, near St Neots. In 1860, he was introduced to Queen Victoria by Sir Charles Wood at a levèe.

He returned to India and served as Barrack Master at Barrackpore in 1862. On 6 September 1864, he was promoted to lieutenant and made Barrack Master at Fort William, Calcutta. On 14 July 1866, whilst en-route to England, he died and was buried in the Red Sea. In 1903, his medals were sold at auction for £54 but their whereabouts is now unknown. A blue plaque was erected in the village of Eaton Socon in Bedfordshire stating: 'On 4 June 1857 Matthew Rosamond, a relative of the Rosamond bakers on this site, won the Victoria Cross during the Indian Mutiny. He died on the Red Sea on 14 July 1866 and was buried at sea.'

John Kirk

The third soldier to receive the VC for his part in the rescue of the Brown family was a private in the British Army. His name and the part he played in their rescue are not mentioned in either of the citations to Gill and Rosamond. It was nearly eighteen months after *The London Gazette* published the award to the two HEIC soldiers that Private Kirk's gallantry was acknowledged on 26 January 1860: 'John Kirk, Private, the 10th Regt. For daring gallantry at Benares on the 4th June 1857, at the outbreak of the mutiny of the native troops at that station, in having volunteered to proceed with two non-commissioned officers to rescue Capt. Brown, Pensions Paymaster, and his family, who were surrounded by rebels in the compound of their house, and having, at the risk of his own life, succeeding in saving them.'

It seems likely that the 10th Regiment interceded on Kirk's behalf to see that justice was done for their man. Also, there was kudos to be gained in having a VC amongst their number. All this must have seemed surprising, for John Kirk was probably one of the most troublesome soldiers in the regiment. There is evidence that he was born in July 1827 in the Liverpool Workhouse. If so, he would have been sent out to work at the age of 10, for when he enlisted in the Army in 1846, he gave his occupation as farm servant.

As soon as he was old enough, Kirk enlisted in 10th Regiment, which was recruiting in Liverpool. He was sent out to India and first saw action in the Second Sikh War of 1848-9 and was present at the Siege of Mooltan and the Battle of Gujarat. The long period of peace that followed saw Kirk and many like him succumb to the readily available cheap alcohol and brothels to compensate for the boredom of Indian garrison life. Kirk became addicted to drink and was often drunk on duty. His service record shows that his name appeared fifty-seven times in the defaulter's book. He spent much time in detention and also hospital being treated for syphilis. It was hardly surprising that he was regarded as a 'bad soldier'.

Then came his one moment of redemption. Some accounts describe that he volunteered and set off alone to rescue the Brown family. Quite why no other member of the 10th accompanied him is not explained. On the way, he met up with Gill and Rosamond and they decided on a rescue plan. The Brown bungalow was surrounded and the thatch ablaze. Captain Brown was holding off the rebels with his revolver but was about to be overwhelmed. Kirk, Gill and Rosamond opened fire and charged into the bungalow. Gathering the family together, they began to pick off the sepoys until they pulled back enabling then to make a dash for the British lines.

Kirk belatedly received his Cross from Queen Victoria at Windsor on 9 November 1860. Sadly it was his last proud moment, for his dissipated life caught up with him and he was discharged as being unfit for further service. He was denied an Army pension because his incapacity was caused by his own vices.

John Kirk died where he was born, in the Liverpool Workhouse, on 31 August 1865 aged 38. He was buried in a pauper's grave, which was properly marked with a memorial stone during the 1980s. His medals are displayed in the Museum of Lincolnshire Life, Lincoln.

INDORE

The next VC action took place 500 miles south of Delhi at Indore, the headquarters of the Central India Agency. Although the State of Indore was ruled by the Holkar Maharaja, Tukoji Rao Holkar II, who remained loyal to the HEIC, the sepoys of his army did not. The British garrison was too small to deal with the increasing discontent and requested a detachment of the Bhopal Contingent to come and help. Acting Agent Henry Durand called for the Europeans in the town to take refuge in the Residency, situated about two miles away. Despite his warning, thirty-nine European men, women and children chose to remain in their homes and were subsequently murdered. After a few days of being exposed to the influence of the rebelling sepoys, the Bhopal Infantry decided to throw their lot in with the Holkar rebels. Finally, on 1 July, the rebel sepoys opened fire on the Bhopal Cavalry.

James Travers

Major James Travers, commanding the Bhopal Contingent, was about to enter the orderly room when grapeshot came whistling through the lines. He hastened to the picquet in the Residency Stable Square, called for those sowars he could find to form up and gave the order to charge the enemy's guns. Travers rode forward, but only half a dozen sowars followed him, the rest refusing. The native gunners prepared to fire, so Travers decided to at least cause a diversion to allow Europeans to take shelter in the Residency. Incredibly, he escaped injury although his accoutrements and uniform were riddled with musket balls. In a letter he wrote on 4 July 1857, he described the action:

'As I cast my eye back, and found only six or seven following me, and not in good order, much as I despise the Mahrattas as soldiers [the Holkar sepoys], I saw we could not by any possibility make an impression. Still, at it I went; to draw rein or turn after giving the order to charge was too much against the grain.

'I came in for a large share of the most polite attention. My horse was wounded in three places; I had to parry a sabre-cut with the back of my sword; but God in His great mercy protected me and the dastardly gunners threw themselves under their gun.

'Had I thirty or forty good sowars at the time, with their hearts in the right place, I would have captured their three guns and cut their 200 infantry to pieces; but what could half a dozen do against so many?'

With hundreds of mutineers augmented by a howling rabble from the bazaar heading for the Residency, the surviving Europeans retreated in to the large building. The odds were not hopeful. To defend the Residency, there were nine officers, including Travers, two doctors, two sergeants, fourteen native gunners from the Bhopal Contingent and five civilians, including women.

At first, the two Bhopal guns were operated effectively by the loyal gunners and the two sergeants, disabling one of the rebel guns. The Bhopal Cavalry had not gone over to the mutineers and reported to Travers. It was clear that the defenders could not hold out for long and it was decided to abandon the Residency via the rear of the building. The small group managed to get away with Travers and his horsemen acting as a rearguard. After two days, they reached safety at Ashta in Bhopal territory.

James Travers was recommended for the Victoria Cross which he received from the C-in-C, General Sir Hugh Rose at a ceremony at Gwalior on 3 June 1862.

James Travers came from a distinguished Anglo-Irish military family. He was one of eight sons born to General Sir Robert Travers, who in turn was one of six brothers who all had long military careers. Like James Travers, all his seven brothers served in India. Born on 6 October 1820 in Cork, he passed out of Addiscombe College and commissioned on 11 June 1838. Travers joined the 2nd BNI, taking part in the First Afghan War 1840-42 and the First Sikh War. He was appointed adjutant to the Bhopal Contingent and was its commander by the start of the Mutiny.

He eventually retired from the Army in 1881 as a full General and died at Pallanza, Lake Maggiore, Italy on 1 April 1884.

PUNJAB

On the North-West Frontier, Sir John Lawrence, the Chief Commissioner of the Punjab, learned of the Meerut mutiny and took steps to prevent it happening in his province. He was helped by having an exceptionally talented staff including John Nicholson, Herbert Edwardes, Neville Chamberlain and a young Frederick Roberts. In the most important garrison at Peshawar, Colonel Edwardes disarmed the 24th, 27th and 31st Native Infantry and 5th Light Cavalry without firing a shot and John Nicholson's 'Punjab Moveable Column' moved rapidly to suppress any revolts as they occurred. The final acts of rebellion occurred when a brigade of mutineers at Sialkot began to move to Delhi. Nicholson intercepted them as they tried to cross the Ravi river. Unable to make headway, they fell back and were surrounded on an island, where Nicholson's men killed 1,100 of the trapped sepoys.

JHELUM

William Connolly
William Connolly was born in Liverpool in May 1817. A tall, well-built youth, he worked as a stableman and groom but at the age of 20, he enlisted in the HEIC and joined the 3rd Bengal Horse Artillery. He saw his first action in the Second Sikh War of 1848-9 when the Bengal Horse Artillery came in for special praise for its performance at the bloody battle of

Chillianwala and the final battle at Gujarat. His regiment remained stationed at Rawalpindi in the Punjab when news was received that the 14th Regiment NI had mutinied at Jhelam seventy-five miles to the south-east. Colonel Charles Ellice of the 24th (Warwickshire) Regiment was ordered to take 300 men of his regiment, a squadron of cavalry and three guns from 3rd Bengal Horse Artillery, and assist in disarming the rebellious sepoys.

Unfortunately, the commander at Jhelum misinterpreted the plan and paraded the 14th before dawn on 7 July. When they learned that the Rawalpindi force was close by, the rebels occupied the fortified stronghold that contained the treasury and armoury, preparing to repel the force that had come to disarm them. With little option but make a frontal attack, Colonel Ellice brought his three guns forward in front of the infantry exposing the crews to a deadly fire from the strongpoint. In the ferocious thirty-minute battle, the sepoys were forced out and retired to a nearby village.

The British force was exhausted, for it had marched all night and immediately been thrown into a fierce battle. Colonel Ellice had been dangerously wounded and the command devolved on Colonel Gerrard who, instead of allowing his men to recover, insisted they attack the village right away. The result was that the soldiers were in no state to engage in street fighting, losing thirty-five killed until they were forced to withdraw. The gunners sited at such short range were particularly vulnerable and suffered greatly. Gunner William Connolly rose to the occasion and was recommended by his commander, Lieutenant Cookes, for the Victoria Cross. On 3 September 1858, *The London Gazette* published an exceptionally lengthy citation usually reserved for officers, but which gave a full description of Connolly's gallantry:

'This soldier is recommended for the Victoria Cross for his gallantry in the action with the enemy at Jhelum on the 7th July 1857. Lieutenant Cookes, Bengal Horse Artillery, reports that: About daybreak on that day, I advanced with my half-troop at a gallop, and engaged the enemy within easy musket range. The sponge-man of one of my guns having been shot during the advance, Gunner Connolly assumed the duties of second sponge-man, and he had barely assisted in two discharges of his gun, when a musket-ball through the left thigh felled him to the ground; nothing daunted by pain and loss of blood, he was endeavouring to resume his post when I ordered a movement in retirement, and though severely wounded, he was mounted on his horse in the gun-team, and rode to the next position which the guns took up, and manfully declined going to the rear when the necessity of his so doing was represented to him. About 11 o'clock a.m., while the guns were still in action, the same gunner, whilst sponging, was again knocked down by a musket-ball striking him on the hip thereby causing great faintness and partial unconsciousness, for the pain appeared excessive, and the blood flowed fast. On seeing this I gave directions for his removal out of action; but this brave man hearing me staggered to his feet and said "No, sir, I'll not go there whilst I can work here", and shortly afterwards he again resumed his post as sponge-man.

'Late in the afternoon of the same day, my three guns were engaged at 100 yards from the walls of a village with the defenders, viz, the 14th Native Infantry Mutineers, amidst a storm of bullets with did great execution.

'Gunner Connolly, though suffering severely from his two previous wounds, was wielding his sponge with an energy and courage which attracted the admiration of his comrades, and while cheerfully encouraging a wounded man to hasten in bringing up the ammunition, a musket-ball tore through the muscles of his right leg; but with the most undaunted bravery he struggled on; and until he loaded six times did this man give way, when through loss of blood he fell in my arms, and I placed him on a wagon, which shortly afterwards bore him in a state of unconsciousness from the fight.'

Connolly must have possessed an incredibly strong constitution, for he survived his terrible wounds in the vermin-infested hospital in the heat of summer. He received his Cross in India in February 1859 before returning to Britain and being invalided out of the Army. Now an out-of-work cripple, Connolly's prospects were not good. In order to stave off total beggary, he sold his VC which fetched just £10 at Sotheby's auction on 9 February 1886. He was taken in by a kind neighbour who cared for him until he died of bronchitis on 31 December 1891.

The purchaser of the VC bequeathed it in 1914, along with other items, to an auctioneer friend. On the auctioneer's death, the VC was rediscovered and declared by experts to be a Victorian copy. It appears that Connolly reported he had lost his VC, for he claimed a replacement, when, in all probability, he had pawned it. The engraving shows the name to be 'Conolly', which is probably an engraver's error or a lack of space which caused the loss of an 'n'.

KOLAPORE

As with the Punjab, the instances of mutiny elsewhere were few and quickly suppressed, thanks to the prompt action of its civil servants and military officers. Both the Bombay and Madras armies remained remarkably quiescent, either through good discipline or a dislike for the Bengal Army, who were perceived as receiving preferential treatment by the Company. The only serious instance of mutiny occurred at Kolapore in July 1857 when the part of the 27th Native Infantry rebelled.

William Kerr

William Alexander Kerr was born on 19 July 1831 at Melrose in Scotland. He joined the 24th Bombay Native Infantry in June 1849 before transferring to the South Mahratta Horse.

Lieutenant Kerr was stationed at the princely state of Satara in the Deccan when a telegram arrived to say that the 27th Native Regiment had mutinied at Kolapore. The European civilians and officers had taken refuge in the Residency and were protected by a few loyal sepoys. They were without food and could not be expected to last long. The Commanding Officer was somewhat hesitant about sending native troops as a relief force because of the fear of them changing sides in the prevailing uncertain climate.

Lieutenant Kerr expressed faith in his men and volunteered to lead them to Kolapore, about seventy-five miles distant. It was the middle of the monsoon season and the fifty horsemen had to cross several rivers swollen with rain. The roads were muddy quagmires but, after twenty-six hours in the saddle, Kerr's small force reached their destination on 10 July.

There he found that about thirty-five sepoys had murdered some of their officers and barricaded themselves in the fort. Kerr decided to attack right away despite the exhausted state of his men and the approach of night. Selecting seventeen troopers as a storming party, he approached the massive teak door backed with rocks and earth. His most trusted sowar was Daffadar Gunput Rao Dekur, who joined Kerr with a crowbar and, ignoring the musket fire, made a gap large enough to crawl through. As the pair emerged into the fort, about twenty rebels opened fire but, as they were stooping, the bullets flew over their heads. Then joined by the rest of the storming party, Kerr led a charge at the enemy and a fierce hand-to-hand fight ensued. Some of the sepoys were killed and the remainder were driven into a small loop-holed lodge at the entrance to the next large door. Kerr wasted little time in trying a frontal attack and set fire to the building, which flushed most of the rebels, who escaped into the inner part of the fort, where they were joined by the rest of the garrison.

With Gunput Rao's help, Kerr wielded the crowbar and made another opening in the second door. Once again they braved the bullets and emerged untouched. Before the sepoys could reload, Kerr and his Mahrattas were among them. Driven into a corner, the rebels fought desperately; one of the bullets cut the chain of Kerr's helmet and another musket discharge temporarily blinded him. He thrust at the shooter and was unable to withdraw his sword. He was struck on the head with a rifle butt and was on the point of being bayoneted when Gunput Rao shot the assailant.

Finally, the few surviving rebels took refuge in a temple, barricading the door and keeping up a heavy fire. As the crowbar could not open the barricaded door, hay was piled up and set alight. Finally the door fell in and Kerr's men rushed in and finished off the surviving rebels. The stiff fight had taken its toll. Kerr was wounded, eight of his sowars had been killed, four later died of their wounds and of the remaining five, not one escaped unhurt from this remarkably intense fight. The 27th Bombay NI was subsequently disarmed.

Lieutenant Kerr was one of the first HEIC officers to be recommended for the Victoria Cross, which was initially turned down mainly through prejudice against non-Imperial servicemen on the part of the War Office. It was accepted after an appeal and published in *The London Gazette* on 24 April 1858. Kerr's *Daffadar* (sergeant) was included in the recommendation but was refused because he was eligible for, and was indeed awarded, the Indian Order of Merit. Kerr received his VC on 4 September 1858 from Major-General F.T. Farrell, Commander of the Southern Division of the Army at Begaum, India.

William Kerr was appointed second in command of the Southern Mahratta Horse on 16 July 1858 and took part in the Central India Campaign and the pursuit of Tantia Topi.

At the conclusion of campaigning, Kerr learned that the Southern Mahratta Horse was to be disbanded and resigned from the army. He returned to England and married Harriet Atty. One of the presents given his wife was a bracelet found on the body of the Rani of Jhansi. He spent his retirement writing books about horsemanship and lived until he was eighty-seven, dying on 19 May 1919 at Folkestone, Kent.

PATNA

News of the Mutiny spread east to the District of Patna on the south bank of the River Ganges. For nearly three weeks there was considerable unease amongst the Europeans wondering if the local native troops would rebel and join the rioting that had broken out in Patna city. By mid-June all women and children had moved from outlying towns and gathered at the military cantonment at Dinapore. Finally, on 25 June, the sepoys of the 7th, 8th and 40th Bengal Native Infantry mutinied and, in a body, travelled south. In their path was Arrah, a small town about twenty-four miles from Dinapore where six officials and three railway engineers had decided to remain at their posts having sent their wives and children to Dinapore.

One of the railway engineers, Vicars Boyle, had taken the precaution of fortifying a two story building which was destined to be his billiard room. When they learned of the mutiny, the British moved into Boyle's small fortress, stocking up with cases of port and sherry to augment the large supply of rice, grain, biscuits, water, brandy and beer that was already stored there. Fortunately, their number was increased by the arrival of fifty loyal men of Rattray's Sikhs.

The mutineers from Dinapore entered Arrah on 27 July 1857. Having released some 400 prisoners from the jail, they began to besiege Boyle's isolated house.

The Relief Column

The authorities at Dinapore hurriedly organised a relief force to lift the siege. One of those who took part was William Fraser McDonell, of the Bengal Civil Service, the Assistant Magistrate and Collector for Sarun. He was born in Cheltenham on 17 December 1829 and studied at Haileybury School before joining the Bengal Civil Service in 1850. With the outbreak of the Mutiny, he found himself without definite employment in Dinapore and readily grabbed the chance to join the expedition for the relief of Arrah.

On 29 July, a 200-strong relief force left Dinapore by steamer but it ran aground on a sandbank during the night, stranding the column. The local general, Lloyd, was persuaded not to withdraw these men but to send a further 150 British and Sikh soldiers under the command of Captain Charles Dunbar of 10th Regiment. When the force finally landed at Berara Ghat it consisted of 150 men of 10th Regiment, 200 of 37th (Hampshire) Regiment and fifty Sikhs. William McDonell volunteered as a guide for he knew the route to Arah. Amongst the party was a fellow civil servant, Ross Mangles, the Assistant Magistrate of Patna. Both McDonell and Mangles left detailed accounts of the disastrous chain of events that followed their landing.

In a letter of 3 September 1857, McDonell wrote: 'About two miles from the Ghat was another river, after crossing which you get onto the public road to Arah, a distance of about 12 miles. As I was not sure I would find boats, as we were in an enemy's country, I offered to go with a small party of Sikhs, and secure the boats while the Europeans had their dinner at the bank ... On reaching the river's bank we found all the boats drawn up on the other side, and about 200 men assembled. They had four or five of those long native guns … and began blazing away at us … We immediately set to work and blazed across the river, and soon set all the fellows running. Two Sikhs swam across and got a small boat.'

The relief column could now be ferried across the river and at 4 p.m. began the long hot march towards Arah. After about four miles, a dozen horsemen were spotted in the distance, obviously enemy scouts for they galloped back towards Arah.

McDonell again: 'The men got very footsore, and we halted at the Kaimnugger Bridge, about three miles from Arah at 10 pm., and here we ought to have remained for the night, but after stopping about half an hour, on we marched. I fancy poor Dunbar thought it useless halting, considering his men had nothing with them, and that it would be better to push on. What possessed us, I know not; up to this time we had made the Sikhs throw out skirmishers, but we now marched in a body … After marching to within half a mile of Arah, we arrived at a thick tope of trees, and the moonlight hardly showed through; in fact the moon was setting.

'Well, we had got nearly through. When, like a flash of lightening, all along our left side came one blaze of musketry, and then another, and a third volley. By the light the firing made, we could see we were surrounded. We got behind the trees and tried to return the fire; Dunbar, myself, three of the 10th, and two Sikhs got together and blazed away … I fancy our firing showed where we were. Poor Dunbar fell against me mortally wounded; I was covered in blood. A ball hit me in the thigh, cutting it slightly only; at the same time two of the 10th and one Sikh also fell … We then tried to join the main body, and ran from tree to tree; the Europeans seeing us coming, all Sikhs, nearly, thought we were the enemy, and fired into us, killing several; in fact, I fear as many of our men were killed by their own comrades as by the enemy. In the night it was difficult to tell friend from foe …

'After daylight, we counted our forces, and found we were 350 strong, 100 missing; afterwards about 50 of these joined us, being concealed in a village close by; the rest were killed. We could see the enemy and tried to make out their numbers; there were the three Dinapore regiments drawn up in order, with bugles sounding the advance. About 2,000 men, with long matchlocks, belonging to and headed by Baboo Koor Singh, and more than 1,000 of the disbanded Sepoys who had managed to join him, and a large rabble army … not formidable in themselves, but who made themselves useful, killing all the wounded, beating them like dogs.'

Ross Mangles wrote: 'We held a consultation and determined to retreat … The whole distance, 18 miles, we walked under a most tremendous fire, the ditches, the jungle, and the houses, in fact every place along the road was lined with sepoys. We kept up a fire as we went along but ... we could see no enemy, only puffs of smoke ... Dozens of poor fellows were knocked over within a yard of me ... The last five miles I carried a wounded man who begged me not to leave him.'

At last the battered remnants of the relief force reached the river, where they hoped the boats would take them across to safety.

McDonell continued: 'By the time we reached the boats 100 must have been killed, and then commenced the massacre. The boats, which we expected to have been taken away, were all there, so with a cheer we all rushed to them, when, to our dismay, we found they (the sepoys) had fastened them securely to the shore, and had dragged them up out of the water and had placed about 300 yards off a small cannon, with which they blazed into us. The men, to escape the shot, got into the boats, and of course, as long as they were in them, it was impossible to push the boats off. So a number of men stripped themselves, throwing away their rifles and everything, and some of them managed to reach the other side. The wounded men, of course, could not swim, and some of us knew we could never reach the shore, so out we jumped, and managed to get two of the boats off; well, then we were at the mercy of the wind and stream, for not an oar had they left us. The wind was favourable, and we started off splendidly, when lo and behold, we gradually turned towards the shore, and I then saw they had tied our rudder, so as to bring it in again. I told the men to cut it, but no one moved, and so I got a knife and climbed up to the rudder. It was one of those country boats, covered in except just at the stern. The moment they saw what I was at they blazed at me, but God in His mercy preserved me. Two bullets went through my hat, but I was not touched. The rope was cut, and we were saved; but about halfway across we struck on a sandbank, and then the bullets poured in so fast that nearly everyone jumped overboard. One young officer jumped over as he was, with his sword on and down he went; another, Ingleby was shot in the head and either drowned or killed. I threw my pistol overboard; my coat I had thrown away early in the morning, as, being a coloured one, it made me conspicuous among the soldiers who were all in white. How I swam on shore I know not, as it is not an accomplishment I am a "dab" at. When once on shore we were pretty safe, and 250 out of 450 reached the steamer alive. Since then, nearly 100 more, from wounds, exposure etc., have died making a loss of 300 out of 450 – the worst that has befallen us yet; nearly every one was wounded ... Of the eight volunteers who went with the troop, six were killed. Young Mangles, John Lowis's brother-in-law, was knocked on the head and stunned for some ten minutes. He had a great lump on his head, but the bullet did no more damage; it must have glanced off.'

General Lloyd made no further effort to relieve Arrah but a more enterprising officer, Major Vincent Eyre, an elderly Bengal Artillery officer, took the responsibility upon himself. When passing through Buxar, he learned of the plight of the garrison at Arrah. Taking his battery and 150 men of the 5th (Northumberland) Fusiliers, he marched seventy miles to Arrah, routed the mutineers and relieved the small besieged garrison, who had held out for ten days.

Once he had recovered from his ordeal, William McDonell took part in another expedition, this time in command of 150 Sikhs. Although there was little fighting, his punitive force burned several villages along the route of the terrible retreat.

With the ending of the Indian Mutiny in 1858, it was time to distribute awards. It also put the War Office in a quandary for the names of three civilians had been submitted for the Victoria Cross, an award specifically created for military personnel. The first two names submitted were Thomas Kavanagh for Lucknow and Ross Mangles, who had saved Private Richard Taylor of the 37th Regiment. Taylor told the surgeon at Dinapore about Mangles's deed, and this passed to higher authority resulting in the announcement of a special Warrant pertaining only to the Indian Mutiny which allowed the award to civilians under the command of the military. Kavanagh and Mangles were gazetted on 8 July 1858 and received their VCs from Queen Victoria at Windsor Castle on 4 January 1860.

William McDonell

A little belatedly, McDonell's name was put forward by the Government of India and his name appeared in *The London Gazette* on 17 February 1860. He took a three-year leave and returned to England where he received his Cross from the Queen at Home Park, Windsor on 9 November 1860.

On his return to India in 1863, William took up the appointment of Magistrate and Collector at Nuddea. He enjoyed the lifestyle of a servant of the Raj, indulging his passion for horses including riding to hounds and pig-sticking. In 1874, he was made Judge of the High Court of Judicature in Calcutta, a position he filled until his retirement in 1886. During this time, he was a Steward at The Calcutta Turf Club. In 1878, his VC was stolen and he was sent a replacement.

After returning to Britain, he resided for a while in London and became a member of the Oriental Club. Finally, he moved to his home town of Cheltenham, no doubt attracted by the comradeship of the many retired

Indian Army and Civil Service officers resident in the town. His health began to fail and he died at the family home on 31 July 1894 having fallen sick after attending a cricket match at the East Gloucestershire Cricket group.

Ross Lewis Mangles

Born on 14 April 1833 in Calcutta, Mangles joined the Bengal Civil Service at the age of twenty. After his heroic part in the retreat from Arrah, he was appointed Magistrate in the Chunparun District, North Behar. He had a narrow escape in early 1858 when the Jewan station he was holding with a few natives was suddenly occupied by rebels. He managed to escape through the back as the rebels entered the front and after a ride of forty miles, he reached the safety of Chuprah.

After the Mutiny, he served in various legal-related positions and retired as Secretary to the Government of Bengal. He died on 28 February 1905 at Pirbright, Surrey.

The VCs of both McDonell and Mangles are displayed in the Imperial War Museum's Lord Ashcroft Gallery.

Denis Dempsey

Another Irishman, Private Dempsey was born in County Wicklow in 1826. He enlisted in the 10th Regiment in 1844 and spent sixteen years in India. Stationed at Dinapore, he was one of the soldiers sent to relieve the Europeans trapped at Arrah. During the retreat to the river, he went to the aid of Ensign Erskine and carried him for five miles to little avail for the mortally wounded officer died the following day.

Dempsey went on to perform two other gallant acts, which were noted in his Victoria Cross citation published on 17 February 1860:

'For having at Lucknow, now on the 14th March 1858, carried a Powder Bag through a burning village, with great coolness and gallantry, for the purpose of mining a passage in rear of the enemy's position. This he did, exposed to a very heavy fire from the enemy behind loop-holed walls, and to an almost still greater danger from the sparks which flew in every direction from the blazing houses.

'Also, for having been the first man who entered the village of Jugdispore on the 12th August 1857, under a most galling fire.

'Private Dempsey was likewise one of those who helped to carry Ensign Erskine, of the 10th Regiment in the retreat from Arrah in July 1857.'

Dempsey returned to England and was presented with his Cross by the Queen at Windsor Castle on 9 November 1860. When he left the Army, he moved to Canada, where he died on 10 January 1886.

NEEMUCH

The early months of the Mutiny were desperate for the British who were thinly spread over huge distances. The news of uprisings quickly infected the native soldiers amongst small military stations hundreds of miles from the mutiny's epicentre. One such was Neemuch in Rajputana situated on the Scind border, north-west of Indore. When the outbreak occurred at Nusseerabad in June it spread to the native regiments stationed at Neemuch. By mid-July, the mutineers controlled a large area from Neemuch to Saugor, and from Gwalior to Mhow. A further problem which restricted the British ability to counter the mutinies was the onset of the monsoon season which rendered the countryside impassable.

The troops stationed at Neemuch were the Bengal Native Horse Artillery, 1st Bengal Cavalry, 72nd BNI and 7th Infantry, Gwalior Contingent. It was not unusual to garrison the stations in Rajputana with Bengal troops as most of the Bombay troops had been withdrawn for service in the recent Persian War. On the night of 3 June, a few sowars of the 1st Bengal Cavalry called to the sepoys of the 72nd to take up their arms and a signal from two guns announced the start of the revolt. Armed with torches, the sowars set fire to the officers' bungalows and released prisoners from the jail. With loyal troops protecting them, the British officers made their escape. Within eleven hours of the mutiny, the rebels had sacked the cantonment before setting it on fire and marching to join other mutineers at Agra.

Neemuch was reoccupied by the Bombay Army, with Colonel Jackson of 2nd Bombay Cavalry in command. A much smaller mutiny broke out on 12 August which led to the awarding of a second Bombay Army VC.

James Blair
James Blair was born at the military station of Neemuch on 27 January 1828, the son of Captain E.M. Blair, Bengal Cavalry. When he was 16, he was commissioned in the Bombay Army and joined the 2nd Bombay Light Cavalry. During the Indian Mutiny he performed two acts of gallantry which are reflected in his citation published on 25 February 1862. This late gazetting was regarded by the War Office as a final clearing up of Mutiny claims, although one or two more were later accepted.

'For having on the night of the 12th of August, at Neemuch, in volunteering to apprehend seven or eight armed mutineers who had shut themselves up for defence in a house, the door of which he burst open. He then rushed in among them, and forced them to escape through the roof; in this encounter he was severely wounded. In spite of his wounds he pursued the fugitives, but was unable to come up with them, in consequence of the darkness of the night.'[3]

In the second action he was part of the column sent from Nasirbad to retake Neemuch, one of two hard-fought actions en route. The citation read:

'On the 23rd October 1857, at Jeerum, in fighting his way most gallantly through a body of rebels who had literally surrounded him. After breaking the end of his sword on one of their heads, and receiving a severe sword-cut on his right arm, he rejoined his troop. In this wounded condition, and with no other weapon than the hilt of his broken sword, he put himself at the head of his men, charged the rebels most effectively, and dispersed them.'

After the Mutiny, Blair progressed through a series of promotions until he became Colonel of the only regiment in which he served for over forty years. He was promoted to Brigadier-General and appointed Political Resident in Aden. He eventually retired as a full General on 1 April 1894 and died in Melrose on 18 January 1905.

FATEHPUR SIKRI

Following the diversion of Colonel Greathed's Flying Column to relieve Agra's non-existent siege, Colonel Henry Cotton took over from the dismissed Brigadier Polwhele. Cotton, commanding the 3rd European Fusiliers, had led the attack on the mutineers' camp after the surprise attack which initially caught Greathed's men unprepared. Cotton then set about strengthening the fortress with increased artillery and volunteers. The town would still be vulnerable if the mighty Gwalior Contingent turned its attention on them. With the rebels being driven out of Delhi there were now plenty of roving bands in the area. One nearby town occupied by detachments of mutineers was Fatehpur Sikri.

James Miller

James Miller was born on 5 May 1820 in Glasgow. He enlisted in the HEIC in 1841 and was a Gunner in the Bengal Artillery. He was promoted to Sergeant in 1846 and transferred to the Ordnance Department in 1856. In 1857, he was a Conductor at Agra and took part in Colonel Cotton's assault and capture on Fatehpur Sikri. His presence at the battle was not explained but, with his artillery experience, he probably was a volunteer. His act of gallantry was noted and belatedly appeared in *The London Gazette* on 25 February 1862:

'For having, on the 28th of October 1857, at great personal risk, gone to the assistance of, and carried out of action, a wounded officer, Lieutenant Glubb of the late 38th Regiment of Bengal Native Infantry. He also was himself subsequently wounded and sent to Agra. Conductor Miller was at the time employed with heavy howitzers and ordnance stores attached to a detachment of troops commanded by the late Colonel Cotton C.B., in the attack, on the abovementioned date, on the rebels who had taken up their position in the serai at Futtehpur Sikri, near Agra.'

James Miller rose to become Honourable Captain and Deputy Commissary in 1879 and retired in 1882. He seems to have had trouble in obtaining his Cross, for Colonel Cotton, who appears to have sanctioned the award, died.[4] Like many Indian Mutiny VCs there are no details of date or place where Miller received his VC, except 1862 and India.

DACCA

Now the capital of Bangladesh, Dacca was the easternmost extent of the Mutiny. The Mutiny threatened to engulf the whole of Bengal, but in the event only Dacca and Chittagong were temporarily affected. The 73rd Bengal NI was stationed at Dacca with two companies at Jalpaiguri, when a rumour spread in July that the sepoys at the latter had mutinied. This and similar rumours proved false but it heightened tension between the British and the sepoys. The Chittagong sepoys finally mutinied on 21 November, plundered the treasury and marched on Dacca. Learning of this, the officers decided to disarm the Dacca sepoys and Native Guards; the latter, however, laid down their arms without resistance. Not so the 73rd, which prepared to resist.

Arthur Mayo
17-year-old Arthur Mayo had arrived in India in 1855 as a Royal Navy Midshipman on HMS *Wellesley*, before transferring to the Indian Navy. He was serving on the steam paddle frigate *Punjaub* when the officers and men were formed into No.4 Detachment of the Naval Brigade and sent from Calcutta to Dacca to help suppress the mutiny in East Bengal. By 22 November, they had reached Dacca. Led by Lieutenant T.E. Lewis, five officers and eighty-five men stormed and captured the Treasury. Then they went on the Lall Bagh, a large enclosure, where they found the mutinous sepoys already drawn up in front of the magazine with two 6-pounder guns in the centre. The Lall Bagh had a domed mosque in the centre, a hospital and other buildings. The barracks on top of a hill had been loopholed and was heavily defended by between 300 and 400 sepoys.

The Bluejackets deployed into a line as the sepoys opened fire with muskets and canister shot. Fortunately, they aimed too high and the sailors replied with a volley before charging up the hill to the barracks. Quickly they broke down the door and rushed inside. In the desperate close-fighting struggle, many sepoys were bayoneted, while the rest escaped into the jungle. With the barracks secure, the sailors charged down the hill and took the remaining rebels in the flank. In this last charge, Midshipman Mayo placed himself some twenty yards in front of his men and led the charge with a great cheer, and captured one of the 6-pounder guns. This action snuffed out any further mutinies in East Bengal.

Mayo remained with the Naval Brigade and was later Mentioned in Despatches for his part in an expedition into the Arbor Hills in the far north-east of India. The Adi tribe had been causing trouble with their raiding and a small punitive expedition was sent in February 1859. In the capture of a native stockade, Mayo received a wound in his hand from a poisoned arrow and was invalided home.

Lieutenant Lewis praised Mayo's conduct at Dacca and as a result he was awarded the Victoria Cross, which he received by registered post in 1862. Another version mentioned in John Winton's book *The Victoria Cross at Sea* states that he received his Cross from the Prince of Wales on 22 June 1864, while he was an undergraduate at Oxford studying Theology.

When he graduated, Mayo was ordained Deacon in 1866 and was Curate in 1867. He converted to Catholicism and resided at St.Mary's, Torquay. He died in 1920 at the age of 80.

NARNAUL

The village of Nasipur lay near the town of Narnaul in Haryana, to the west of Delhi. It was learned that the rebel Jodhpur Legion, which had mutinied at Erinpura, was marching towards Delhi. Lieutenant John Gerrard, commanding 1st Bengal Fusiliers, set out from Delhi with a column of 2,500 men to intercept the mutineers. They reached Narnaul on 16 November 1857 and learned the enemy was encamped at the nearby village of Nasipur.

Marching towards the camp, Gerrard halted his men so they could eat. Shortly a cloud of dust was spotted and soon they saw masses of horsemen approaching. When they came under cannon-fire, Gerrard immediately ordered the advance. The British artillery replied and the Carabiniers and Guides Cavalry charged into the dust. With the flash and scrape of swords, the cavalry combat began. Soon the enemy sowars gave way and the British cavalry swooped on the gunners, followed by the Bengal Fusiliers to complete the rout. The British lost seventy killed, including their commander, Colonel Gerrard, who insisted on wearing a bright red jacket which made him an irresistible target.

Francis Brown

Born at Bhagalpur, India on 7 August 1837, Francis David Millet Brown entered the Bengal Army in December 1855. He was a lieutenant by the time he performed his heroic act at Narnaul. His citation, published on 17 February 1860, was a brief one:

'For great gallantry at Narrioul [sic], on the 16th Nov.1857, in having, at the imminent risk of his own life, rushed to the assistance of a wounded soldier of the 1st European Bengal Fusiliers, whom he carried off under a heavy fire from the enemy, whose cavalry were within forty or fifty yards at the time.'

He remained in India and in 1864, joined the Bengal Staff Corps. Brown was presented with his Cross by General Sir Hugh Rose, C-in-C Indian at Mooltan in December 1860.[5] His subsequent career was unexceptional as he climbed the promotion ladder to reach Colonel (Unemployed Supernumerary). He died at Sandown on the Isle of Wight in 1895.

CHOTA BEHAR

At the end of September, the Ramgarh Light Infantry Battalion mutinied at Chota (Chutra or Chuttra) close to the border between Chota Nagpore District and Behar in West Bengal. A mixed force of about 280 made up of the Left Wing of the 53rd (Shropshire) Regiment and the Bengal Military Police, under the command of Major F. English of the 53rd, confronted about 1,000 mutineers. Although completely outnumbered, English's small force completely routed the mutineers, capturing their guns and treasure. Two Victoria Crosses were awarded for this largely forgotten action.

John Daunt and Denis Dynon

John Charles Campbell Daunt was born on 8 November 1832 at Autranches, Normandy. After attending the Addiscombe College, he was commissioned in the 70th Bengal Native Infantry before transferring to the Bengal Military Police in July 1857. In the fight against the mutineers of the Ramgarh Battalion, he shared his citation with Corporal (later Sergeant) Denis Dynon of the 53rd Regiment. Published in *The London Gazette* of 25 February 1862, it read:

'Lieutenant Daunt and Sergeant Dynon (53rd Regiment) are recommended for conspicuous gallantry in action, on 2nd of October, 1857, with the mutineers of the Ramgurgh Battalion at Chota Behar, in capturing two guns, particularly the last, when they rushed at and captured it by pistolling the gunners, who were mowing the detachment down with grape, one-third of which was hors de combat at the time.'

In fact, this was just half of John Daunt's citation, for he performed another gallant act at Gopalganj in Bihar. His citation went on to read:

'Lieutenant Daunt is also recommended for chasing, on 2nd of November following, the mutineers of the 32nd Bengal Native Infantry, across a plain into a rice cultivation, into which he followed them with a few of Rattray's Sikhs. He was dangerously wounded in the attempt to drive out a large body of these mutineers from a large enclosure, the preservation of many of his men, on this occasion, being attributed to his gallantry.'

After Daunt received his VC through registered post, he wrote to the War Office claiming he should have received both Cross and Bar as his citation which was for two separate actions. In reply, the War Office said his claim did not come within the statutes as 'no person is entitled to a bar unless, after having received the cross, he shall again perform an act of bravery'.[6]

Daunt then served as Baggage-Master with a column commanded by Lieutenant-Colonel Fisher. He was elevated to Interpreter and Secret Service Operative as they sought to put down any signs of rebellion in West Bengal. He returned to England on sick leave but went back to India, rejoining the 70th BNI, which became the 12th BNI in 1861. Later he served as a District Superintendent of Police and remained with the Bengal Police, retiring in 1882 as a Colonel. He returned to Britain and died at Bristol in April 1886.

At the end of the Mutiny, Denis Dynon returned home with his regiment and was discharged in 1861. Like John Daunt, he received his VC through the post in 1862 and shortly afterwards died in Dublin aged just forty.

Chapter 4

Delhi's Flying Columns
September to October 1857

Delhi had been captured, but because so many mutineers escaped before its fall, there was no time to delay in bringing these groups to battle. In their weakened state, the victors could only muster a small flying column numbering 750 British and 1,900 native soldiers. In command was Colonel Edward Greathed of the 8th Regiment, a surprise, though not altogether popular, choice over the experienced Colonel James Hope Grant.

Frederick Roberts described the leaving of Delhi: 'Nicholson's funeral was taking place as we marched out of Delhi at daybreak on the morning of the 24th September ... That march through Delhi in the early morning light was a gruesome proceeding. Our way from the Lahore gate by the Chandni Chauk led through a veritable city of the dead; not a sound was to be heard but the falling of our footsteps; not a living creature was to be seen. Dead bodies were strewn about in all directions, in every attitude that the death-struggle had caused them to assume, and in every stage of decomposition. We spoke in whispers, as though fearing to disturb those ghastly remains of humanity.'

On the morning of the 28th, the cavalry sent ahead to scout and came under fire from enemy videttes at a crossroads. Greathed was informed that the main body of the enemy was located two miles away in the town of Bulandshahr.

BULANDSHAHR

The battle quickly evolved. The mutineers occupied a strong position behind a breastwork at the entrance to the town with six cannon including two 9-pounders. Their left flank was covered by enclosed gardens and ruined buildings but a charge by 8th Regiment and the 2nd Punjab

Regiment soon cleared that area of the enemy. The 75th Regiment, supported by the Royal Horse Artillery, charged the centre and captured two of the 9-pounders. The enemy began to pull back and were followed by a small body of the 9th Lancers, already basking in the nickname given to them by the mutineers – the Delhi Spearmen. The Lancers, led by Captain Drysdale, were joined by Frederick Roberts and his friend Augustus Anson, of the 84th (York and Lancaster) Regiment, eager to join in the pursuit.

Augustus Anson
The Honourable Augustus Henry Archibald Anson was born on 5 March 1835, the third son of the 1st Earl of Lichfield. He was commissioned into the Rifle Brigade on 27 May 1853 and two years later was sent to the Crimea where he was promoted to captain. He exchanged to the 84th Regiment and was made ADC to his uncle, General the Honourable George Anson, Commander-in-Chief India. On his way to take command of the Delhi Column on the Ridge, General Anson succumbed to cholera. His nephew was then appointed ADC to Colonel Hope Grant. Anson joined Greathed's Flying Column and attached himself to the cavalry. He rode his late uncle's horse described by Captain Garnet Wolseley as 'a big, flea-bitten, greyish Gulf Arab that had belonged to his uncle, General Anson … Augustus was an indifferent horseman and a bad swordsman, [but] never lost the chance of taking part in any cavalry charge that was going on in his neighbourhood.'

When the mutineers began to withdraw into Bulandshahr town, the infantry refused to move, fearing they would suffer the same experience they had endured in the streets of Delhi. Anson wrote: 'They could not be got to look round a corner or to advance in any way.'

He now joined the charge into the main street. 'I went through with them [the 9th Lancers]. We passed through a shower of musketry from both sides of the houses. We met with no loss till we got to the other side of the city. There the enemy had made a stand for a moment, but with the head squadron charging, the rebels took flight.'

The 9th Lancers reformed and prepared to rejoin the main body but found their way blocked by a number of carts that had been dragged across a gateway so trapping them in the *serai*. Anson took the initiative, grabbing a lance and knocking the drivers from their carts.

During the Delhi siege, Anson had the forefinger of his right hand shot off by a bullet that had then passed through his left arm. This had weakened his grip so he was not in complete control of his horse, which plunged into a group of mutineers, who fired a volley at him. His horse galloped on and he was lucky to escape with just one ball passing through the flap of his coat.

Anson went onto perform other brave deeds, including joining the storming party at the taking of the Secundra Bagh during the Second Relief of Lucknow. Wolseley recalled: 'During the course of the Mutiny he had a large number of hand-to-hand encounters with individual sowers, in which he generally killed his man. I can see him now in my mind's eye, with his mouth firmly closed and determination marked on every feature of his face. He was in every sense a soldier, absolutely indifferent to danger; he revelled in these hand-to-hand encounters ... He charged with Fraser of the 7th Hussars [at Nawab-Gunge 15 June 1858] and joined in this mêlée to his heart's content. When I saw him after the charge, his flea-bitten grey was bleeding from many a sabre-cut.'

Augustus Anson was gazetted on 24 December 1858 and he received his Cross from the Queen at Buckingham Palace in 1859. He also married the same year before returning to the Far East and acting as ADC to General Sir James Hope Grant during the China War. Once again he was in the thick of the fighting and cut the ropes holding a drawbridge at the North Taku Fort. To show his appreciation, Hope Grant sent him back to the UK with his despatches announcing the capture of Peking.

Now a Lieutenant-Colonel, Anson entered Parliament as a member for Lichfield. He died at the early age of 42 in Cannes, France, where he was buried.

James Reynolds Roberts
Born in Bow, London, in 1826, Private Roberts was part of the group that followed Captain Anson through the streets of Bulandshahr. Despite being wounded in the bridle hand, Roberts rode to the rescue of Farrier Stillman, who had been shot off his horse. Immediately the two soldiers were surrounded by sepoys, but Roberts managed to hold them off until help arrived. Unfortunately, Stillman died of his injuries but his rescuer was recommended for the Victoria Cross, which was gazetted on 24 December 1858. Sadly, Roberts died on 1 August 1859 at Marylebone, London and his VC was sent to his next to kin.

Robert Blair and Patrick Donohue
Robert Blair was born on 13 March 1834 in Linlithgow, Scotland, and was an academically gifted student who gained honours at the University of Glasgow and later, Balliol College, Oxford, where he studied Law. He was expected to follow his father's footsteps and become a lawyer; instead he chose a career in the Army. Whether or not his father was disappointed with his son's change of career, he did purchase a commission for him in the

70

9th Lancers. In late 1856, Blair exchanged to the 2nd (Queen's Bays) Dragoon Guards but, as the regiment was scheduled to be posted to India, he elected to remain with the 9th Lancers until his new regiment arrived.

Blair and his close friend and fellow officer, Alfred Jones, resolved to win the new gallantry award as a means of standing out from the rest of the young officers.

During the cavalry action at Bulandshahr, Captain Blair was ordered to bring in an abandoned ammunition wagon. Taking a sergeant and twelve men, he approached the wagon when suddenly about sixty enemy horsemen appeared from behind some buildings. Despite the heavy odds against him, Blair led his men in a charge against the enemy and managed to kill three of them. In the process, he received a sabre-cut across his left shoulder.

Private Patrick Donohue saw Blair was disabled and about to be hacked to death so moved to defend him and lead him to safety. The small party fought their way clear, leaving nine dead, including Blair's tally, before making it back to their lines. Blair was found to be severely injured as the sword-blow had nearly severed his arm from his shoulder very close to the joint. The regimental surgeon had little alternative but to amputate the damaged arm.

Both Blair and his rescuer, Donohue, were recommended for the Victoria Cross. Robert Blair's was announced in *The London Gazette* on 18 June 1858 and Patrick Donohue's on 24 December 1858.[1] Donohue received his from the Queen on 4 January 1860 at Windsor Castle.

When he was well enough, Blair returned to England and received his Cross from the Queen at an investiture at on 2 August 1858 at Portsmouth. Almost immediately afterwards, Blair returned to India but died of smallpox on 28 March 1859 at Cawnpore.

Robert Kells

Born the son of a serving soldier in Meerut on 7 April 1832, Robert Kells was destined to serve the Queen. On 22 October 1844, at the age of 12 years and 9 months, Kells was attested as boy soldier to the 9th Lancers. He took part in the Second Sikh War and was present at Chillianwala and Gujarat. At Bulandshahr, Kells was orderly to Captain Drysdale, who was leading the charge when his horse was shot under him. Falling heavily, Drysdale's collar bone was fractured and he lay helpless. Lance Corporal Kells and Private Jordan reined in and went to Drysdale's assistance as the mutineers closed in for an easy kill. Kells and Jordan managed to keep the sepoys at bay until further assistance arrived. Jordan was severely wounded by a musket ball and did not survive. Kells was nominated for the Victoria Cross, as was Captain Drysdale. The award was approved for Kells but not for Drysdale.

Kells' citation appeared in *The London Gazette* on 19 December 1858. He had to wait some time before he received his Cross as it was one of fifteen forwarded by the Secretary of State for War for presentation in India. By the time the Crosses arrived, the 9th Lancers were already on the voyage back to Britain. In error, Kells' VC was included with those of the 9th Lancers and returned to London, despite Kells remaining in India and transferring to the 1st Bengal European Light Cavalry.[2]

Finally, the much-travelled VC journeyed back to India and Kells received it at Allahabad in 1860.

He was medically discharged from the Army after a fall from his horse and whilst suffering from one of the many tropical diseases prevalent in India. Electing to live in London, Kells travelled to England, a country he had never seen. He applied for and was appointed a Yeoman of the King's Body-Guard at the Tower of London in 1881 and was present at many State occasions. He died in London on 14 April 1905.

The Battle of Bulandshahr resulted in the awarding of five Victoria Crosses to men of the 9th Lancers. By the end of the Mutiny campaign, the Regiment had won twelve VCs, more than any other cavalry regiment.

Also taking part in this battle were three HEIC Cavalry officers, John Watson and Dighton Probyn of the 2nd Punjab Cavalry and Hugh Gough leading a squadron of Hodson's Horse – all of whom were destined to receive the Victoria Cross during the following year.

At the beginning of the battle for Bulandshahr, two of the guns of the Bengal Horse Artillery had advanced too far forward and came under very heavy musketry fire from the enemy. The exposed crews were either killed or disabled but two men continued to operate their gun despite the withering fire, finally managing to cause the sepoys to retreat. Their steadfastness was noted by Major Frank Turner in his despatch and both men were recommended for the Victoria Cross.

Richard Fitzgerald

Born in Cork, Ireland in 1831, he enlisted in the Bengal Horse Artillery in December 1851. After the Mutiny, he transferred to the Royal Artillery as 'Local in India' and was pensioned off in 1872. He drew his pension until 1884 when, it is presumed, he died, though the actual date and place are unknown.[3]

Bernard Diamond
Diamond was born in 1827 in Co. Antrim. He worked as a labourer until the age of twenty when he enlisted in the Bengal Horse Artillery in 1847 in time to take part in the battles of the Second Sikh War. In 1854, he was promoted to sergeant and married a widow named Mary Collins. Both he and Gunner Fitzgerald were gazetted on 24 April 1858 but when and where their received their Crosses is unknown.

Sergeant Diamond went on to fight at Agra, Cawnpore and the Relief of Lucknow. He received three wounds, one of which was to the head. This resulted in him losing the sight in one eye and he was medically discharged in 1861. In 1875, Diamond and his family immigrated to New Zealand and settled at Masterton on the North Island, where he died in 1892.

In total, seven Victoria Crosses were awarded for an action which lasted just three hours.

AGRA

During July and August, the city of Agra with its imposing Red Fort was a very isolated British outpost surrounded by a country in a state of rebellion and anarchy. A large rebel force had assembled at the old Mogul capital of Fatehpur Sikri, only twenty-three miles distant and the Europeans at Agra withdrew to the protection of the Red Fort. On 4 July, it was learned that this force had advanced to Sassiah, just five miles away, and a small force of 742 men under the elderly Brigadier Polewhele was sent to disperse them.

The inadequacy of Polewhele's force was quickly exposed when it was outgunned by the rebel artillery and soon running low on ammunition. After nearly three hours, Polewhele ordered a withdrawal back to the fort – a severe blow to British prestige in the area. The rebels, instead of following up their victory, chose to join their fellow mutineers in Delhi, leaving a small force to enforce a half-hearted siege.

The authorities at Agra sent an urgent appeal requesting relief from the anticipated attack by the Gwalior, Mhow and Delhi insurgents. Greathed's column had camped at Bolandshuhu for six nights before continuing its march. During the course of the march, the Flying Column learned of the situation at Agra and when they arrived at Bijaigarh on 9 October, Greathed had to make a decision.

The Flying Column's priority was to link up with the forces assembling at Cawnpore for the relief of Lucknow, but Agra's plight sounded so urgent that Greathed ordered a forced march of forty-four miles in twenty-four hours to rescue the desperate defenders. Dusty and exhausted, the column reached Agra on the morning of 10 October only to find to their disgust that there was no sign of the rebels. To add to their annoyance the female residents were heard to remark: 'Was ever such a dirty-looking lot seen?' Another assumed that the bearded and sun-burnt soldiers of the 8th Regiment must be Afghans!

Greathed's men were assured that the rebel army was nowhere in the vicinity and had moved on towards Gwalior. Tents were pitched on the parade ground where many of the troops immediately fell asleep. Others prepared breakfast and large numbers of the inquisitive population came to look upon their rescuers. Having been assured that there were no rebels in the area, no picquets or patrols were posted. The camp took on a carnival atmosphere and tradesmen came from the city to sell their wares.

Then four jugglers appeared and prepared to entertain a party of Sikhs and 9th Lancers. Suddenly they threw off their cloaks, drew their *tulwars* and began to attack their audience. The relaxed scene was violently transformed when a large rebel force emerged from the high growing crops at the edge of the camp supported by two heavy guns. The civilians who had come to look at the men of the Flying Column made a panicked dash for the fort, impeding reinforcements hurrying to the camp. To complete the confusion, rebel cavalry galloped into the camp hacking at the bewildered mob. Fortunately, some troopers of the 9th Lancers managed to get mounted and confront the rebels.

Led by Captain French and Lieutenant Alfred Jones, the Lancers managed to hold the rebel horsemen and buy precious time for the reinforcements to arrive.

Captain French was killed and Lieutenant Jones was shot and fell from his horse. The rebel horsemen hacked at the helpless officer until Private John Freeman rode to his rescue, killing the leader of the rebel cavalry and keeping the sepoys at bay. For this act of gallantry, Freeman was recommended by General Sir James Hope Grant for the Victoria Cross, which was gazetted on 24 December 1858.

John Freeman

John Freeman was born in 1833 in the village of Barming near Maidstone in Kent. He followed his father as an agricultural labourer, but when he was 24, he enlisted in the 9th Lancers and joined them in India. Little is known of his service career. Apart from the affair at Agra, he was involved in many more battles during the Mutiny campaign and was dangerously wounded during the Battle of Bareilly in May 1858 – the only British casualty. Freeman was invested with his VC by the Queen on 4 January

1860 at Windsor Castle. He was invalided out of the Army but lived until he was eighty and died in Hackney, East London, on 1 July 1913.

Dighton Probyn

Three squadrons of Punjab Cavalry, under the command of Captain Dighton Probyn and Captain Younghusband, were in the saddle and hurrying to reach the enemy's right flank. Charging on ahead of his men, Probyn dashed into a party of six sepoys, cutting two down before his men caught up with him. Soon afterwards he was bayoneted in the chest but managed to slay his assailant. He then spied a rebel standard-bearer surrounded by a guard of sepoys and sowars and charged the group. One sowar managed to get the better of Probyn and was about to deliver a telling blow. Probyn's orderly, who kept close to him, saw the danger and thrust his arm in the path of the descending blow, practically severing his arm. The devoted orderly died two days later. Probyn captured his standard and the Punjabis drove off the rebels who abandoned two guns.

It was largely for Probyn's courageous behaviour at Agra that he was later awarded the Victoria Cross. He did continue to perform acts of gallantry throughout the Mutiny and his citation, published in *The London Gazette* on 18 June 1858 (Waterloo Day), reflects this with a concluding comment: 'These are only a few of the gallant deeds of this brave young officer.' In fact, Probyn was Mentioned in Despatches a further four times.

The squadron of the 2nd Punjab Cavalry which he commanded was frequently referred to as Probyn's Horse and identified by their khaki dress and blue turbans. Later he was to command the 1st Sikh Irregular Cavalry, and they, too, were commonly referred to as Probyn's Horse.[4] Continuous campaigning, with its frequent hand-to-hand fighting, caught up with Dighton Probyn and he displayed the symptoms of combat fatigue. On medical advice, he was withdrawn from the campaign and sent home to England.

Dighton Macnaghton Probyn was born in Marylebone, London, on 21 January 1833, the son of Captain George Probyn RN. Commissioned in the 6th Bengal Light Cavalry in 1849, he was appointed Adjutant three years later in the newly-raised 2nd Punjab Cavalry. He took part in the assault on Delhi, the Second Relief of Lucknow and many other fights and skirmishes during the height of the Mutiny.

When he arrived back in Britain, he received his Cross from the Queen at a parade on Southsea Common on 2 August 1858.[5] The reverse of the suspension bar was inscribed, 'Capt. Dighton M. Probyn 2nd Punjab

Cavalry'. The centre in the reverse of the Cross, however, is undated as his gallantry covered many different dates.

With his health now restored, the Press noticed that he cut a dash in fashionable society attired in his splendid uniform. An old friend remarked: 'He could not help being showy in appearance – nature made him so.'

He returned to India and persuaded General Sir James Hope Grant to take his irregular cavalry to the Second China War. Each member had to indicate his willingness to serve abroad by signing his name and without exception, every man signed.

Probyn's Horse was in the field again for the campaigns against the troublesome tribes on the North-West Frontier including the Umbeyla Campaign of 1863. In 1870, Probyn was promoted to major-general and appointed ADC to the Viceroy, Lord Mayo. Two years later, he returned to the UK to become equerry to Edward, Prince of Wales and thereafter his life became entirely involved with the Royal Family. In 1877, he was appointed Comptroller and Treasurer of the Prince of Wales Household, a function he carried out until his death.

He was made a full general and received many royal honours. When King Edward died in 1910, Probyn, at the age of seventy-seven, was looking forward to a well-earned retirement. Instead, out of loyalty, he stayed on as Comptroller to Queen Alexandra who, if anything, was even more profligate with her finances than the late King. In 1911, Probyn was paid a unique tribute by being advanced to G.C.B (Knight Grand Cross of the Order the Bath Military Division), becoming the only non-royal to hold this highest grade of the Order.

In August 1911, he fell seriously ill with heart problems and was not expected to live. He did pull through and once more took up the onerous task of trying to control Queen Alexandra's spending. She was recklessly extravagant when it came to charitable organisations and a total stranger to household economy. It became even more serious when the First World War broke out as there many more deserving causes for her to sponsor. Probyn wrote about the Queen: 'The Blessed Lady's generosity knows no bounds, hundred and thousands she is spending on all sorts of war charities.'

Besides his heart condition, Probyn began to suffer from gout in his neck which contracted the muscles so that he could not lift up his head or turn it from side to side. For his 80th birthday treat Queen Alexandra took him to the Hendon Air Show, but he was so afflicted that he had to be lain on the ground to see the aircraft overhead. When he commanded Probyn's Horse he had been made an honorary Sikh and in deference to this singular honour, never cut his long white beard, which had the effect of covering his VC when he was in uniform. In June 1924, he was taken ill at Sandringham and died in Queen Victoria's room. He was buried in Kensal Green Cemetery, London.[6]

Chapter 5

Against The Odds:
Havelock's March
June to September 1857

For six months in the year before the Mutiny, the British Army had been involved in a short-lived war against Persia. This had ended with a peace treaty signed on 4 March 1857 – though news of the signing did not reach Persia until a month later. The campaign commander was Major General James Outram, with Brigadier General Henry Havelock commanding the 2nd Division, both of whom were to operate together in the First Relief of Lucknow.

As the expeditionary force returned to India over the next few months, they became immediately engaged in the outbreak of the Mutiny. Arriving in Calcutta on 17 June, Havelock learned that he had succeeded the deceased General Anson as commander of a Moveable Column being sent to restore British authority at Allahabad and the districts beyond. Events were moving swiftly and he was further ordered to march on to Cawnpore and Lucknow to give support to Sir Hugh Wheeler and Sir Henry Lawrence respectively.

Havelock's appointment was sharply criticised by some who regarded him as too old and hardly a high-flyer: 'An old fossil, dug up and only fit to be turned into pipe-clay.' Lady Canning damned him with faint praise, saying: 'General Havelock is not in fashion, but all the same we believe he will do well. No doubt he is fussy and tiresome, but his little old, stiff figure looks active and fit for use as if he was made of steel.' This 'little old, stiff figure' was to prove to be a very good military leader in his effort to relieve Lucknow.

There were many problems to overcome before Havelock could begin marching up the Great Trunk Road, amongst which were a lack of transport, a shortage of gunners to man the six gun battery, too few cavalry and the worse season of the year to embark on a campaign, with its debilitating heat interspersed with torrential rain. One redeeming note was that Havelock would have the 64th (Staffordshire) Regiment and the 78th (Ross-shire) Highlanders who had served him well in Persia.

The transport problem was sorted out and the shortage of gunners was resolved with the transfer of infantrymen who had some knowledge of working the guns. Besides the thirty Sikh irregular cavalry, another eighteen former officers of mutinied regiments, a couple of infantrymen and a few civilians volunteered as horsemen. The only difficulty over which he had no control was the extreme conditions in which his men had to march.

Finally, on 25 June, Havelock's Moveable Column left Calcutta on a march to Cawnpore that would see them fight a series of battles and defeat an enemy many times larger. This scratch column consisted of about 600 men of the 64th Regiment, 600 men of the 78th Highlanders, a 6-gun battery, thirty Sikh irregulars and eighteen mounted European volunteers. Passing first through Benares and then on to Allahabad, Havelock's men were marching in the wake of Colonel James Neill's avenging force. Along the route was evidence of the terrible indiscriminate retribution Neill and his men had wreaked on the mutineers and the largely innocent villagers. The route was lined with trees and hastily made gallows which still displayed their grisly human remains. Finally the column caught up with Neill at Allahabad on 30 June and the two forces were combined under Havelock.[1]

On 3 July news was received of the terrible massacre at Cawnpore where the male survivors of General Wheeler's defence had been tricked and slaughtered at Satichaura Ghat. This spurred on the Moveable Column which left Allahabad and forced marched its way towards Cawnpore, fighting a series of battles as they approached their destination: Khaga on the 11th, Fatepore on the 12th and Aong and Pandu Nadi on the 15th.

On 16 July, the column reached the village of Aherwa about four miles from Cawnpore. Here they were confronted with the large force commanded by Nana Sahib, one of the prominent rebel leaders, but far from their most skilful. In a fierce fight lasting several hours, Havelock's exhausted command managed to drive the enemy from the field. In doing so, the first of several Victoria Crosses was won in highly controversial circumstances.

CAWNPORE

Henry Marshman Havelock

Brigadier General Henry Havelock had employed his son, also named Henry but familiarly called Harry, as an aide of his staff in the Persian War and did so again in the current conflict. Harry was born on 6 August 1830 at Cawnpore. When he was just 15, he was commissioned as ensign with the 39th (Dorset) Regiment before becoming a lieutenant by purchase with 86th (Royal Ulster) Regiment. He then transferred to the 10th Regiment as Adjutant in 1852 and was appointed to his father's staff for the Persian War and the Indian Mutiny.

Towards the end of the battle at Aherwa, which is more commonly referred to as the First Battle of Cawnpore, Nana's force had pulled back to a position where they were supported by a 24-pounder. The British attack began to falter as casualties mounted from this well-sited gun. With the 64th and 78th taking cover after their huge efforts in pushing back the enemy, General Havelock called for one last charge to take the 24-pounder which stood between them and Cawnpore.

Accounts of what happened next widely differ. The 64th was chosen to head the attack, led on foot by their commander, Major Thomas Stirling, whose horse had been shot.[2] Harry Havelock, the General's ADC, also placed himself in the front of the regiment on horseback and at walking pace headed directly for the enemy's cannon. All the time the regiment was under heavy fire but when it got within range, the men charged with the bayonet and soon captured the gun putting Nana's men to flight.

For his prominent involvement in the advance, Harry Havelock was provisionally recommended for the Victoria Cross by his father. This was later endorsed by General James Outram, who arrived in Cawnpore on 16 September to take overall command.

Lieutenant Havelock's citation, published in *The London Gazette* on 15 January 1858, reads:

'In the combat at Cawnpore, Lieutenant Havelock was my Aide-de-camp. The 64th Regiment had been under much artillery fire, from which it severely suffered. The whole of the infantry were lying down in line, when, perceiving that the enemy had brought out the last reserved gun, a 24-pounder, and were rallying around it, I called up the regiment to rise and advance. Without another word from me, Lieutenant Havelock placed himself on his horse, in front of the centre of the 64th, opposite the muzzle of the gun. Major Stirling, commanding the regiment, was in front, dismounted, but the Lieutenant continued to move steadily on in front of the regiment at foot pace, on his horse. The gun discharged shot until the troops were within a short distance, when they fire grape. In went the corps, led by the Lieutenant, who still steered steadily on the gun's muzzle until it was mastered by a rush of the 64th. (Extract of a telegram from the late Major-General Sir Henry Havelock to the Commander-in-Chief in India, dated Cawnpore, August 18th, 1857).'

Lieutenant Harry Havelock later recalled the battle and his part in it: 'Eager to get ahead of the Highlanders, the 64th had got a little in advance of their front lines when all at once a shrapnel shell from the 24-pounder in their front struck their No. 5 Company, burst, and knocked over six men, one of whom was killed and the other five awfully mutilated. At this, someone shouted out that they were to lie down. They got into confusion. Many broke their ranks and ran back into the village for shelter, and it looked as if they were going to break into a general rout ... I rode up, dismounted, and got the men out of the village by abuse and entreaties. I then got them to lie down in the front line. There the wounded men were left groaning a few paces in advance of the line; and Major Stirling, the commander, instead of sending a few men to remove them, kept beckoning and calling out to me, in the presence of his regiment, "For God's sake, get some help for these poor fellows ..."

'I at last went over and quietly spoke to him about it, and he left off his whining and the men were removed as I suggested. I had noticed earlier in the day that his nerves were badly shaken, and now the thing was critical enough in itself without his making it worse. And I confess that I thought it was all up with us ...

'I must confess that I felt absolutely sick with apprehension; and if I looked calm, I never was before and hope never to be again in such a funk in my life ...

'Just then, the General rode bareheaded to the front. He was the only man who dared raise his head, so close and thick was the fire that rained down upon us; but he had a charmed life, and had come out of some thirty actions without a scratch, though he had lost many a mount. He pulled up with his back to the fire; and smiling, he said clearly and calmly, "The longer you look at it, men, the less you will like it. We must silence those noisy guns. Rise up! The brigade will extend in skirmishing order to the left, in battalion echelon from the left."

'I think I was the first on my feet, shouting, "Get up, men, and take those damned guns!"

'I rode on the right flank of the 64th ... However, contrary to the General's wishes and the rules of the Service, these same officers dismounted and were advancing on foot so as to be less exposed. They were hardly visible to their men and consequently lost in the ranks as far as example or leadership was concerned.

'Major Stirling later claimed that he was on foot because his pony was rendered unrideable by a shell bursting close by. If this was the same animal he was riding the day before, I can understand its excitability. For I saw it on the loose and advancing on its hind legs, determined to bite some other horse if possible, and I had to draw my sword to defend my own mount if necessary. But it doesn't explain the Major's allowing his subordinates to dismount. And worst of all, he was merely grazed on the left shoulder and immediately went to the rear. I then asked each of the three other senior officers of the regiment to take his place; but they all declined, saying it was not their duty to do so. This was poppycock, of course, and they knew it; but there was no time to argue the matter; so I rode forward at once and led the regiment myself, shaming and ridiculing then into steadiness over those twelve hundred yards of level ground, with the enemy blazing shot and shell into us the whole way ...

'To say nothing of the other officers, this action of mine was in itself highly irregular; and I got criticised for it afterwards, especially as I did it without orders; but I had no regrets, considering the irregular conduct of the other officers, and the General thought it was an action worthy of the Victoria Cross; for if it didn't save India, at least it saved the day.'

There is little dispute that Harry Havelock performed an act of gallantry, something he was to often repeat. In response to the accusations of nepotism, his father issued a disclaimer stating that: 'On this spontaneous statement of the Major-General [Sir James Outram] the Brigadier General [Havelock] consents to award the Cross to this officer which, if originating from himself, might from the near relationship Lieutenant Havelock bears to him, assume the appearance of undue partiality.'

It certainly did reek of nepotism and caused much resentment among other officers, particularly those of the 64th. When the wording of the citation reached India, the officers of the 64th felt that it badly reflected on them and wrote to Sir Colin Campbell, the new Commander-in-Chief. Never an advocate of the Victoria Cross, he sent the officers' letter to the Adjutant-General with his own pithy comments:

'This instance is one of many in which, since the institution of the Victoria Cross, advantage has been taken by young aides-de-camp and other staff officers to place themselves in prominent situations for the purpose of attracting attention. To them life is of little value compared with the gain of public honour, but they do not reflect, and the Generals to whom they belong do not reflect, on the cruel injustice thus done to gallant officers, who, beside the excitement of the moment of action, have all the responsibility attendant on the situation. By such despatches as one above alluded to, it is made to appear to the world that a regiment would have proved wanting in courage except for an accidental circumstance; such a reflection is most galling to British soldiers, indeed it is almost intolerable, and the fact is remembered against it by all other corps in Her Majesty's service. Soldiers feel such things most keenly. I would, therefore, again beg leave to dwell on the injustice sometimes done by General officers when they give a public preference to those attached to them over the officers who are charged with the most difficult and responsible duties.'

The troops, nearly dropping from exhaustion, pursued the enemy to the edge of Cawnpore before Havelock called a halt. At the beginning of the battle, Brigadier Havelock passed his watch to his orderly to time the duration of the fight. At its conclusion, the orderly announced that that victory was achieved in two hours and forty-five minutes. In nine days from 7 to 16 July, the Column had marched 126 miles and fought four actions – all in the heat of an Indian midsummer. It was, however, twenty-four hours too late to avert the cruel fate of the 120 women and children slaughtered and dismembered at the Bibighar.

Promoted to captain, Harry Havelock took part in the First Relief at Lucknow. On 25 September, he joined the Volunteer Cavalry in their charge to take the Charbagh Bridge, but a shower of grapeshot left only Havelock alive although badly wounded[3]. Moving on and taking terrible casualties, the column finally reached the Residency and Lieutenant Havelock and his father thus joined the defenders until Campbell's Relief Column reached them in November. Once relieved, Harry Havelock continued campaigning and commanded the 1st Hodson's Horse and, by the end of the Mutiny, had been brevetted Lieutenant-Colonel at the age of thirty.

Havelock received his Victoria Cross from the Queen on 8 June 1859. He also succeeded to the baronetcy bestowed on his father, who died of dysentery at Lucknow within hours of the Residency being relieved by Campbell's force. Parliament also awarded annual pensions of £1,000 to both Harry and his mother.

Havelock went on to serve in the New Zealand War, Canada and Dublin. He had a gift for writing and took a leave of absence to act as a war correspondent in the Franco-Prussian War 1870-71 and the Russo-Turkish War 1877.[4] Ill health forced his retirement in 1881 but when the Anglo-Egyptian War broke out in 1882, he made his way to the British Headquarters in Ismailia, telling a war correspondent he knew: 'Don't for goodness sake mention me in your despatches, for my wife thinks I'm somewhere on the Riviera, but I could not resist coming here to see the fun!'

He petitioned the British commander, Sir Garnet Wolseley, for a role on the staff, but the general refused. Publicly, Wolseley had described Havelock in the Mutiny as the bravest man in India but was his usual waspish self when he wrote in private to his wife: 'Havelock is still here as mad as ever; I received a letter from him yesterday, begging to have it sent home as it was a request to be re-employed, etc, etc., in his usual strain. I am extremely sorry for him, and I feel for him very much, but still feel that he can never be employed again: he is not sane enough to argue with.'

Despite this rejection, Havelock somehow managed to take part in the Battle of Tel-el-Kebir, following the Highland Brigade and riding into the Egyptian defences armed with just a riding crop. He is also said to have joined the Cavalry Brigade in their ride into Cairo. He became a Liberal Unionist MP in South East Durham and championed the local coal miners. He inherited the estates near Darlington from his cousin, Robert Allan, as a condition of which he changed his name to Havelock-Allan.

At the age of sixty-seven, Havelock, now created colonel of his old regiment, the 18th (Royal Irish) Regiment, visited them on the North-West Frontier. They were part of the Malakand Expedition under General Sir William Lockhart, who provided an escort for his visitor. Promising not to take any unnecessary risks, but unable to resist the thrill of danger, Havelock rode on ahead of his escort and was shot dead by Afridi tribesmen on 30 December 1897 and later buried at Rawalpindi.

SLAUGHTER AT CAWNPORE

When the rebels in Cawnpore heard that the column was approaching they murdered all the British women and children held captive, slaughtering them with swords and throwing the bodies down a well. (The men had been killed the previous month after being promised safe passage.) The rebels then blew up the magazine and abandoned the city, which was occupied by the British on 17 July. The British troops were shocked and disgusted by the scenes of carnage and took immediate reprisals against captured rebels. Most were hanged, but many were killed by being blown from guns.

Havelock, now promoted to major-general, was anxious to move onto Lucknow as soon as possible. His Moveable Column had fought itself to a standstill and suffered fatalities through battle and sickness. Even in its reduced state, news from Lucknow made it imperative that the column should make the effort. First, Cawnpore had to be made secure otherwise Nana Sahib would reoccupy the city and deny Havelock a way back over the Ganges.

Havelock chose a defensive position close to the ferry and bridge across the river and left just 300 men – a number he could ill afford – for its

Above: Thomas Flynn (his VC action is recounted in the chapter entitled 'Second Relief of Lucknow').

Above right: Clement Walker Heneage (The Tide Turns).

Below: Henry Marsham Havelock (Against the Odds).

Below right: Duncan Home (The Capture of Delhi).

Above: Henry Ward, on the right, with 78th Foot comrades (Against the Odds).

Below left: William George Hawtry Bankes (Lucknow Taken).

Below right: Thomas Cadell, pictured in 1855 (The Siege of Delhi).

Above left: Stephen Garvin (The Siege of Delhi).

Above right: Alfred Heathcote (The Capture of Delhi).

Left: Herbert Mackworth Clogstoun (Mopping Up).

Below left: Cornelius Coughlan (The Siege of Delhi).

Below right: Thomas Hancock, circa 1858 (The Siege of Delhi).

Above left: Dighton Probyn, circa 1866 (Delhi's Flying Columns).

Above right: Francis Edward Henry Farquharson (Lucknow Taken).

Below left: Harry North Dalrymple Prendergast, circa 1860 (The Tide Turns).

Below right: Nowell Salmon (The Second Relief of Lucknow).

Above left: Valentine Munbee McMaster (Against the Odds).

Above right: James Hollowell (Against the Odds).

Below left: Francis Cornwallis Maude (Against the Odds), on the right.

Below right: Samuel Hill Lawrence (The Defence of Lucknow).

Above left: James Hills, circa 1860 (The Siege of Delhi).

Above right: Herbert Taylor MacPherson (Against the Odds).

Below left: Hugh Henry Gough (The Second Relief of Lucknow).

Below right: John Christopher Guise (The Second Relief of Lucknow).

Above left: Patrick McHale (The Defence of Lucknow).

Above right: Thomas Kavanagh (The Defence of Lucknow).

Below left: Kunoujee (also spelt Kanouji) Lal, the guide of Thomas Kavanagh (The Defence of Lucknow).

Below right: William Edward Hall (The Second Relief of Lucknow).

Above left: Joseph Petrus Hendrik Crowe (Against The Odds).

Above right: Joseph Charles Brennan (The Tide Turns).

Below left: James Blair (Other Outbreaks).

Below right: Augustus Henry Archibald Anson (Delhi's Flying Columns).

defence. In torrential rain, Havelock's remaining force of 1,500 men advanced into Oudh and its capital, Lucknow.

UNAO

They did not have to wait long before they met their first opposition. On 29 July, at the town of Unao they found a strong force of rebels barring their way. With the enemy's right flank covered by a swamp and the left flank by flooded country, Havelock had little option but to attack directly against the centre.

The 78th and Madras Fusiliers advanced up the road and cleared the enemy from the strong points they had made in a series of enclosures. The 64th stormed the nearby village and captured some guns and forced out the defenders. News was received that 6,000 mutineers with artillery were moving into Unao from the Lucknow side. It became a race between Havelock and the rebels who would occupy the town first.

Pushing through the streets Havelock's men made it first and occupied the outskirts which commanded the road along which the rebels were moving. In a brief but fierce exchange, the rebels were beaten off leaving 300 dead and abandoning fifteen guns which had become bogged down.

With the enemy in retreat, Havelock's men chased them another six miles to the walled-town of Bashiratguni. Although the rebels occupied the walls, the sight of the British moving to surround the town was enough to frighten them into further retreat.

Andrew Bogle

One of nine children, Andrew Cathcart Bogle was born on 20 January 1829 in Glasgow. Educated at Cheltenham College, he was commissioned by purchase into the 78th Regiment, following his brother Robert, who joined three years earlier. He took part in the Persian War before joining the Moveable Column.

When the gates were blown at Unao, Lieutenant Bogle led a few men in an attack on a strongly held house that was holding up the advance. Forcing their way in, the 78th became involved in hand to hand fighting during which Bogle was badly wounded. For his action, he was recommended for the Victoria Cross, which was gazetted on 2 September 1859.

He recovered enough to take part in the final assault on Lucknow when he became one of the defenders. Sadly, he learned of the death of his brother Robert during the attack of 25 September.

In 1859, he transferred to the 13th (Somerset) Regiment as a captain and then to the 10th Regiment. Bogle received his Cross on 4 January 1860 at

Windsor Castle. He retired from the Army as a major in 1868 and died at Sherborne House, Dorset, on 11 December 1890.

George Lambert
Lambert was born on December 1819 in Co. Armagh and joined the Army on 6 June 1840. He rose swiftly through the ranks and was serving as a sergeant-major with the 84th Regiment at the start of the Mutiny. He was recommended for the Victoria Cross for gallantry in three separate actions and his brief citation dated 18 June 1858 reads:

'George Lambert, Sergt.Major (now Ensign), 84th Regiment. For distinguished conduct at Oanoa on 29 July; at Bihoor on 16 Aug; and Lucknow on 25 Sept.'

There is no information as to when he received his Cross, but this may have been due to his premature death. During the assault on Lucknow on 25 September, he suffered a severe blow to the head, which may have contributed to his demise. Newly promoted to lieutenant, he returned to England. For a few days he was not feeling well. During a parade at Hillsborough Barracks, Sheffield, he suffered a fatal broken blood vessel and died on 10 February 1860. He was accorded a full military funeral at Wardsend Cemetery and his fellow officers erected a fine gravestone.

BASHIRATGUNI

After two victories in one day (29 July), the Moveable Column rested. Havelock was greatly concerned that his force had been reduced to 850 effectives and the casualties from wounds and disease were occupying all his transport assigned to the sick. Furthermore, he was running short of artillery ammunition. Reluctantly, he pulled back to Mangalwar on the right bank of the Ganges. His request for reinforcements was barely fulfilled; a company of the 84th and a half battery of guns. Although he was hardly any better off, Havelock decided to advance once more. When he reached Unao he learned that the enemy had reoccupied Bashiratguni. On 12 August, Havelock's column prepared to attack the town once more.

Joseph Crowe
The first South African-born recipient of the Victoria Cross was Joseph Petrus Hendrik Crowe, born on 12 January 1826 at Uitenhage, Cape Colony. His Irish father, Joseph Crowe, had been an officer in the 60th Rifles garrisoned in the Cape when he fell in love with, and married, an Afrikaans girl, Clasina Magdalena Vermaak, in March 1815. Placed on half-pay, Crowe

settled in South Africa, starting to farm at Uitenhage. When his son, Joseph, was at an age when he wanted to join the Army, his father applied to Major General Sir George Napier on the strength of his previous service and his request was granted. On 27 October 1846, Joseph Crowe was appointed ensign in the 78th Regiment and joined his regiment in India.

On 12 August 1857, the column came up against the enemy in the village of Boursekee Chowkee about a mile and a half in front of Bashiratguni. The enemy redoubt, on a hill some 400 yards from the main road, was heavily defended by artillery. A deep and wide marsh protected its front and heavy rain had made the surrounding area impossible to move the guns. Without support from their artillery, the infantry formed up ready to storm the redoubt under heavy fire from the mutineers. Lieutenants Crowe and Campbell stood just ahead of their troops waiting for the order to charge through the thick mud. The order was given and both officers engaged in a race to be the first to reach the breastwork.

Crowe reached the redoubt just ahead of Campbell and clambered over the wall, sword swinging and ploughed into a group of mutineers. The troops soon followed and in no time all the rebels had been killed. The rest of the column chased the rebels out of the village and then out of Bashiratguni. The only wound Crowe received was the loss of the end of his little finger to a *tulwar*'s stroke. Both Crowe and Campbell were recommended for the Victoria Cross, but sadly Campbell died of cholera four days later. Crowe's citation appeared in *The London Gazette* on 15 January 1858, but there is no record of when or where Crowe received his Cross. At the same time he was promoted to captain and transferred to the 10th Regiment.

In 1860, his regiment proceeded to the Cape for garrison duty, which gave the newly-promoted Major Joseph Crowe the opportunity to see his family for the first time in thirteen years. A further posting to Malaya and Singapore saw Crowe's health undermined by tropical disease. He sailed to the UK and, in January 1876, ill-health forced his retirement from the Army with the rank of lieutenant-colonel. He lodged with his niece in Upper Norwood, South London and soon after died there on 12 April 1876. This was brought on by a chill he caught while snipe shooting in Ireland which caused lung congestion. Joseph Crowe left his Victoria Cross to his sister but it was destroyed in a fire some years later at his sister's farm in the Cape.

MANGALWAR

Once again Havelock was forced to withdraw having sustained more casualties. Crossing back to Cawnpore, he learned that General Sir James

Outram had been given command of the relief column. Furthermore, on 17 August, General Sir Colin Campbell had taken over as commander-in-chief and he wrote to Havelock advising him to stay until reinforced by Outram's column.

Outram arrived at Cawnpore on 16 September, bringing with him the 90th (Cameronians) Regiment, the 5th (Northumberland) Fusiliers and a battery of 18-pounders. The force now amounted to 3,179 men, but was still destined to be outnumbered by the rebels. Although Outram was fully entitled to take over command, he generously allowed Havelock to complete his task in relieving Lucknow. In the event, there was to be much interference from Outram but their disagreements did not divert their main aim of reaching Lucknow as soon as possible. Outram offered to serve with the Volunteer Cavalry, now numbering 109, a move that Harry Havelock thought was a way of placing himself in a prominent position to get the Victoria Cross; a statement that smacked of the pot calling the kettle black.

A more effective floating bridge had been constructed over the Ganges over which the Moveable Column made their third attempt to advance on Lucknow. On a rain-sodden 21 September, Havelock again approached Mangalwar and found the enemy in prepared positions, with their right flank resting on a loop-holed village with high standing corn acting as a screen to the front. The centre and left were covered by breastworks behind which six guns were placed. As Havelock's men advanced along the road through the heavy drizzle and mist, the rebel's guns opened up on the elephant-drawn heavy British guns. One of the elephants had the lower part of its trunk carried away and, crazed with fear and pain, rushed through the battery causing panic amongst its fellow beasts.

After a long delay, the battery was deployed and returned fire. With the 5th Fusiliers acting as skirmishers, Havelock sent his main force, including the 90th, to attack the enemy's right flank. As the rebels fell back, the cavalry were let loose and went in pursuit. General Outram, mounted on his huge roan horse, was in the thick of the chase wielding a gold-topped Malacca cane, with which he whipped the fugitives. The pursuit went on for eight miles to Bashirhatgani with the rebels losing two guns and 120 men.

William Rennie
Born on 1 November 1821 at Elgin, William Rennie was the son of the Duke of Sutherland's gamekeeper. He enlisted in the 73rd (Black Watch) Regiment and served in South Africa in the Sixth and Eighth Frontier Wars of 1846-47 and 1850-53 respectively. Promoted ensign on 11 August 1854

and lieutenant on 30 November 1855, he transferred to the 90th and served in Havelock's Column. At Mangalwar, Rennie charged the enemy's guns ahead of the skirmishers and set about attacking the gunners and sepoys guarding the guns with his fists and caused such great confusion that the guns were taken with a minimum loss of life.

In the charge at Charbagh Bridge, Lucknow, he again repeated his action and forced the rebels to abandon their guns. Havelock is quoted as saying: 'To do once was bravery. To do it twice was madness.' Rennie was recommended for the Cross and his double citation was gazetted on 24 December 1858. He received his VC in February 1859, presumably by registered post as there is no record of an investiture.

Rennie was promoted to captain and when the regiment returned to Scotland in 1869, he received his majority. He was finally advanced to lieutenant-colonel in 1874 before retiring in 1875. He died in Elgin in August 1896 at the age of 75.

Patrick Mahoney
Born in 1827 at Waterford, Patrick Mahoney enlisted with the HEIC Army and served as a sergeant in the 1st Madras Fusiliers. With his former knowledge of working with horses, he eagerly applied to join the Volunteer Cavalry.

He was recommended for the VC and his brief citation dated 18 June 1858 read: 'For distinguished gallantry (whilst doing duty with the Volunteer Cavalry) in aiding in the capture of the Regimental Colour of the 1st Regt. Native Infantry at Mungulwar on 21 Sept. 1857. (Extract from the Field Force Orders of the late Major-General Havelock dated 17 Oct.1857).'

Sadly Mahoney was not able to enjoy the fruits of his gallant action for he was killed on 30 October within the walls of the Residency.

ALAMBAGH

The next resistance that the Moveable Column met was on the southern outskirts of Lucknow at the Alambagh, a large garden house with strong walls and turrets at each angle encompassing a garden of 500 square yards.[5] The rebel force numbered about 10,000 and extended along a two-mile front with their left posted on Alambagh. They had the advantage of being slightly elevated on a dry plateau, while the British were crowded on a road surrounded by an impassable marsh. With case-shot causing casualties, the column pressed on until drier ground was found. The artillery was now able to reply and soon the British heavy guns silenced the rebel guns.

With the centre being pressed, Havelock employed his familiar tactic of attacking the flank, which was the Alambagh. The 5th Fusiliers, led by Lieutenant Johnson, was ordered to clear the enclosure which they managed to do and in about ten minutes all the sepoys had either been killed or had retreated.

Robert Grant

Yorkshireman Robert Grant was born in Harrogate in 1837 and joined the 5th Fusiliers in 1854 at the age of 17. By 1857, he was made up to corporal and performed his act of gallantry within the walled enclosure of the Alambagh. His citation published in *The London Gazette* of 12 October 1860 states: 'For conspicuous devotion at Alumbagh, on 24th September 1857, in proceeding under a heavy fire to save the life of Private E. Deveney, whose leg had been shot away, and eventually carrying him safe into camp, with the assistance of the late Lieutenant Brown and some comrades.'

Promoted to sergeant, he received his Cross from Lady Hersey at Fort William, Calcutta on 12 December 1860.

When Grant left the Army, he joined the Metropolitan Police as a constable and served in the Y Division, Holloway area, until his death in 1874 from consumption. He was buried in an unmarked pauper's grave in Highgate Cemetery. In 2008 a headstone was unveiled by Sir Ian Blair, the then-Commissioner of the Metropolitan Police. Robert Grant's VC is displayed at the Lord Ashcroft Gallery in London's Imperial War Museum.

ENTRY INTO LUCKNOW

The column began the relief of Lucknow on 25 September 1857. Advancing towards the Charbagh Bridge which crossed the canal that ran from the River Gumti and formed the southern boundary of the city, they were confronted with a well-entrenched enemy. Havelock's men came under immediate fire from a rebel battery of six guns, including a 24-pounder gun which was protected by an earth parapet on the bridge itself. The bridge had to be taken as it was the only way to reach the Residency, for the surrounding countryside was waterlogged from the torrential rains.

CHARBAGH BRIDGE

The town side of the bridge and canal was lined with musketry and well-sited guns guarding the crossing. In order to combat these guns, Captain Francis Maude's battery was called up to within 150 yards under a murderous fire which inflicted many casualties amongst his crews. Lieutenant George Blake of the 84th recalled that he saw Maude, 'standing by his guns, calmly smoking a cheroot, with sixteen dead gunners lying around him. He said to me, as I was passing by with my company, "Lend me some of your men, old fellow, until some more of mine can come up".' One of the volunteers performed so well he was awarded the VC.

Joel Holmes

Joel Holmes was born in Gomersal, Yorkshire in 1821 and was a private in the 84th. His officer, Captain Frederick Willis, wrote: 'At one of our guns, five men were knocked over in as many seconds. I am happy to say, however, that one of my old company (Private Jack [sic] Holmes) was first to volunteer as a "number" at the gun in place of the poor fellow who had been killed; and he remained working at it until it limbered up, for which I recommended him for distinguished conduct. With his and the help of others of my regiment, Maude worked his guns very bravely and steadily.'

Holmes was recommended for the VC which was gazetted on 2 August 1858 and he received his Cross from the Queen at Portsmouth. Little is known of his subsequent life except that he died on 27 July 1872 and is buried in All Souls Cemetery, Halifax.

Francis Maude

Francis Cornwallis Maude was born in London on 28 October 1828 and attended Rugby School and the Royal Military Academy at Woolwich. He was commissioned in the Royal Artillery in 1847 and served in Ceylon until news of the Mutiny brought him and his battery to join Henry Havelock's Column at Allahabad. He had already proved to be an effective artilleryman and was several times Mentioned in Despatches.

In his memoirs, Maude described the action at the Charbagh and quoted from a letter written by Captain Willis, of the 84th Regiment, who wrote:

'Maude's battery followed the 84th to the Char Bagh (Four Gardens), and I shall never forget seeing the two leading guns unlimber, and come into action on the road at very close range (150 yards) opposite the Char Bagh Bridge, under a murderous fire from the enemy's guns in position on the further side of the bridge ... The first discharge from one of the enemy's guns disabled one of Maude's guns, the greater portion of the detachment serving it being killed or wounded. It was then I offered to assist him, by calling for volunteers from the regiments, many men of which, for some time, whilst lying inactive in Cawnpore, had by order been instructed in gun-drill … The gun was again served, the men remaining with it the remainder of the day … A portion of the Madras Fusiliers came up to the Char Bagh in support, and they, with the 84th charged across the bridge, and captured the four guns in position.'

Captain Maude later reported the gallantry of his men to General Outram, who assumed command once the Residency was reached. Outram later ordered a ballot to decide which member of the battery should be awarded the VC. Two ballots were held, and on both occasions Maude was unanimously nominated by his men.

Maude played his part in the defence of the Residency until relieved by Campbell's column in November. He went on to receive two brevet promotions and was made a Companion of the Bath. His Victoria Cross citation, dated 18 June 1858, reads:

'This officer steadily and cheerily pushed on with his men, and bore down the desperate opposition of the enemy, though with the loss of one-third of his Artillerymen.

'Sir James Outram adds that this attack appeared to him to indicate no reckless or fool-hardy daring, but the calm heroism of a true soldier, who fully appreciates the difficulties and dangers of the task he has undertaken; and that, but for Captain Maude's nerve and coolness on this trying occasion, the Army could not have advanced. (Extract from Field Force Orders of the late Major-General Havelock, dated 17th October 1857.)'

He received his VC in India in 1858, although the details of exactly how and when are not recorded. Maude's VC was in a batch of sixteen Crosses sent to Sir Colin Campbell by the War Office on 20 July 1858, with instructions for presentations to be made at the earliest fitting opportunity. Francis Maude was the cousin of another VC recipient – Frederick Francis Maude of the 3rd (East Kent) Regiment who was awarded for gallantry at the storming of the Redan, Sebastopol.

Although he was highly regarded, he must have had serious financial problems for he sold his VC group to an American collector. This came to light when Maude applied for a loan of a VC from the War Office in 1897. A statement was made by the Commander-in-Chief that 'he much regretted that an officer should sell such an honourable distinction'. The American buyer allowed Maude to wear his group during his lifetime but a provision in Maude's will deemed it should be returned to the collector on his death.

Colonel Maude was made a Military Knight at Windsor Castle and on the evening of 23 October 1900, while returning home, he collapsed and died within the castle walls.

His funeral took place at St George's Chapel, Windsor Castle and he was buried in nearby Windsor Cemetery. Despite the honours bestowed on him, Francis Maude left an estate worth just £63.15.6.

Abraham Boulger

Born in Co. Kildare on 4 September 1835, Abraham Boulger joined the 84th in India. His citation dated 18 June 1857, covers his bravery during the whole of Havelock's advance on Lucknow and reads: 'Date of Acts of Bravery, from 12th July to 25th September, 1857. For distinguished bravery and forwardness; a skirmisher, in all twelve actions fought between 12th July, and 25th September, 1857. (Extract from Field Force Orders of the late Major-General Havelock, dated 17 October).'

An example of his bravery occurred on 24 September in the crossing of the Charbagh Bridge where they were held up by an enemy 68-pounder. Captain Willis of the 84th recalled: 'I was in a front house at the crossroads when a gallant young lance corporal named Boulger came running up and said, "Oh, sir! The Madras Fusiliers are ordered up to take the battery. We can't let them go in front of the 84th!"

'"Certainly not," I said, although the Madras men had not yet had their turn in front. "If you will collect eight or ten men, I will go over the bridge with you."

'He got some men; and as the Fusiliers came up, we all charged together. As we rushed into the road, we received a shower of grape, which took five men on my right and cut the legs right from under them. The leading officer of the Fusiliers (Lieutenant Bailey, who was at my side) had his left foot shot off at the ankle.

'I was struck above the left knee and came down, but picked myself up, and finding no bones broken, rushed on for my bare life; and we were all cheering like madmen, and that one round was the last the enemy fired from those guns. The battery was ours in an instant; and Corporal Boulger, always in front, shot down a gunner just as he was going to fire another round. (I recommended him for the VC and he got it).'

Lance-Corporal Boulger received his Cross on 8 June 1859 from the Queen at Buckingham Palace. He remained with his Regiment and served with them as Quartermaster in the 1882 Anglo-Egyptian War. When he retired in 1887, he was made honorary lieutenant-colonel. He died in Westmeath, Ireland on 23 January 1900.

Patrick Mylott

Born in 1820 at Claremorris, Co. Mayo, Patrick Mylott is one of the many early VCs who left behind very little in the way of information about their life other than their moment of heroism. Mylott enlisted in the 63rd (Suffolk) Regiment on 18 May 1839 before transferring to the 84th on 1 January 1847. He was with the regiment when it joined Havelock's Column on 12 July and was involved in every engagement up to the Relief of Lucknow. Afterwards, when the ballot was taken amongst his comrades, he was voted to receive the Cross. His citation dated 24 December 1858 states:

'For being foremost in rushing across the road, under a shower of balls, to take an opposite enclosure; and for gallant conduct at every engagement at which he was present with his regiment from the 12th July 1857, to the relief of the Lucknow garrison. Elected by the Private soldiers of the regiment.'

He later achieved the rank of Sergeant and in December 1860 was pensioned off after twenty-one years of service. He received his Cross from the Queen on 4 January 1860 at Windsor Castle. On 22 December 1878, he died in Brownlow Hill Workhouse, Liverpool and was buried in a pauper's grave at Anfield Cemetery. In 1994, a handsome memorial stone to Mylott was erected within the cemetery.

William Olpherts

Another Irishman who constantly performed acts of gallantry was William Olpherts from Armagh. Born on 8 March 1822, he received a nomination to attend Addiscombe College and entered the Bengal Artillery on 11 June 1839. He saw much active service during the 1840s, campaigning in Burma, Saugor, Gwalior, the First Sikh War of 1844-45 and the North-West Frontier in 1851. During the Crimean War, he served in the Caucasus with General Sir Fenwick Williams at the Defence of Kars and Erzeroum. He then went to the Crimea where he commanded a brigade of *bashi bazouks* in the Turkish contingent,

At the start of the Indian Mutiny, he was involved in the disarming of mutineers at Benares and joined Havelock's column at Allahabad. Known as 'Hell-fire Jack', Captain Olpherts revelled in danger. Garnet Wolseley, who served in the 90th during the Mutiny, described Olpherts: 'His battery was a sort of military curiosity in every way. His gun-carriages were old, and always on the verge of absolute dissolution; and as for his harness, it seemed to be tied together with pieces of string. First came dear old Billy himself, clad in garments he had used in the Crimean War, a fez cap and a Turkish grego [a rough jacket], the latter tied round his waist with a piece of rope. About fifty yards behind him came his well-known battery sergeant-major, in a sort of shooting coat made from the green baize of a billiard table; then a gun, every driver flogging as hard as he could; then another, a long distance in the rear ... Some of the spokes had gone; they all rattled.'

Olpherts accurately described himself as 'an old smooth-bore, muzzle-loader, hopelessly behind the times'. An example of his dash was apparent when he joined the 90th in their dash across the Charbagh Bridge to capture a two-gun battery posted at the end of a street. Olpherts, who had charged with them, galloped back under a severe fire of musketry, and brought up the limbers and horses to carry off the captured guns. For this and many other actions, he was elected by his regiment for the Victoria Cross. He was awarded the VC in his citation dated 18 June 1858 and received his Cross from Major-General Sir Sidney Cotton at Lucknow on 4 May 1859.

When the Residency was reached, Olpherts acted as brigadier of artillery and, after Sir Colin Campbell's column relieved Lucknow, he was left to defend the Alumbagh as the British advanced position.

William Olpherts finally returned home and retired as a full general in 1883, to being further honoured by an appointment as Colonel Commanding the Royal Artillery. He died at his home in Upper Norwood in 1902 at the age of 81. His VC group is displayed at the National Army Museum, Chelsea.

Herbert Taylor MacPherson

Born on 27 January 1827 at Ardersier, Inverness-shire, Herbert MacPherson joined the 78th as an ensign in 1845. He first saw action during the Persian War.

During the march on Lucknow, Lieutenant MacPherson was wounded at Unao but recovered sufficiently to lead a charge which captured two brass cannon. While he was besieged in Lucknow, MacPherson was promoted to captain and soon after, brevet major. His citation was published on 18 June 1858 and he received his Cross in November 1858. He later transferred to the Bengal Staff Corps and took part in the various expeditions against the troublesome tribes on the North-West Frontier. He commanded the 1st Brigade of the 1st Division in the Afghan War of 1878-80 and in 1882, he commanded the Indian Contingent in the 1882 Anglo-Egyptian War. His final campaign was in the Burma War of 1886, where he contracted a fever and died. He was buried in the Military Cantonment Cemetery in Rangoon.

Joseph Jee

A third member of the 78th involved in the fight at Charbagh Bridge was a non-combatant. He was the Regiment's surgeon, Joseph Jee, who had been born on 9 February 1819 at Hartshill, Warwickshire. After qualifying MRCS in 1841, he was commissioned as assistant surgeon in the 15th Hussars and soon transferred to the Royal Dragoons. In 1854, he was promoted to surgeon and joined the 78th.

His VC citation dated 9 November 1860 is more detailed than most: 'For most conspicuous gallantry and important Services on the entry of the late Major-General Havelock's relieving force into Lucknow, on 25 September 1857, in having during action (when the 78th Highlanders, then in possession of the Char Bagh, captured two 9-pounders at the point of a bayonet), [see MacPherson] by great exertion and devoted exposure, attended to the large number of wounded in the charge, whom he succeeded in getting removed on cots and the backs of their comrades until he had collected the Dooly bearers who had fled. Subsequently, on the same day, in endeavouring to reach the Residency with the wounded men, Surgeon Jee became besieged by an overwhelming force in the Mote-Mehal, where he remained during the whole night and following morning, voluntarily and repeatedly exposing himself to a heavy fire in proceeding to dress the wounded men who fell while serving the 24-pounder in a most exposed situation. He eventually succeeded in taking many of the wounded, through a cross fire of ordnance and musketry, safely into the Residency, by the river-bank, although repeatedly warned not to make the perilous attempt.'

Surgeon Jee was invested with his Cross by the Queen at Windsor Castle on 9 November 1860. He returned to the Royal Dragoons in 1864 and became Deputy Inspector of Army Hospitals in 1868. He retired the same year as Deputy Surgeon General. He died at the age of 80 at his home near Leicester on 17 March 1899.

Valentine McMaster

Surgeon Jee's Assistant Surgeon was Valentine Munbee McMaster who was born on 16 May 1834 at Trichinopoly, India. He graduated from the Edinburgh Medical School and joined the 78th as they took part in the Persian War. His VC recommendation came through the ballot method and was almost a last measure. General Havelock called for recommendations for the Victoria Cross and the only regiment not to forward one was the 78th. When asked why, they stated that no one of their number had more particularly distinguished himself than another. When further pressed, they sent in the name of one of their medical officers, Assistant Surgeon Valentine McMaster.

Francis Maude tells what may be an apocryphal story that rings true. Two private soldiers were discussing who they would vote for in a ballot.

One said he would vote for the Doctor because he was the most likely man to live to wear it. When asked why he thought that, the private replied: 'Because he takes such f...... good care of hisself!'

McMaster duly received his cross in 1858 from Lieutenant General Henry Somerset at Bombay.

He went on to take part in the 1863 Umbeyla Campaign and in 1869, he and the 78th were posted to Halifax, Nova Scotia, where he became involved in the city's social life. He met and fell in love with Eleanor Burmester, fifteen years his junior. They were married in June 1870 and had a son. The new family were soon on the move when the 78th were posted to Belfast, Ireland in November 1871. Tragedy struck when McMaster died on 22 January 1872 from heart disease aged 38. He was buried in Belfast City Cemetery where his widow erected a cross over his grave.

Eleanor, expecting another child, returned to her family in Halifax to give birth to her second son. She met another surgeon, Canadian-born Campbell Millis Douglas VC of the Royal Artillery, and married him on 10 August 1874. Uniquely, she married two men who were surgeons and recipients of the Victoria Cross.[6]

Henry Ward

Born in Harleston, Norfolk, in 1823, Henry Ward joined the 78th in 1845. During the intense street fighting suffered by Havelock's men as they slowly made their way to the Residency, a part of the 78th which had been instructed to wait for the heavy guns found that it was forming the rearguard. As night fell, General Outram ordered that the force should hold the ground they had won until first light the following day. The halt would allow the wounded and the heavy guns to close up with the main column. The wounded were helpless in their covered stretchers (*dhooly*) and men of the 78th were assigned to protect them. Private Henry Ward stood guard over the wounded Lieutenant Harry Havelock through the night. In the morning, he rounded up four *dhooly*-bearers to carry Havelock and another wounded private to the Residency.

An officer of the 78th wrote: 'Lieutenant Harry Havelock, with his left arm shattered at the elbow, and a wounded Highlander lying beside him, was in the leading litter and would have suffered the same fate had it not been for Private Ward of the 78th, who forced the bearers to go on at bayonet point. For that he was awarded the Victoria Cross.'

Havelock appointed Ward as his personal servant. He was recommended for the VC by General Outram and received his Cross in late 1858 without a presentation. Later he was promoted to quartermaster-sergeant, before leaving the Army in 1865. He did not survive civilian life long and died on 12 September 1867 at Malvern, Worcestershire. He was buried in a pauper's grave but when Harry Havelock learned of this, he had a handsome gravestone erected.[7]

TO THE RESIDENCY

Havelock's column had not kept together as a body but was spread out along the route. With nightfall fast approaching, General Outram proposed a halt, but Havelock, who was still in command, insisted they press on as they were only a half a mile from the Residency. With the 78th and a regiment of Sikhs in the vanguard, the two generals and their staffs fought their way through the final heavily defended street. As they fought their way through the bazaar, Brigadier Neill was shot and killed. Finally, they reached the Baillie Guard Gate, the entrance of which was filled with earth and rubble. However, on the right of the gate was a wicket doorway from which the muzzle of a big gun protruded. Quickly, this was pulled back and the first of the relief party entered the Residency to great cheering.

One of those who entered was Ensign Tweedie, who later recalled: 'But the cheering was over when we counted the cost: 196 killed and 535 wounded, or nearly a third of the force – to which 522 more casualties would be added before the garrison was finally relieved. The 78th Highlanders lost the most of any regiment: over one third of about four hundred.'

With a couple of groups still defending their positions during the night, the following day, the 26th, brought another six VC actions.

Thomas Duffy

Thomas Duffy was born in Athlone, Co. Westmeath in 1806 – making him, at 51 years, one of the oldest privates in Havelock's column. He joined the 1st Madras European Fusiliers and was one of the party, which included Captain Olpherts's battery, that spent the night outside the Residency. At dawn on the 26th, Olpherts saw that a 24-pounder, which had been used against the enemy the previous day, was in danger of being captured by the rebels. It was standing in a very exposed position and any attempt to approach it was met by heavy fire. Three men made the attempt; Olpherts, Crump of the Madras Artillery and Private Duffy. With a combination of daring and guile, Duffy managed to fasten a rope to the tail of the gun, which was then pulled back to the Olpherts battery. The gun then was effectively used to clear the road to the Residency. Captain Olpherts recommended Duffy for the Victoria Cross, which was gazetted on 18 June 1858. He received his Cross in 1859 from Lieutenant-General Marcus Beresford at a parade in Mysore. There is no further information of his subsequent life except that he died in Dublin in 1868.

THE LUCKNOW RESIDENCY: SAVING THE WOUNDED

The following five Victoria Cross recipients were all involved in the struggle to save the many helpless wounded left along the route to the Residency. Many had been abandoned to be mutilated or burned alive. An account written by one of the VCs, Surgeon Anthony Home of the 90th, gives a vivid impression of the terror endured by the invalid party as they endeavoured to reach the safety of the Residency.

'The 25th: Our sick and wounded were very numerous and were brought on with great difficulty. Litter bearers fell or deserted in large numbers, and eventually it was necessary to place invalids on the limbers of the guns. At this critical time, our advance was also sorely impeded by most of the guns having to be dragged by hand, as large numbers of horses and oxen and elephants who were pulling them and the ammunition wagons were deliberately killed by the enemy ... Altogether I lost eighty litter bearers that day killed or wounded; this out of three hundred and ninety-four. Of course, many invalids were killed in the litters as we went along: and whenever the bearers of a particular litter were shot down or deserted and there was no room in another litter, as only two men could fit in each, the poor occupants had to be abandoned. It was heart-breaking. All the more so because the officers took precedence over the men, who cheerfully gave place and were left with rifles and pistols in their hands to defend themselves as best they could ...

'At four in the afternoon, we got into comparative safety with the rest of the column in a palace having a large oblong square, where we were very much crammed together; a veritable pandemonium of men and animals. A council of war voted to press on at once to the Residency, and the headquarters wing of the 90th Regiment was ordered to remain behind with the invalids and two of the heavy guns and some ammunition wagons ... So there we stayed the night; and a night of great horror it was, what with the unceasing cries and groans of men and animals and almost incessant fire from the enemy, which rattled on the outer walls of the palace ... We were like rats in a trap, and there was nowhere to hide for shelter.

'The 26th: Our situation was now more critical than ever. The enemy were pressing very close all around us and kept up a storm of shot, shell and musketry on us. We were cut off from the main body of our force by nearly a mile ...'

A message received from Outram ordered Colonel Campbell of the 90th to fight his way into the Residency, which meant abandoning the invalid party. He did, however, leave a barely adequate escort of 150 men. A guide was sent to them who said that the way to the Residency was clear. Leaving the comparative safety of the palace, the invalid party made for the apparently deserted bazaar, but after 200 yards, the rebels began firing on the helpless party.

'Our escort preceded us, firing all the way, but they had really no chance. They were shot down right and left by unseen assailants behind loopholed walls. When I got to the entrance of the main street of the bazaar, I found a number of them lying wounded or dead; and most of the others rushed on with their lives ... The bazaar, which twenty minutes ago seemed deserted, was now occupied by the enemy, who poured out a heavy fire from the roofs and windows, killing both invalids and bearers alike ...

'The gateway at the far end of the main street was now blocked by heavy fire from that direction. There was no other accessible outlet besides the one we had entered, and so there was no hope but to turn back as many of the litters as possible which happened to be near that entrance and bypass the loopholed walls through a small gate on the left.

'Under the able conduct of Assistant Surgeon Bradshaw of my regiment ... some litters were saved and finally reached the Residency by a path along the river. (One of the litters contained Lieutenant Havelock, the General's son and adjutant, his left arm badly broken by a musket ball). For most of the litters in the street, however, the case was hopeless. The bearers were either shot down or had saved themselves by running ...

'All hope seemed gone; but there was one last resource, I ran back with four others into a small empty gatehouse at the entrance through which we had come. Other fugitives then joined us; some stragglers from the main column and some soldiers from the escort who had escaped, and two badly wounded officers.

'The enemy now commenced yelling fearfully. I calculated their numbers at from 500 to 1,000. Their leaders tried to get them to charge down on us, but as often as they came on in swarms of 50 or so, we gave them a volley from the windows and doorways and off they went leaving many dead and wounded behind – some of them nearly at our feet ...

'At this time, we expected instant death. It seemed incredible that 10 effective men could resist 1,000, who were firing a fearful hail of shot through the open windows and doorway. Three of our number were struck down wounded, and this diminished our fire. Worse, the enemy all the time were massacring the invalids in the litters. 'They killed perhaps forty of them by firing volleys at the litters. A little later on, they set fire to some of them – a further attempt to terrorise us – and all who were not already dead perished. But we managed to rescue two more wounded officers and five more wounded men …

'Just as there were no shutters to the windows, there was no door to the doorway; so we made a barricade of sandbags by digging up the floor with swords and bayonets and using the dead rebel's clothes to hold the dirt. These we had to drag in off the portico at great risk, but their pouches replenished our supply of ammunition. We also piled up the dead so as to keep men from rushing in on us …

'After a while, we saw that most of the remaining enemy were tired of rushing us. We had killed over twenty of them, and must have wounded many more. This put a damper on them. But a few were still game, and we had to be ready for them; so we now told off one man to fire from each window. I had only one revolver with only five shots.

'Sure enough, one of the game rebels came creeping up to fire as usual through my window – quite unconscious that at the time an equally game opponent had him covered with a revolver. When he got about three yards from me, I shot him dead; and another, who was coming up, was shot down by one of the men …

'After about half an hour … they set the thatch roof on fire. But we were able to escape by a back window and rushed into a shed behind the house and outside the walls of the quarter, carrying our wounded with us. Three of them were mortally wounded whilst we were carrying them; and strange to say, we sound men did not get a scratch.

'It was now three in the afternoon, and our position seemed hopeless. Surely the enemy would set the shed on fire as well. But just as they had not fired the house immediately, they played cat-and-mouse with us here as well. Imagine our horror when we found that the shed was loopholed all around … and the enemy now came creeping up to the loopholes, firing in suddenly, and then off they went again. We now put a man at every loophole … and this soon checked the second assault. We then had a worse alarm.

'The enemy brought some ladders and got onto the roof, bored holes through it, and fired down on us. The first two shots were fired at me – the muzzles of the muskets being, perhaps, four feet from me – but neither shot hurt me …

'The shed being a very long one, we had a great deal to defend; but luckily the enemy found out that if they could fire through the roof, so could we – with the advantage of knowing exactly where they were by the noise of their feet – so they kept off the roof.

'We now organised our defence: told off each man to his alarm post, and told off the sentries and reliefs. Including wounded, there were nine men fit for sentry and seven men fit to fight; and of these seven, six were unhurt, including myself. It was agreed that if the enemy forced the shed, we should rush out and die outside … there was an anger and resentment against those, as we thought, had left us to perish without any attempt at rescue; uncertainty as to where and how the enemy would next attack us; and added to this, the exhaustion produced by want of food and rest, and the heat and anxiety.'

Home's group had been defending themselves for twenty-two hours without a sign of any help reaching them. Then, suddenly they heard the sound of firing which was identified as the sharp crack of Enfield rifles. 'Up we got; and now I said, "Men, cheer together!" In return, they heard their rescuers give a cheer and within five minutes the men of the rear guard appeared. Now unencumbered with litters, Home's party and the rear guard made its way to the Residency and comparative safety.

Anthony Home

Anthony Dickson Home was born on 30 November 1826 at Dunbar, Scotland. He gained his medical degrees and joined the Army Medical Service in 1847. During the Crimean War he was Regimental Surgeon to the 8th Hussars and the 13th Light Dragoons, both participants in the Balaklava Charge. He then joined the 90th Regiment and was sent to India. His epic defence deep in the enemy-held part of the city has been largely overlooked, in part maybe because no rescue party was sent to look for them and it was the rear guard that rescued them. Certainly, Anthony Home did not raise questions as to why no party came to search for them and the loss of so many undefended wounded.

Deservedly, Home was recommended for the Victoria Cross and it was gazetted on 18 June 1858. He received his Cross from the Queen on 8 June 1859 at Buckingham Palace. He went on to serve in the China Campaign 1860 and the New Zealand Wars 1863-65. In 1873, he was appointed Deputy Surgeon General and took part in the Ashanti Campaign of 1873, for which he was appointed a Knight Commander of the Order of the Bath. He retired as Surgeon General and died at his home in London on 10 August 1914.

William Bradshaw

William Bradshaw was born on 12 February 1830 in Tipperary and qualified LRCS before joining the Army in 1854. He served in the Crimea with the

50th (West Kent) Regiment before being transferred to the 90th. During the chaotic attempt to reach the Residency, Assistant Surgeon Bradshaw became separated from the rest of the party but managed to bring twenty litters to the Residency via a path along the river bank. He was recommended for the VC on 18 June 1858 and was received his award from the Queen, along with Surgeon Home, at Buckingham Palace on 8 June 1859.

He retired from the Army and returned to Ireland, where he died on 9 March 1861 aged 31 years.

Peter McManus and John Ryan

Two Irishmen who shared the same VC citation were Peter McManus, born March 1829 in Co. Armagh, and John Ryan born in 1823 at Kilkenny. McManus joined the 5th Fusiliers and Ryan enlisted in the 1st Madras Fusiliers. Both men were mentioned by Surgeon Home in his account: 'Private Ryan, a straggler from the Madras Fusiliers, could not be prevented from attempting to save his officer, Lieutenant Arnold, who was lying wounded in a litter at some distance. [He had both legs fractured by grapeshot whilst leading the charge at the canal bridge.] Private McManus, a straggler from the 5th Fusiliers, though hurt in the left foot, joined Ryan in dashing into the street under heavy musketry fire, dragging Arnold out of his litter, and carrying him into the gatehouse. They escaped unhurt, but Arnold was shot through the right thigh whilst in their arms. Another sortie was then made and a disabled soldier brought in. He also was mortally wounded – twice – whilst his rescuers remained uninjured. They didn't give up, however until another officer and four more men were saved.'

Both men received a citation published in *The London Gazette* on 18 June 1858, which only refers to their rescue of Lieutenant Arnold. Sadly, neither man survived for long. Ryan, promoted to sergeant, was killed in action at Cawnpore on 4 March 1858. McManus, also promoted to sergeant, died of smallpox at Allahabad on 27 April 1859.

James Hollowell

Londoner James Hollowell was born in 1823 and enlisted in the 78th, and took part in the Persian War. Once again Surgeon Home, who wrote about a number of individual acts of heroism in his account, mentions Hollowell: 'Private Hollowell, a straggler from the 78th Highlanders, was the crack shot of our little band. Whenever the enemy came forward to storm the house, he repeatedly killed the foremost man; and the rest fell back. At last, he had the opportunity of taking a long shot at their chief leader – a vociferous old man with a red beard and turban, and armed with a sword and shield – who died on the spot. After that, most of the enemy went away. And none too soon, as we had only seven rounds left to fire.'

Hollowell was recommended for the VC and his citation dated 18 June 1858 reads: 'A party, on 26th of September 1857, was shut up and besieged in a house in the city of Lucknow, by rebel sepoys. Private James Hollowell, one of the party, behaved, throughout the day, in the most admirable manner; he directed, encouraged and led others, exposing himself fearlessly, and by his talent in persuading and cheering, prevailed on nine dispirited men to make a successful defence, in a burning house, with the enemy, firing through four windows. (Extract from Divisional Orders of Major-General Sir James Outram, GCB, dated 14 October 1857)'. Promoted to Lance-Corporal, Hollowell was presented with his Victoria Cross by General Outram in 1858.

Archibald Forbes, a famous war correspondent started a new journal in 1867 entitled *The London Scotsman*. He was not only the proprietor but also its only contributor. He wrote everything from sketches, reviews, births, deaths and marriages.

In order to fill up the pages, he also serialised an unpublished novel he had written about the Indian Mutiny. Having no first-hand experience of either India or campaigning, Forbes employed a veteran who worked as a commissionaire outside a gentleman's outfitters in Oxford Street. The old soldier was none other than James Hollowell. He was paid five shillings an interview for giving detailed and colourful descriptions of his experiences, which Forbes was able to weave into a very readable story.

Hollowell died in London on 4 April 1876 and was buried at Brookwood Cemetery.

Chapter 6

The Defence of Lucknow
June toNovember 1857

News of the Meerut mutiny reached Lucknow, the capital of the newly annexed province of Oudh. Brigadier Sir Henry Lawrence, the Chief Commissioner, had been aware of discontent amongst the native soldiers and had already disarmed the 7th Oudh Irregular Infantry.

The headquarters of the military command for Oudh was at Cawnpore, whose commander was the elderly Major-General Hugh Wheeler, but the only European regiment, the 32nd, was garrisoned at Lucknow. Sir Henry Lawrence got wind of mutiny a week before it broke out at Meerut and began to make preparations to withstand any attack by stockpiling stores and preparing defences at the British Residency in Lucknow. He also assumed military command of all troops in Oudh, which left Wheeler deprived of most of his force. Wheeler began to make preparations of his own to shelter the large numbers of non-combatants in a badly sited and inadequate defensive position on open ground. He appealed to Lawrence to send some men of the 32nd and eighty-five unlucky men were detached.[1]

It was on the evening of 30 May that the 71st Native Infantry mutinied and rampaged through the cantonment three miles from Lucknow. The 32nd was called out and positioned between the cantonment and the city. There were several outbreaks of firing but it was not until daybreak that the 32nd advanced into the camp where they found murdered British officers and burnt-out bungalows. The sepoys of the 71st had moved away and joined a larger body of mutineers.

Over the following weeks there were risings throughout Oudh and neighbouring Rohilkhand. British civilians from the surrounding area were urged to seek protection at the Lucknow Residency and, by the end of June, there were 1,280 non-combatants including hundreds of women and children who had heeded the call. Lawrence's preparations eventually saved the garrison from annihilation. The Residency was constructed in 1780 and occupied the highest point in the city. The grounds covered some sixty acres and were hemmed in to the south, east and west by tightly packed city streets and native buildings, including palaces and mosques, all of which were good vantage points for the rebels. The engineers demolished the mud-walled buildings and enclosures close to the perimeter, but Lawrence initially refused permission for the mosques to be destroyed urging them to 'spare the holy places'. It took a mounting casualty toll before this order was withdrawn. With few soldiers to call upon, Lawrence summoned the help of known loyal native troops, including pensioners, Sikhs and some Hindu sepoys numbering 712. The only British troops stationed at Lucknow were 855 officers and men of the 32nd (Cornwall) Light Infantry. Officers from rebellious native regiments, some artillery gunners and civilian volunteers made up the rest of the effective male defenders.

Lucknow was fast becoming a rallying point for the rebels and during June there were mutinies at Sitapur, Faizabad, Sultanpore and Salon. So far the increasing population of the Residency had not come under fire and the weeks were spent preparing the barricades and gun emplacements with an assortment of materials ranging from packing cases, bedsteads, books and even an old harmonium.

When the rebels heard of the events at Cawnpore, they decided to move on Lucknow. Sir Henry Lawrence learned of this on 29 June and decided to send a force to prevent any further advance on the city. What happened the following day condemned the population of the Residency to 139 days of hellish incarceration in what was an overcrowded and insanitary prison.

CHINHAT

Sir Henry Lawrence was to be commended for his foresight in preparing defences and amassing stores and provisions. Unfortunately, he lost all credit by his handling of an unnecessary battle. Acting on dubious information that an enemy force of fifty cavalry and 500 infantry with one gun was approaching the city, Lawrence assembled an expedition consisting of 300 men of the 32nd, 170 Native Infantry, thirty-six Volunteer Horse, eighty-four Oudh Irregular Cavalry and eleven guns.

During the night of the 29th, many of the soldiers had drunk raw spirits and, in the morning, the majority were suffering severe dehydration. Because of a misunderstood order, the start was delayed. When the column finally started, the men were marching with the sun in their eyes as it approached its mid-day zenith. The men of the 32nd had not eaten breakfast and the native *bisti wallahs* (water carriers) had deserted. In another oversight, Lawrence did not order a reconnaissance and his small force blundered into the mutineers at Chinhat. Instead of the small force he had expected, Lawrence was confronted by a well-organised enemy of 800 cavalry, 5,500 infantry and fifteen guns.

Outnumbered ten to one, Lawrence's native gunners and cavalry deserted. The soldiers of the 32nd were in no fit state to fight, suffering dehydration from excess drinking and debilitated from lack of food and water. Lawrence sent in skirmishers as he deployed his artillery. In an exchange of fire lasting about fifteen minutes, the enemy appeared to pull back. In fact they were sending a flanking force of cavalry around the British right flank.

The 32nd was ordered to take a nearby village but having occupied it, were too weak to resist the counter-attack. The enemy threatened to completely overwhelm the British force. Lawrence belatedly handed the command to Colonel Case, commanding the 32nd, and returned to the Residency to organise its defence. With little option but to retreat, the British made their way to a bridge over the Kukrail stream, the only way back to Lucknow. The rebel cavalry raced to cut off this retreat, but were confronted by the thirty-six Volunteer cavalrymen who threw the rebels into confusion, allowing a significant part of the force to cross.

The retreat was a shambles, but several rearguard actions enabled the survivors to reach the safety of the Residency. Exhausted, dehydrated men were helped along by comrades but several died of heatstroke. The sepoys loyal to the British, especially the 13th BNI, saved many British soldiers, even at the cost of abandoning their own wounded men. One such selfless act led to the award of the Victoria Cross.

When at last they reached the Residency, the 32nd had left behind almost half their number dead or wounded, including their colonel, William Case. The command of the regiment and the whole of the military defence now devolved on Lieutenant-Colonel John Inglis.

Morale fell further on the morning of 2 July when Sir Henry Lawrence returned from his inspection of the posts and batteries. As he lay on his bed dictating his notes, an enemy shell hit his room and exploded with a huge roar, mortally wounding him. Lawrence lingered another two days before dying. The man to replace him was John Inglis, now elevated to the local rank of brigadier.

William Cubitt

William George Cubitt was born on 19 October 1836 in Calcutta to Major William Cubitt of the HEIC Army. In 1853, he joined the 13th BNI and was serving at the cantonment at Lucknow when mutiny broke out. During the retreat from Chinhat, he saved the lives of three soldiers of the 32nd. As a mounted officer, he was able to take one seated behind him and the other two holding on to his stirrups as they made their slow way back to Lucknow. The survivors of the abortive Chinhat expedition staggered back to the Residency, which must have dispirited the refugees. While William Cubitt deservedly received the VC, there were many similar such acts with soldiers carrying comrades on their backs and the Volunteer cavalry with two or three exhausted or wounded soldiers on their mounts.

Lieutenant Cubitt's single sentence citation appeared in *The London Gazette* on 18 June 1858, and he received his VC from the Queen at Windsor Castle on 4 January 1860.

He transferred to the 16th (The Lucknow Regiment) NI and was appointed adjutant in 1862. By 1879, he had become lieutenant-colonel before becoming commandant of the 43rd (Assam) Regiment in Afghanistan. He was awarded the DSO for his service during the Burma War 1886/7 and retired in 1889. He married the sister of James Hills-Johnes VC and retired to Camberley, where he died on 25 January 1903.

As Havelock's final advanced reached its destination, the relief force came under close fire from doors, windows and rooftops as they passed. In the twisting streets some men got lost but managed to reunite with the main party. When the battling soldiers came into view of the Residency the defenders on the roof erupted with cries of joy and support to those who had come to their aid. When the gates were, at last, opened and the ragged troops poured through men and women alike were reduced to tears of gratitude. Over 200 of the 1,000 that attempted the perilous journey were lost.

Almost as soon as the gates were closed and the cheers subsided spirits sank a little. Welcome as the relief force was, it was not large enough to turn the tide. The new combined force numbered around 1,500 and there were still around 10,000 Sepoys on the other side of the wall thirsting for blood. They were still prisoners but now with even more mouths to feed.

Robert Aitken

There were many cases of original defenders prepared to involve themselves in the thick of the action other than for advancement or glory-seeking. One such was Scotsman, Robert Hope Moncrieff Aitken. He was born on 14 April 1828 in Culper, Fife. Having qualified at Addiscombe, Aitken was commissioned in 1847 and joined the 13th BNI. He took part in the Second Sikh War and was present at Ramnugger and Gujarat. His conduct during the Lucknow siege resulted in a five-part citation which was published some six years after the event. Dated 17 April 1863, it reads:

'For various acts of gallantry performed during the defence of the Residency of Lucknow from June 30th to November 22nd 1857.

'On three different occasions Lieutenant Aitken went into the garden under the enemy's loopholes in the "Captains Bazaar". On two of these occasions he brought out a number of bullocks which had been left in the garden. Subsequently, on the 3rd of July, the enemy having set fire to the Bhoosa stock in the garden, and it being apprehended that the fire would reach the powder magazine which had been left there, Lieutenant Aitken, accompanied by other officers, went into the garden, and cut down all the tents which might have communicated the fire to the powder. This was done, close to the enemy's loopholes, under a bright light from the flames. It was a most dangerous service.

'On the night of the 20th August, the enemy having set fire to the Baillie Guard Gate, Lieutenant Aitken was the first man in the gateway, and assisted by some sepoys and a water-carrier of his regiment, he partially opened the Gate, under very heavy fire of musketry, and, having removed the burning wood and straw, saved the Gate.

'On the evening of the 25th September, this officer led twelve sepoys of his regiment for the purpose of attacking two guns opposite the Gate referred to, in order to prevent them from being turned on the late Major-General Havelock's second column. Having captured them, he then attacked and took the Terse Kotee [Tehri Koti], with a small force. [These guns had been left by Maude's battery when the crew's had been killed or disabled, and were in danger of being captured by the rebels].

'On the morning of the 26th September, with a small party of his regiment, he assaulted and captured the barricaded Gateway to the Furreed Buksh Palace, and the Palace itself. On this occasion he sprang up against a small wicket-gate on the right, and prevented the enemy from shutting it, until, with assistance, it was forced open, and the assaulting party were thus enabled to rush in. The complete success of the attack was solely owing to this officer's distinguished bravery.

'In a subsequent sortie, on the 29th September, Lieutenant Aitken volunteered to take a gun which still continued firing, taking with him four soldiers through the houses and lanes to the gun. The enemy fired on this party from the houses, but they held their ground, until, a stronger party coming up, the gun was upset from its carriage, and taken into the Residency. Another gun was subsequently taken.'

Aitken was Mentioned in Dispatches ten times and appears in Colonel John Inglis' reports: 'Lieutenant Aitken, with the whole of the 13th NI, which remained to us, with the exception of the Sikhs, commanded the Baillie Guard, perhaps the most important position in the whole of the defences. With respect to the native troops, I am of the opinion that their loyalty has never been surpassed. They were indifferently fed and worse housed. They were exposed, especially the 13th Regiment, under the gallant Lieutenant Aitken, to a most galling fire of round shot and musketry, which materially decreased their numbers. They were so near the enemy that conversation could be carried out between them, and every effort, persuasion, promise, and threat was alternatively resorted to in vain, to seduce them from their allegiance to the handful of Europeans, who, in all probability would have been sacrificed by their desertion.'

On the evening of the Relief, a work party of Aitken's men had been led out to level a rebel's battery. Suddenly they were attacked by the advancing 78th Highlanders who, mistaking Aitken's sepoys for rebels, charged them with the bayonet. Aitken rushed up, crying: 'For God's sake, don't harm these poor fellows. They've saved all our lives!' His timely intervention restricted the casualties to three wounded sepoys.

Aitken not only had to wait an excessive time for his Cross to be approved, but the actual presentation was something of a farce. Although it had taken six years for his award to be gazetted, Aitken had to wait a further two years, until May 1865, before its presentation. This was due to the Commander-in-Chief, General Sir Hugh Rose, breaking his ribs in a hunting accident and delaying his tour of inspection.

In May 1865, he and his staff arrived in Lucknow to present Major Robert Aitken of the Oudh Police with his long-overdue VC. A general parade was ordered on the very spot where Aitken had performed so gallantly. Just before parade, members of the staff searched for the Cross but it was nowhere to be found until it was realised that it had probably been left behind in Simla. The hope was expressed that someone in the garrison might be a VC recipient and perhaps prepared to lend his Cross for the duration of the ceremony, but this proved fruitless. There was no alternative but to inform the Commander-in-Chief of the blunder; predictably, General Rose was less than pleased. When he had cooled down, it was suggested that Colonel Stewart, who broke the bad news, would lend Rose his Companionship of the Bath from his breast as the troops and assembled company would not be near enough to distinguish the difference. The parade went ahead but at the ball held in honour of the occasion, Aitken wore a painted leather imitation VC.

110

There was a further complication: the Cross was not at Simla and had been lost. When it did arrive, Aitken was billed by the War Office for a replacement for the one he had lost! As the Cross had been lost before he received it, the War Office finally waived the charge and Aitken received his replacement on 5 April 1866.

Retiring with the rank of colonel in 1876, Aitken lived quietly in St Andrews where, when he died in 1887. Those that knew him had no idea that he was a VC recipient.

William Oxenham

The first VC action by a member of the 32nd occurred on 30 June, the same day as the disastrous Chinhat battle. William Oxenham was born on 15 October 1821 in Tiverton, Devon. In 13 March 1841, he married Hannah Harris and soon had a daughter named Charlotte. It is likely that poverty drove William to enlist in the Army for in April 1842 he joined the 32nd Regiment. In May 1846, the Regiment sailed to India aboard *British Sovereign* and arrived in Calcutta on 23 August 1846. Oxenham took part in the Sikh War of 1848-49 and in 1853, was promoted to corporal.

When the survivors from Chinhat reached the Residency, they were closely pursued by the rebels who were quick to establish firing points. One of these was opposite a position which came to be known as Anderson's Post. According to Captain Birch, ADC to Colonel Inglis: 'The principal means of defence of this side, commanded by and named after Captain Anderson, 25th Native Infantry. It was severely handled, and almost destroyed by the enemy. It was, perhaps, the most exposed post in the whole garrison, and the only one called by the name of its own commander during the siege. Mr W.C. Capper of the Bengal Civil Service, was the second in command of this glorious Anderson's post.'

The rebels positioned a six-pounder which hit the outer veranda of Anderson's Post. The position consisted of ten men from the 32nd Regiment and ten civilians trained by sergeants of the 32nd. The house belonged to William Capper of the Bengal Civil Service, who was one of the volunteers. He was standing behind one of the pillars when the enemy's fire brought down the veranda and buried him under six feet of timber and masonry. The enemy's round shot continued to pour over the collapsed veranda. Captain Anderson at once called for assistance in digging out the buried man who most thought was probably killed. Setting an example, Anderson was soon joined by Corporal Oxenham, a Frenchman, Monsieur Geoffroi, Signor Barsatelli, an Italian and two Post Office workers, Lincoln and Chick.

Captain Anderson recalled in his journal: 'The enemy's round shot continued to pour over the place where Capper lay, and to be able to work, the six men I have mentioned were forced to lie on their stomachs and grub away in that position. At length they succeeded in extricating Capper's body, but his legs still remained buried. The situation for him was now replete with danger, for to stand up was almost certain death. In this dilemma, Oxenham, obeying a signal from Anderson, who was supporting the head, dashed round the other side, and extricated at a supreme effort the buried legs. This done, Capper was hauled in by the other five men and was saved.'

For this act, which had taken three quarters of an hour, Oxenham was awarded the Victoria Cross. Later, Capper was adamant that he owed his life mainly to Anderson and lobbied for the same award. Unfortunately, it was not until 1868 that a recommendation was received by the War Office, but was turned down on the grounds that it was over ten years and a limit for applications had been passed.

For Oxenham, the action was probably just one of many dangerous incidents that he experienced during the Siege. On 1 August, he received a serious wound to his forearm but survived. Oxenham's award was announced in *The London Gazette* dated 22 November 1858 with a citation that read: 'For distinguished bravery in saving the life of Mr Capper of the Bengal Civil Service, by extricating him from the ruins of a veranda which had fallen on him, Corp. Oxenham being for ten minutes exposed to a heavy fire while doing so.'

There was no mention of Anderson and the others; such is the lottery of awarding the VC. William Oxenham received his Cross from Queen Victoria at Windsor Castle on 4 January 1860.

The following month Oxenham remarried as during the thirteen years spent in India, Hannah Oxenham had died. It did not, however, take him long to court and marry Caroline Pulman of Exeter. He was discharged from the Army on 25 August 1862 and lived in Bodmin, Cornwall. The couple moved to Exeter where he lived out his final years, dying of meningitis on 29 December 1875. His VC was sold for £70 in 1910 and it now held by the Duke of Cornwall's Light Infantry Museum, Bodmin.

William Dowling
One of the soldiers who had been active in sorties against the enemy guns and survived was Private William Dowling. He was born in 1825 at Thomastown, Kilkenny, and in 1845 was probably one of the thousands of Irishmen forced to enlist in the British Army by the ravages of the Irish

Potato Famine. Posted to the 32nd, he was soon on his way to India and fought at Mooltan and Gujarat in the Second Sikh War.

When the Residency was surrounded on 30 June, he took part in one of the first sorties against the enemy. On 4 July, Dowling and two other men rushed a gun position killing a native officer, before the two guns were successfully spiked. He was not so successful five days later when he led another sortie but found the spike too small. On 27 September, he made another raid and succeeded in spiking an 18-pounder. During the entire raid, he was subjected to heavy enemy fire.

Dowling was also actively involved in the mining and counter-mining operations that went on throughout the siege. These were very difficult and dangerous operations requiring a great deal of physical stamina and courage. At the end of the siege, Captain Crommelin, the chief engineer wrote a report to the Governor General in which he said: 'I cannot close this report without noticing, in the most favourable manner, the important services performed by the under mentioned soldiers, as superintendents of the miners – A/Sergeants Cullimore, Banetta and Farrer; and Corporal Dowling, all of the 32nd Regiment' By the end of the Siege he had been promoted to Sergeant.

Dowling was recommended for the VC and received his Cross from the Queen at Windsor Castle on 4 January 1860. When he left the Army, he joined the Customs and Excise Service and was living in Lancashire, where he died of bronchitis in February 1887. He was buried in an unmarked grave in the Ford Roman Catholic Cemetery, Liverpool.

Samuel Lawrence

Samuel Hill Lawrence was born on 22 January 1831 in Cork, Ireland. His father, also named Samuel Hill, served with the 32nd Regiment of Foot and was wounded at the Battle of Quatre Bras fought on 16 June 1815. His mother was Margaret Macdonald and the family lived at Belmont Cottage, Douglas, Cork.

The young Lawrence joined the 32nd as an ensign on 12 December 1847 and was immediately sent to India to join his regiment. He was present at the Punjab campaign of 1848-49, taking part in the battles at Mooltan, Cheniste and Gujarat.

On 22 February 1850, he was promoted to lieutenant before receiving a promotion in the field to captain at Lucknow. The early preparations for withstanding a siege included the dilapidated fort of Machchi Bhawan, some three miles from the Residency. It had been provisioned and stocked with munitions, but it soon became clear that it was not possible to hold such a position so far from the main garrison. Days were spent transferring the stores and magazine from the crumbling fort to the Residency. With the defeat at Chinhat, Sir Henry Lawrence ordered the complete evacuation of Machchi Bhawan. Captain Sam Lawrence was amongst the few members of the 32nd in the fort as charges were laid for its destruction. In an enormous explosion, some 240 barrels of gunpowder and 594,000 rounds of ball and gun ammunition added to the complete demolition of the old fort.

On 1 July, Colonel Inglis' wife, Julia, recorded in her journal: 'At twelve o'clock (midnight) a tremendous explosion which alarmed us much. I thought the Residency house was destroyed, but we soon heard that the Muchee Bowun [*sic*] fort had been evacuated by Sir H. Lawrence's orders and blown up, and the whole force with their sick, prisoners and treasure had made their way from thence to the Residency without encountering one of the enemy. It was a splendidly managed affair and strengthened our garrison considerably.'

Sam Lawrence's first action that made up part of his recommendation for the Victoria Cross occurred on the night of 7 July. An enemy position called Johannes House stood opposite one of the crucial defensive posts. It was suspected that there was a mine shaft being dug. Julia Inglis wrote: 'They rushed into Johannes House, Ensign Studdy being the first to go through the wall, [they] bayoneted some thirty men they found there and then, reckless as soldiers are, were running down the Cawnpore Road when John [Inglis] called them back ... Captain Lawrence had one of the legs of his trousers blown to pieces but was not touched. This little affair raised our spirits as it had been so thoroughly successful and showed what we could do.' Lawrence was also singled out for praise for great personal gallantry.

Lawrence commanded a very strong battery named the Redan which commanded the iron bridge over the Goomtee river. He was convinced that a mine was being dug from an earthwork about forty yards away. Naturally cheery and jolly, he told Inglis that he 'expected very shortly to be up amongst the little birds'. One of the engineers went out one night and was able to assure Lawrence that there was no tunnel being dug from that position.

On 25 September, the first relief column under Generals Outram and Havelock fought its way into the Residency. On 27 September, Captain Lawrence led a sortie and managed to spike an enemy gun despite being under heavy fire. Colonel Inglis protested that the 32nd was being overused in leading dangerous sorties. He was particularly upset at the death of

Captain McCabe, who had shown constant bravery on the many occasions he had attacked the enemy's guns. It is highly probable that had McCabe lived, then he would have been awarded the Victoria Cross. Despite Inglis' protest, Outram insisted that the men of the 32nd knew the layout of the enemy's positions better than the newly arrived troops.

Sam Lawrence survived the siege and returned home. He was not, however, free from jeopardy. On 10 February 1858, he boarded a ship at Calcutta along with other survivors of the siege. One of these was Julia Inglis who later recalled:

'We weighed anchor about 4 pm. We were told that we were to run into Trincomalee, Ceylon, to land treasure, but the captain said he would go in and out as quickly as possible, and allow no one an opportunity of landing. We expected to reach there the next evening. We made good progress all that day (Tuesday). It was eight o'clock, a beautiful night, and we were running along at a great pace. Mrs Case and I, finding it very hot in the saloon after tea, had come on deck, and were sitting on the bulwarks behind the wheel.

'Suddenly we were startled by a loud grating sound something like the letting down of an anchor, and just then saw a large rock close to us. I said, "We must have touched that". Several men rushed to the wheel, and then again we heard the same sound, only louder, and a quivering of the whole ship. She then remained stationary, only heaving backwards and forwards. We ran below and found the saloon filled with ladies and children, evidently just out of bed.

'Meeting Captain Lawrence of the 32nd, he seized my hand and said, "Don't be afraid, Mrs Inglis". This decided me that there was some cause for fear, but I thought we had run ashore. I begged him to ascertain what was to be done, and, going into my cabin, roused up my nurse Mrs Campbell, and told her to be prepared to leave the steamer.

'My cabin was forward; I was getting something for the children to put on, when Captain Lawrence rushed in and said, "Don't wait a minute! Come on deck at once!" … On going on deck we found the boats were being lowered. The captain, Kirton by name, a young man of twenty-eight, was giving his orders in a quiet, calm manner; the greatest order prevailed, no one appeared to have lost his presence of mind, and not even a child cried.

'The first boat was launched in about twenty minutes, and Captain Lawrence and Captain Foster came and said that I was to go in it. I objected at first, not liking to be the first to leave the scene of danger, but they pressed me and said all would follow immediately, so I made no further remonstrance. As I left the steamer, the captain said, "This is only a

115

precautionary measure." Captain Lawrence had run down to my cabin, and brought me up my cash-box, containing £40 and my writing-desk.'

The night was spent rowing backwards and forwards near the wrecked ship. Distress rockets had been fired but these were not answered. Finally, at daybreak, the seven heavily-laden boats made for Trincomalee, about ten miles distant. Fortunately, there had been no loss of life and eventually all were transferred to *Himalaya* and continued their journey to Britain.

Lawrence was awarded a brevet majority and recommended for the VC which he received from the Queen at Windsor Castle on 4 January 1860 along with William Oxenham and William Dowling.

The rest of his life is shrouded in mystery. Within the space of three years, he exchanged to the 25th (The King's Own Scottish Borderers) Regiment before briefly transferring to the 8th The King's Royal Irish Hussars then finally into the 11th Prince Albert's Own Hussars.

In 1868, he travelled to South America and died on 17 June near the provincial city of San Jose de Mayo about fifty miles from the Uruguayan capital Montevideo. He was buried initially in the Old British Cemetery but reburied in 1884 at the British Cemetery, Avenue General Rivera in Montevideo.

Henry Gore-Browne

The fourth member of the 32nd to receive the Victoria Cross for the defence of the Lucknow Residency was another Irishman. Born on 30 September 1830 in Newtown, Holywell, Co. Roscommon, Henry George Gore-Browne came from a noble family. He was educated at Trinity College, Dublin, but did not enter the Army until the comparatively late age of twenty-five. He was commissioned into the 32nd on 31 August 1855 and sent to join the regiment in India. On 15 October 1856 he was promoted to lieutenant and to captain eight months later.

Major Wilson (13th Native Infantry) had been appointed assistant adjutant-general and kept a diary. On 21 August he wrote: 'At daybreak all was prepared and ready for blowing up our mine and the simultaneous sorties of fifty Europeans under Captain McCabe and Lieutenant [*sic*] Browne divided into two parties for the purpose of spiking the enemy's guns which fired into the mess house and in order to hold Johannes' house while the engineer officers blew it up. Precisely at 5 pm the mine containing 400 lbs of powder was sprung and as soon as the dust and smoke had in a measure subsided, the party ran out.'

Captain Browne was the first man to enter the enemy battery, which was protected by high palisades, the embrasures being closed with sliding shutters.

Browne pulled aside the shutters and leapt into the battery and drove out the gun crews. The two guns were successfully spiked and the enemy position demolished. For this act, Browne was recommended for the Victoria Cross.

Browne, like all the officers of 32nd, took part in many sorties, which were not always regarded with favour. Julia Inglis later wrote of one such raid on 1 October after General Outram had taken command with the first relief: 'Mr Browne led the 32nd today in the sortie. Mr Browne returned untouched, contrary to our, and I fancy his own expectations. John [Inglis] was much annoyed at the 32nd being made to lead all the sorties.'

Captain Birch wrote in his diary of these sorties: 'Parties of twenty men of the reduced 32nd were told off to lead each column of attack and on them fell the brunt of the loss that ensued. The other regiments did not in the least want to be shown the way but the general seemed to think that enough loss had been sustained in relieving us ... The batteries were all taken but only temporarily silenced, they were soon at work gain; indeed it was a most useless waste of life to leave our entrenchments unless we meant to hold the outside position.'

Julia Inglis wrote on 8 November: 'Mr Browne of 32nd was wounded slightly in the leg – hardly an officer of the regiment had escaped; one and all did their duty nobly.' Captain Browne was again wounded, more severely, on 11 November.

The end of the siege did not mean the end of service in India for the 32nd. When he had recuperated, Henry Gore-Browne joined his comrades as part of Major-General Edward Maxwell's Moveable Column. This was one of the various formations that criss-crossed Oudh and Rohilkhand during August to October 1858 in an effort finally to defeat the rebels.

In 1859, the regiment returned to the UK and Browne transferred to the 100th (Prince of Wales' Royal Canadian) Regiment, raised and commanded by Alexander Dunn VC of Light Brigade fame, which was stationed at Gibraltar. For some reason, his recommendation for the VC was not submitted until 1862 by which time the Commander in Chief, the Duke of Cambridge, had stated that a time limit should be enforced for claims in relation to the Indian Mutiny. Fortunately, he had second thoughts and, along with other claimants, Gore-Browne did receive his Cross at an investiture parade at Gibraltar in July 1862.

In 1867, Browne was promoted to Major and went on half pay. He was made a lieutenant-colonel on 27 February 1877 but was unattached in 1881 and finally discharged in 1888. The Regimental Depot of the 100th had been on the Isle of Wight at Parkhurst, which may be the reason why

Browne chose to live his retirement on the island. He died on 15 November 1912 and was buried at St Mary the Virgin Churchyard, Brook near Shanklin.

During the siege, the 32nd Regiment lost fifteen officers and 364 other ranks killed and eleven officers and 198 other ranks wounded. Colonel Inglis' service was recognised with a promotion to Major-General and a KCB. His health, however, had suffered and he died on 27 September 1862.[2]

Jacob Thomas

The son of a farmer, 20-year-old old Jacob Thomas joined the Bengal Artillery at Cardiff in 6 July 1853. He was a member of the only artillery company to be present during the whole of the siege. On 27 September he was part of a mixed detachment of men from the 32nd and Madras Fusiliers, who had arrived with Havelock's column. The small party of artillerymen were along to destroy any guns that they could capture.

From the start, there was a lack of discipline and planning, and several men became lost in the narrow lanes leading towards the battery. The infantry managed to reach the guns but had to wait until the gunners managed to find them.

The most effective method of destroying a gun was to ram powder down the barrel and block the muzzle with clay rendering the gun unusable. Unfortunately, because the day was so hot, the soldiers had drunk all their water so the clay could not be moistened. The guns had to be abandoned, undamaged, and the party began to make its way back to the Residency perimeter. By this time, the rebels were fully alerted and lined the escape route as the British ran a gauntlet of musket fire, sustaining several casualties.

One of the Fusiliers was shot and fell. Thomas ran to him, picked him up and carried him to safety over his shoulder. Miraculously, the pair reached safety without being hit. Thomas remained on the barricades for the rest of the siege until it was lifted in November.

His bravery was noted and his citation appeared in *The London Gazette* on 24 December 1858. He received his VC from the Queen on 4 January 1860 at Windsor Castle. After the Mutiny, he transferred to the Royal Artillery but elected to remain in India.

He was eventually promoted to quartermaster sergeant but was medically discharged in 1866 due to injuries when a horse fell on him. He became a fitter, which he had been before he joined the Army, and died on 24 April 1896 at Hooghly, India.

Patrick McHale

The first member of Havelock's column to be recommended for the Victoria Cross was Irishman, Patrick McHale. Born in Co. Mayo in 1826, the 6ft 2in recruit enlisted in the 5th Fusiliers on 18 December 1847. Six months later, the Regiment sailed to the island of Mauritius in the Indian Ocean, where it stayed until the outbreak of the Mutiny nine years later. The 5th was one of the regiments closest to India and were soon attached to the columns that relieved isolated European posts. One such defensive setting was the small garrison at Arrah where eight British and sixty Sikhs held off 2,000 rebels for ten days. On 3 August, led by Major Vincent Eyre of the Bengal Artillery, the 5th Fusiliers attacked and drove off the mutinous sepoys.

The regiment joined Havelock's column and were part of the relief force column that forced their way into the Residency on 25 September. Private McHale performed two acts of bravery which were recognised in his citation dated 19 June 1869:

'Dates of Acts of Bravery: 2 Oct. 1857 and 22 Dec. 1857. For conspicuous bravery at Lucknow on the 2nd Oct. 1857, when he was the first man at the capture of one of guns at the Cawnpore Battery; and again on the 22nd Dec. 1857, when, by a bold rush, he was the first to take possession of one of the enemy's guns, which had sent several rounds of grape through his company, which was skirmishing up to it. On every occasion of attack, Private McHale has been the first to meet the foe, amongst whom he caused such consternation by the boldness of his rush as to leave little work for those who followed in support, By his habitual coolness and daring, and sustained bravery in action, his name has become a household word for gallantry among his comrades.'

After the Second Relief of Lucknow in November, McHale and his regiment stayed with General Outram at the Alumbagh from where the men could harry the enemy until Sir Colin Campbell's main force returned in March 1858.

McHale received his Cross from Lady Hersey at Fort William, Calcutta on 12 December 1860. He returned to England and died on 26 October 1866 while on duty at Shorncliffe, Kent. He was buried in Shorncliffe Military Cemetery and his comrades erected an impressive gravestone.

John Sinnott

One of the six members of the 84th Regiment to receive the VC during the Indian Mutiny was Private John Sinnott. He was born at Wexford in 1829 and enlisted on 29 October 1849 in Dublin. The 84th was sent to Burma after the war of 1851 and was one of the first units to respond to the outbreak of the Indian Mutiny. Joining Havelock's Column at Calcutta, it fought in every engagement until it reached the Lucknow Residency. Corporal Sinnott performed his act of valour on 6 October 1857 and was elected by his comrades as being a worthy recipient of the Victoria Cross. His citation dated 24 December 1858 reads:

'For conspicuous gallantry at Lucknow, on the 6th Oct., in going out with Sergts. Glynn and Mullins, and Private Mullins, to rescue Lieut. Ghibaut, who, in carrying out water to extinguish a fire in the breastwork, had been mortally wounded, and lay outside. They brought in the body under heavy fire, L.-Corpl. Sinnott was twice wounded …

'He had previously repeatedly accompanied Lieut. Ghibaut when he carried out water to extinguish the fire.'

In performing this act, Sinnott was twice wounded. He received his Cross on 4 January 1860 from the Queen at Windsor Castle. He took his discharge on 22 March 1870 with the rank of sergeant. He died on 20 July 1896 in London.

Thomas Kavanagh

Perhaps the most celebrated Mutiny VC and certainly one that caught the British public's imagination was that of Thomas Henry Kavanagh. Born on 15 July 1821 at Mullingar, Co. Westmeath, he was the third son of the bandmaster of the 3rd (Buffs) Regiment.

The family moved with their father when he was posted to India in 1834 where the 3rd Regiment were stationed at Meerut. When he was old enough, young Thomas was employed as a clerk in the office of the Commissioner for Meerut until 1839. He then worked in a Counting House for a merchant at Mussoree until 1843 before becoming head clerk to the Government Treasury at Ambala. Another move found him appointed head clerk at the Board of Administration at Lahore and then assistant magistrate at Jullindur. Despite being constantly in employment and gradually moving up the civil service ladder, Kavanagh was experiencing financial hardship. It was when he transferred to Mooltan that he narrowly escaped dismissal for his increasing debts. It took the intervention of Lord Dalhousie to save Kavanagh and to secure him a position of Superintendent of the Office of the Chief Commissioner in Lucknow. This was a small demotion but more lucrative.

When the siege began, Kavanagh had his wife, Agnes, and four of his ten children with him. He was now in charge of the male civilians and he set about organising them into a fighting unit. He arranged accommodation

120

and issued them with arms. Some felt that this was a foolish move as they were a bigger threat to themselves than the enemy. Kavanagh took great pride in ensuring these new civilian units behaved with as much military discipline as was possible given the circumstances. Some of his charges found his methods overbearing, openly questioning his authority.

By the end of July there was another threat to the defenders. In the constant heat and unsanitary conditions, cholera, fever and smallpox now stalked the compound bringing death just as surely as a sniper's bullet. Thomas lost his eldest child, Cecil, to sickness and was haunted by the fear that a similar fate awaited the rest of his children. It was almost impossible to keep the healthy completely separate from the sick, so Kavanagh encouraged his children to play outside. He preferred to keep them away from the threat of infection even if it meant they were exposed to the danger of enemy snipers.

Throughout August there were constant rumours of imminent relief. Time and again it was imagined the sound of British artillery could be heard on the outskirts of the city, but on each occasion excitement gave way to despair. One despatch that reached the Residency had promised help within four days, but none had arrived. The situation inside was getting more desperate – the heat was stifling, food was low, rats swarmed everywhere and disease continued to extend its grip.

Finally Havelock's troops did force their way into the Residency compound but were too few in number to achieve a relief, though they did reinforce the dwindling number of defenders. Kavanagh decided he must play a prominent role and not just for altruistic reasons. He was determined to use this crisis as a means to pull himself out of the poverty trap in which he had sunk, and by the end of October, he had been appointed assistant field engineer in recognition of his service.

The sepoys were digging tunnels beneath the perimeter in order to plant explosive charges. It was Kavanagh's responsibility to discover these mines and destroy them through countermining. He found crawling through cold, dark tunnels a frightening experience, with the chance he might run into the enemy or be buried if the roof collapsed. Whenever he discovered an enemy digging about to open, he would wait in the shadows for a rebel miner to emerge and then shoot him. On one occasion after killing an enemy miner, he crawled into the tunnel to recover the sepoy's tools. Unable to find them, he went further into the mine until he could hear the sepoys on the other side calling down to their dead comrade. Realising he had crawled too far, he lay still to see what would happen next. Suddenly another sepoy appeared and Kavanagh shot him in the stomach. With only one round left in his revolver he quickly reversed his way out. Suddenly the mine was filled with gunfire and the acrid smell of gunpowder.

Boldly, Kavanagh called out to the enemy miners that he could retrieve the digging equipment. To which the sepoy leader replied he was welcome to them if he could take them. Then Kavanagh began to talk of the excellent state of their provisions and of the rapidly approaching British Army, which momentarily distracted the enemy. Quickly, he jumped into the tunnel and retrieved the tools before the enemy could react. It was such a daring and audacious move that even the sepoys were moved to applaud it and the Sikh soldiers who had remained loyal in the Residency nicknamed Kavanagh, 'Burra Surungwalla' – the Great Miner.

On 29 November Kavanagh learned that Kunoujee Lal, an Indian messenger, had managed to get inside the Residency. He carried with him a despatch from Sir Colin Campbell who had reached Cawnpore and hoped to break the siege within a week. In the preceding few days, senior officers at the Residency had drawn up a plan to assist Campbell, outlining the best route through the city. It occurred to Kavanagh that the plan, on its own, was of little use without someone to explain it. The more he considered the matter, the more convinced he became that someone with local knowledge of the city and of the enemy's positions must reach Campbell before he arrived at the city limits. If the route outlined in the plan should be blocked by the enemy or was otherwise inaccessible what would Campbell do? Hesitation could be fatal and might result in more losses than the 200 suffered by Havelock. The Residency could not afford the luxury of a third attempt – the food was almost exhausted and the sick and wounded were dying for want of medical supplies.

He met with the messenger and outlined his plan to accompany him on his return journey. Kunoujee Lal refused point blank due to the added risk of having to care for an accomplice, especially a European one. In the end Kavanagh convinced him by hinting at the chance of a great reward for such a service. Now he now faced a more difficult task of persuading his superiors to let him make the attempt.

Kavanagh approached Colonel Napier, an officer with whom he enjoyed a friendly rapport, and outlined his idea. It took no more than a couple of seconds for Napier to realise the absurdity and absolute folly of such a mission. How would any European manage to slip undetected though the many enemy patrols and checkpoints, never mind one who was over six feet tall and had blue eyes, a shock of red hair and freckles? Nonetheless, he was impressed with the courage shown by Kavanagh and wanted Sir James Outram to be aware of the offer.

Outram, like Napier, was both astonished and impressed by Kavanagh's determination to undertake such a hazardous undertaking. He saw the logic for a knowledgeable European to act as guide, but the odds of making it through enemy lines were practically zero and so he declined the offer.

Kavanagh, however, did not give up easily. Two strong forces were urging him on. The first was a strong sense of duty and the desire to ease the suffering of his family and comrades. The second was that this might be his only chance to make the impression which could aid his advancement. His persistence and determination paid off and Sir James finally accepted his offer.

On returning to his family, Kavanagh began to feel pangs of remorse. He had been married for twelve years and his wife, Agnes, had stood by him through many tribulations. She had also been badly wounded in the leg from one of the enemy's shells. He knew that if he revealed his plans to her she would beg him to not go and that he would probably surrender to her pleading. At 6 o'clock in the evening he kissed Agnes and the children and left giving the impression he was heading for mine duty as usual. He found a small deserted room and with the aid of a colleague put on a disguise made from native clothing he had acquired earlier. He then applied black colouring to his face and hands to give the appearance of native skin. At first Thomas was not convinced that the colouring was natural but after a quick discussion it was agreed it would be good enough in the darkness of the night. To be sure, a test was needed in order to judge its effectiveness.

It was forbidden for natives to enter the house of Europeans and take a seat without first being invited to do so. When Kavanagh entered the quarters of Sir James Outram, in disguise, he did so and immediately took a seat where he sat in silence. All of the staff on duty knew Kavanagh well but it seemed none of them recognised him. Indeed the atmosphere was one of agitation that a native would be so impudent. They called for Sir James who would soon put this insolent wretch in his place. When Sir James entered he also failed to recognise Thomas immediately. He had passed this simple test, but Sir James and the other officers present made some final adjustments and alterations to complete the disguise. Captain Sitwell presented Thomas with his revolver which was not to be used for shooting his way out of trouble, but to be turned on himself should he be threatened with capture. By 8 o'clock the farewells were made and Thomas left to meet with Kunoujee Lal.

The first task the pair faced was to cross the River Gomti. Thomas removed his clothes, gathered them into a bundle on his head, and slipped into the icy cold water. Reaching the far bank, Kavanagh and Lal dried themselves, dressed again and made their way 100 yards or so inland. Encountering a matchlock man (sentry), Kavanagh decided it was time to try out his native Hindu accent. He casually remarked on how cold the night was, to which the matchlock man replied that it was indeed cold. Having passed this latest test, Kavanagh was feeling even more confident in himself.

A little further along, they came to the Iron Bridge and were called over by a sepoy officer. Recognising the danger of the situation Kavanagh remained in the shadows while his guide approached and explained that they were returning to their homes in the city; they were allowed to continue on their way. Their journey now took them back over the river and into the heart of city. Though Lal wished to use the small side streets, Kavanagh thought it best to stay on the main street with the crowds where they were less likely to stand out.

The gamble paid off, for they were only stopped and questioned once on their journey to the outskirts of the city. The pair continued on for five miles not realising that they were heading in the wrong direction. When Kunoujee Lal finally realised his mistake, they found an old woman who pointed them in the right direction again.

After a couple of hours they came across a man singing at the top of his voice. Despite the noise he was making the man heard them as they approached and immediately sounded the alarm. A party of sepoys came rushing out of a hut and began to ask questions. It was a very dangerous situation and for the first time since they had begun Lal lost his nerve and threw away the despatch he was carrying for Campbell.

Kavanagh stepped forward and explained that the excited behaviour of the soldiers had frightened his poor companion. Accepting the explanation the sepoys allowed them to proceed and even advised them on the best route. After a time they waded across one of the many marshes in the area and became too far in to turn back. Progress was slow as heavy mud sucked on their feet and their clothes grew cumbersome. After floundering in the swamp for almost two hours they reached dry land and rested for fifteen minutes.

Carrying on, they came upon enemy guards spaced about 300 yards apart dozing by their watch-fires. Passing between the two fires, an exhausted Kavanagh succumbed once more to fatigue and decided to lie down and rest for an hour. Kunoujee Lal was not pleased but agreed to try and find some assistance while Kavanagh slept. But the guide managed to walk just a few yards before a challenge of 'Who comes there?' rang out. It quickly became apparent that the two men had run in to a picquet of the Punjab Cavalry on duty near the Alambagh. Kavanagh and Lal explained their mission and were taken to meet the commander-in-chief.

By 5 a.m. they were in Sir Colin Campbell's tent. Campbell was not entirely convinced until Kavanagh removed his turban, taking from it Outram's message which he then handed to Campbell. Finally he accepted the messenger as genuine and pressed him for an account of the journey. Kavanagh was physically and mentally drained and begged that he be allowed to sleep first. Sir Colin agreed and he was assigned a tent in which to rest.

Later that morning over breakfast with Sir Colin, Kavanagh rediscovered the simple and delightful pleasures of bread and butter. It had been months since he had tasted coffee with sugar and the flavour of it too was wonderful. He recounted his adventures to Sir Colin and the other commanding officers, who were full of admiration for him.

The next day the relief force set out for Lucknow. Word reached the Residency that Kavanagh had succeeded in his mission while his wife was informed of her husband's adventure and that all was well. On 14 November, the second attempt to break the siege of Lucknow began. Arriving on the outskirts of the city, Campbell's force came under sporadic fire from the rebels. Their progress was checked when they came to a canal that was crossed by a stone bridge. Unsure of its condition Campbell requested a report and Kavanagh volunteered to take a look. He rode as close to it as he dared and came under fire from the enemy, which badly wounded his horse, but he had seen enough to determine that the bridge was indeed damaged. On receiving the report, Campbell decided it was unsafe to cross and ordered his troops to camp for the night.

The next morning, Campbell continued his cautious advance until the Residency was in sight and Kavanagh decided to try and reach Sir James Outram alone. Running haphazardly through the streets he managed to dodge the enemy's fire until he met with a soldier from the Residency. Together they ran at full tilt until they reached the 'Steam Engine House' where some officers from the Residency were taking cover. With a cry of 'It is Kavanagh! Three cheers for him! He is the first to relieve us!', Kavanagh was quickly shown to Sir James, receiving thanks and praise from all he passed. He then escorted Sir James and Havelock back through enemy fire to Sir Colin Campbell's command post. Finding Campbell inside, Kavanagh announced, 'Sir James Outram is waiting, sir, to see you.' Campbell was incredulous: 'The devil he is! Where is he? Where has he come from?'

Kavanagh outlined his quick visit to the Residency and led him to meet Outram where they congratulated each other on their achievements. Leaving them to organise the evacuation of the Residency, Kavanagh went to meet his family. The daring journey to reach Campbell and his courage during the advance on the city had finally brought the recognition he had craved. His comrades in the Residency called to his house just to glimpse the man who had brought their salvation.

It would appear that Thomas Kavanagh's service was still required for he acted as a mediator between the pockets of rebels who wished to surrender and the rather unforgiving British. He joined Brigadier Barker's column as they approached the fort at Birrwa and offered the rebels the chance to escape with their lives if they surrendered immediately. The mutineers were not sure if they could trust him so he laid down his revolver, walked into the middle of the fort and placed himself at their mercy. This gesture worked and the rebels surrendered.

By 1859, the last remnants of mutiny had finally been quashed and, in May, Kavanagh and his family travelled to England. The two things he had sought had been achieved: fame and fortune. He was indeed famous but the fortune was less than he had hoped. In return for his services during the relief of Lucknow, the Indian government awarded him £2,000. Kavanagh felt this to be a miserly sum considering that his actions had also saved the public treasure, which he estimated at around £300,000. This was to be a sore point that stayed with him until the day he died.[3]

Little is known of Kunoujee Lal, other than that he was rewarded, albeit with considerably less than his companion, and retired to land given him by a grateful government.

When Thomas Kavanagh was first nominated for the Victoria Cross the application was refused on the grounds that the Royal Warrant stated that it could only be conferred on military personnel. A second civilian, Ross Lewis Mangles, had also been nominated for distinguished conduct during the Indian Mutiny and many thought that they both fully deserved the award. A tribute from Sir Colin Campbell must also have contributed significantly. After much lobbying the Royal Warrant was amended:

'War Office, 6 July, 1859 – The Queen, having been graciously pleased by warrant under Her Royal Sign Manuel bearing date 13 Dec,1858, to declare that Non-Military persons who as Volunteers, have borne arms against Mutineers, both at Lucknow and elsewhere, during the late operations in India, shall be considered eligible to receive the Decoration of the Victoria Cross, subject to rules and ordinances already made and ordained for the government thereof, provided that it be established in any case that the person was serving under the orders of a General or any other officer in command of Troops in the Field when he performed the Act of Bravery for which it is proposed to confer the decoration, Her Majesty has accordingly been pleased to signify her intention to confer this high distinction on the under mentioned Gentlemen, whose claims to the same have been submitted for Her Majesty's approval, on account of Acts of Bravery performed by them in India, as recorded against their names.'

Thus, Thomas Kavanagh and Ross Mangles were presented with their Victoria Crosses by Queen Victoria at Windsor Castle on 4 January 1860. Kavanagh also received the Indian Mutiny Medal with clasps for the Relief and Defence of Lucknow. Despite the honour and public adulation, Kavanagh returned to India with the impression that the VC had only been awarded grudgingly and wrote:

'I shall probably be on my way back (to India), reluctantly to resume my duty under a Government that thinks me undeserving of the honour, and to labour hard in a climate from which I cannot hope to escape again to Europe.'

Back in India Kavanagh still courted controversy after the Mutiny by the publication of his book, *How I Won the Victoria Cross*. He was castigated in some quarters for both profiting from his deed and for self-aggrandisement. Whatever bitterness Kavanagh may have felt about the dismissive attitude of his detractors, the British public and media regarded him as one of the greatest heroes of the Victorian age.

In 1882, at the invitation of the Governor of Gibraltar, his old friend from the Residency, General Sir Robert Napier, Kavanagh sailed in the P&O ship *Khedive* and was taken ill on board. On arrival, Kavanagh was taken to hospital where he died on 11 November. In demonstration of the esteem in which he was held, he was given a full military funeral and his coffin was conveyed to the North Front Cemetery by 200 soldiers of the Loyal North Lancashire Regiment.

There is no doubt that he was a man of great personal courage. This was somewhat negated by the self-promotion and ungracious manner that belittled his great achievement.

Chapter 7

The Second Relief Of Lucknow
October to November 1857

When news of the Mutiny reached the UK in early July 1857, Lord Palmerston offered Sir Colin Campbell the command of all British forces in India in place of the recently deceased General George Anson. Campbell accepted and left Britain on 12 July, reaching Calcutta in August. Palmerston must have been persuasive because in March 1857 Campbell had turned down the offer of commanding the expedition to China.

Colin Campbell, real name McLiver, came from humble beginnings and rose to become the greatest commander of the mid-Victorian period. He fought against Napoleon in the Peninsular War and the Indian wars of the 1840s. After his heroics at the Battle of Balaklava with his 93rd Highlanders – the Thin Red Line – his peacetime appointments were in keeping with a 65-year-old senior officer. After the Crimean War, he took over command of the south-eastern district and in September was appointed inspector-general of infantry, the sort of appointments leading to retirement. He confided to his friend, Colonel James Hope Grant at the end of the Second Sikh War in 1849: 'I am growing old and only fit for retirement.'

When Campbell arrived in India, he reviewed the situation. General Havelock had been hurried into marching on Lucknow before he was ready with an inadequate force and bedeviled with terrible logistical problems. Campbell was not going to make the same mistake. With the prospect of receiving some 30,000 troops from garrisons around the Empire he set about organizing an adequate transport and supply system. Instead of the weeks that many had hoped for, it was to be late October before Sir Colin was able move his column to Cawnpore and then Lucknow. On 3 November 1857, unable to wait for the large reinforcements promised, he reached Cawnpore with a force of only 4,500. This included HM 23rd, 82nd, 93rd, 53rd, 8th, and 75th, with EIC 2nd and 4th Punjab Infantry. The mounted troops were mainly Punjab Cavalry, HM 9th Lancers, Artillery and 200 men of the Naval Brigade from HMS *Shannon*.

The strategic situation was complicated as well as critical. Cawnpore, from where the column would cross the Ganges on a bridge of boats, was vulnerable from the Gwalior Contingent under the generalship of the ablest rebel leader, Tantia Topi. The Contingent was gathering more support as it made its way towards Cawnpore. On the other hand, Campbell could not ignore Outram's pleas to come to the Residency's rescue. In the end Campbell calculated that if he could relieve Lucknow, he could return in time to confront Tantia Topi.

Campbell's force was augmented by the men of Greathed's column, so Campbell was able to leave 1,050 men and nine guns at Cawnpore under the command of Major-General Charles Windham with instruction to strengthen the defences. On 9 November, with some reassurance that the crossing would be protected, Campbell led his column across the Ganges into Oudh.

Halting to make camp at Bani, on the banks of the Sai River, the column continued their march to Alambagh on the southern outskirts of Lucknow. It was here that the first VC of Campbell's Column was won.

Hugh Gough

The Goughs came from Co. Tipperary in Ireland and had an outstanding military pedigree, so their paths into the Army and military glory were not entirely surprising. On 22 November 1833, Hugh Henry was born in Calcutta, two years after his brother, Charles (whose own VC-winning exploits are detailed in Chapter Two). Hugh attended the East India College in Hertford Heath, which later reopened as Haileybury College. He passed his exams and, on 4 September 1853, was commissioned cornet in the 3rd Bengal Light Cavalry. It was among the 3rd BLC that the mutiny broke out on 9 May 1857. Lieutenant Hugh Gough was amongst those who were sent to the Delhi Ridge, where he was appointed adjutant of the newly-formed irregular cavalry regiment, Hodson's Horse, named after its leader, Lieutenant William Hodson, the head of the Intelligence Department.

After the fall of Delhi, Hugh was attached to Colonel Greathed's Flying Column and involved in the battles of Bulundshahr and Agra before it made its way to Cawnpore where it was absorbed into Sir Colin Campbell's relieving force.

The advance had met with little opposition and by 12 November it had reached the Alambagh, a large walled estate on the southern approaches to Lucknow. Hugh Gough recalled the events in his book *Old Memories*:

'On 12 November, our whole force under Sir Colin Campbell marched from our base camp to the Alum Bagh [sic] or 'Garden of Beauty' about six miles away ... I, with my squadron, had the post of honour with the Advance guard. It was not expected we should meet with opposition, as several hundred of Havelock's troops still held the Alum Bagh; but suddenly, as our column was advancing up the road, an attack developed itself on the right flank, where a body of the enemy (which we calculated at about two thousand strong, with two guns) had taken up a position. As these guns were troublesome, Brigadier Sir Hope Grant (who was commanding the advance) rode up to me and desired me to take my squadron and see if I could capture the guns.

'With my small body of men, my only chance of success was by making a surprise flank attack; so I made a considerable detour under cover of some fields of tall corn and sugar cane and managed to arrive on the left flank of the enemy perfectly unseen. The guns were posted on a small mound; and a considerable body of the enemy had an admirable position to the rear of the mound. Between us and them lay a strip of marshland with long reedy grass: an unpleasant obstacle, but which served admirably to cove our movements.

'I then advanced my men through this at a trot till we got clear, when I gave the words "Form line!" and "Draw swords!" My men gave a ringing cheer, and we were into the masses of the enemy at once. The surprise was complete; and so the shock to them and victory to us was as if we had been the whole brigade.

'My charger, "Tearaway", carried me like a bird; and I soon found myself well ahead. I had to make a lane for myself as I rode along, and it seemed like cutting one's way through a field of corn as I swung my sword to right and left. The men followed me splendidly, wielding their blades with deadly effect; and in a very short time, the affair was over. The guns were captured, the enemy scattered, and the fight became a pursuit ... Sir Colin Campbell, who witnessed the charge, got me a VC for it.'

Hugh Gough's citation, published on 24 December 1858, covers two events. The second was after the Residency had been relieved and when Campbell was marching on Lucknow the following year with enough men to capture the city. The Alambagh had been garrisoned since the evacuation and had been under almost constant harassment. Once again Hugh Gough later recalled his part in one of the stiffest cavalry actions of that campaign:

'On 24 February, 1858, we received an order to make a forced march of thirty-six miles from our camp at Oonao to the Alum Bagh to reinforce General Outram, who was threatened by a large body of rebels. We marched all that night and arrived at the Alum Bagh on the early morning of the 25th, when we received orders to be ready to turn out at a moment's notice ...

'This was my first day in action with Hodson's Horse as a complete regiment – I might almost call it a brigade! – for by Major Hodson's influence and the magic power of his name amongst the warrior tribes of the north, recruits from the Punjab and beyond had come flocking in; and I should say we were nearly a thousand strong.

'No time was to be lost, as the enemy had already heard of the reinforcements which had come in during the night and were therefore in full retreat to Lucknow. When we now came in view of them, they were passing in rather a disorganised mass right across our front as we advanced. We could see they had a couple of field guns, one gun being about six hundred yards ahead of the other. The main body was almost entirely infantry; and all were mutineer regulars, arrayed in uniform with banners flying.

'Our rapid approach had a great effect upon them. They seemed to make no effort to rally and stand; and as we advanced and then charged, we got well into them, cutting right and left, and the whole affair seemed over almost at once. The rearmost gun was in our possession and the enemy (as far as we had encountered them) in full flight.

'But somehow, owing to the ardour of the charge and the pursuit, our regiment got quite out of hand, lost all formation, and scattered; and the enemy, seeing our condition and probably having a leader with a good cool head, rallied round their remaining gun, regained their formation as we lost ours, and pouring in volleys of musketry with discharges of grape from their gun, rendered our confusion worse confounded.

'Our men, gallant and forward in pursuit or a charge, could not stand being hammered at a disadvantage and began to fall back. There was a din of shouting – officers doing their best to bring the men up and re-form them – but all to no effect, and it looked sadly probable that Hodson's Horse would in their turn retreat.

'Hodson himself, at this crisis, managed to get a few brave spirits together – not more that a dozen. Well I remember him, with his sword arm in a sling from a wound he had received in a recent skirmish, brandishing a hog spear in his left hand and shouting to the men to follow him as he made an attempt to charge. He and I were riding close together; and as we advanced with our small following, I saw his horse come down with him; and the next instant my own charger, my beloved "Tearaway", reared straight up and fell dead.

'The fire was most deadly – the range was short and just suited to the point-blank discharges from the smoothbore muskets to which we were exposed – so that nearly everyone of our small party was killed or wounded. Fortunately, I fell clear of my horse; and catching one whose rider had just been killed, I speedily mounted, and as good luck would have it, was able to rally our men to a certain extent. Seeing our supports (the 7th Hussars and Military Train) coming up, they now came on with a will and a vengeance, and charging the remaining gun, scattered the enemy in all directions, cutting down as many of them as they could.

'My temporary charger – a small gray country-bred mare – carried me well; and we followed the enemy in pursuit, the British cavalry also cutting in. But it was no easy matter, as the enemy had got amongst the trees and low jungle and were guarded by a village, where cavalry were not of much use.

'In the ardour of pursuit, I had got well ahead of my men, when I came upon a couple of sepoys on their way to the village. They had their bayonets fixed, and seeing me unsupported, stood defiantly – one in my direct front and the other to my right. I made for the one in my direct front, but the one on the right took aim at me as I passed and shot me clean through the thigh – the bullet going through my saddle and my horse, striking her dead. Fortunately, I fell clear, though helpless. My opponents were just coming up to finish me off when they were sabered by a couple of troopers of the Military Train …

'My wound placed me out of action for some time. My other leg barely escaped injury by a shot through my scabbard, and a shot through my sun helmet missed my head by a mere hair space.'

In addition to his VC, Gough was five times Mentioned in Despatches. There is no record of any investiture, so Hugh may have received his Cross through the mail. When Hugh recovered from his wound, he was made second in command of the newly-raised 2nd Mahratta Horse, which went in pursuit of Tantia Topi during the last phase of the Mutiny.

After the Mutiny, Hugh Gough was given command of the 12th Regiment of Bengal Cavalry and took part in the expedition to Abyssinia in 1868. He was on the staff of General Frederick Roberts in the Afghan War 1879-80 and retired as a full general and a knight. He was further honoured when he was appointed Keeper of the Crown Jewels at the Tower of London and made Lieutenant Governor of the Channel Islands.

At the age of 75, Sir Hugh Gough died and was buried with full military honours in a parade through the streets of London from the Tower to Kensal Green Cemetery on 12 May 1909. His pall bearers included fellow Mutiny VCs, Earl Roberts and Sir James Hill-Johnes.

CAMPBELL MARCHES TO LUCKNOW

A steady supply of reinforcements had increased Sir Colin Campbell's force to about 8,000 by the time he reached Lucknow. On 14 November, he had made up his mind regarding the route the column should take – a decision based on the information supplied by Thomas Kavanagh. Rather than cross the Charbagh Bridge and following Havelock's example of fighting a way through the narrow and dangerous streets of Lucknow, Campbell opted for a wide flanking attack to the east with Dilkusha Park as his first objective. He was able to do this, whereas Havelock could not, because the ground had dried sufficiently for him to transport his guns and supplies. As a diversion, he detached some of his guns to bombard the area around the Charbargh Bridge, giving the impression that he was going to follow Havelock's route.

For three miles the column moved through the country east of Alambagh without meeting any opposition. When they entered Dilkusha Park they came under a spattering of musket fire, which was quickly silenced by a few rounds from the artillery. Campbell used the house and grounds as the base for the final drive on the Residency.

The fleeing sepoys made their escape to the nearby public school, La Martinière, where the second VC was won.[1]

John Watson
Born in Chigwell, Essex, on 6 September 1829, John Watson entered the Bombay Army in 1848 and served with the Bombay Fusiliers in the Second Sikh War. After two short-lived postings to other Bombay infantry regiments, he began his career as a cavalryman with the 1st Punjab Cavalry. Promoted to adjutant, he was regarded as one of the most promising officers of the Punjab Frontier Force, along with George Younghusband and Dighton Probyn.

He was present during the siege and assault of Delhi and the subsequent battles of Greathed's Flying Column. He was particularly prominent at Agra and captured a gun. In the advance on Lucknow, the British drove the rebels out of La Martinière and the cavalry pursued them as far as the canal. Frederick Roberts recalled:

'A long way ahead of his squadron, he [Watson] suddenly came on a squadron of the enemy. Knowing if he returned to his men to give them orders they would misunderstand his movement, and probably go back themselves, he charged the enemy entirely alone, and was at once engaged with the leader [a Ressalder] and six or seven of the front men. The leader's pistol missed his mark, and Watson ran him through with his sabre. The remainder of his squadron then attacked him; but Probyn, who was not far off with his own and Watson's squadrons, galloped to the rescue, and the enemy fled. For this and other actions, Watson received the Victoria Cross.'

During this fight, Lieutenant Watson received a blow to the head from a *tulwar*, another on the left arm, which severed his chain gauntlet glove, and a *tulwar* cut on his right arm, which disabled him for some days.

In 1864 he was promoted to major and by 1873 was lieutenant-colonel of the Central India Horse. In 1879, he was brigadier in the 2nd Afghan War and commanded the Kurram Field Force. He was knighted and retired as a full general in 1891. He retired to Finchampstead, where his neighboour was Lieutenant-Colonel Alfred Stowell VC, who daughter married Watson's son. Sir John Watson died on 23 January 1919.

SECUNDRA BAGH, FIRST ENGAGEMENT OF 16 NOVEMBER

The city of Lucknow was bordered by the canal which ran north-east to south-west, and the area in which Campbell's column was advancing was countryside with some farms, jungle, marshes and a few sumptuous palaces and pavilions. After the Dilkusha and La Martinière were taken largely without a fight, the next obstacle to overcome was the Secundra Bagh, a far tougher objective which saw some of the fiercest fighting of the campaign.[2] In fact, two battles were to be fought on 16 November, one leading into the other, which saw a record number of Victoria Crosses awarded.

Corporal William Mitchell of the 93rd Highlanders described the advance: 'Before daybreak, we of the Lucknow Relief Force slowly and silently commenced our advance across the canal at a dry ford that was out of range of the enemy's guns and where they could not see us because of the high grass – and which we were surpised to find undefended on the opposite side; and just as the morning broke, by following the winding of the river for about two and a half miles, we had reached the outskirts of a village on the east side of the Secunder Bagh, which was about a mile and three quarters from the Residency. Here, a halt was made for the heavy guns to be brought to the front; while three companies of the 93rd, with some light artillery, were diverted to the left under the command of Colonel Hay, to attack and clear out the old sepoy lines (a cluster of mud huts) and the old 32nd Light Infantry barracks; a large building in the form of a cross, strongly flanked with earthworks, also occupied by the enemy.'

The first VC exploit was undertaken by Captain George Steuart, whose action was witnessed by Surgeon William Munro of the 93rd, who recalled:

'The 53rd skirmishers advanced steadily and, supported by the 93rd, drove the enemy out of the village. While following them in rapid pursuit, the 93rd came unexpectedly out on to an open space, on the opposite side of which stood a large, square-turreted building with loopholed walls – the famous Secunderbagh – from which a tremendous, but not effective, musketry fire was poured on the regiment as, on emerging from the village, it formed into line in the open. To avoid the storm of fire, and to be under cover until artillery could be brought up to breach the wall, Colonel Leith Hay was ordered to move the regiment to the shelter of a long low embankment which ran parallel to the south face of the building and at a distance of about one hundred yards from the wall.

'There, under shelter, the regiment remained until two of Travers' heavy guns having been brought up – a nine-pounder having proved useless – succeeded in breaching the tower at the south-west corner of the building, while our men by a steady rifle fire kept back the enemy from their loopholes, and from showing themselves above the parapet on the top of the walls …

'While the two heavy guns were battering the base of the tower, Colonel Hay, with two companies of the regiment, drove the enemy out of a large square enclosure (the Serai) opposite the western face of Secunderbagh. Captains Cornwall and Stewart [sic], with Nos. 2 & 3 companies and sections from 4 & 8 companies, were sent out to the left front to keep down a flank fire from two guns, which the enemy had brought forward and with which they were raking the road … and interfering with the breaching operations.

'But Stewart, perceiving the annoyance which these two guns were causing, called upon his company, and at the head of it … dashed forward in a most gallant style, captured the guns at the point of the bayonet, turned them on the flying rebels.'

With his left flank secure, Campbell examined the breach made in the wall, which a man could just squeeze through.[3] He decided that the honour of leading the charge should go the 4th Punjab Infantry who were 'like cats when it came to getting into tight places'. Closely supported by the 93rd Highlanders, the two regiments cheered and raced each other to be the first to enter. The winner to squeeze through the gap was a Sikh, who was immediately killed. He was followed by a succession of 93rd and Punjabis, all of whom were either killed or wounded.

The first man to enter and survive was Lance Corporal John Dunlay, who was wounded in the left leg. All around him, men and officers were being killed or wounded, but finally the weight of numbers pushed aside the defenders. With the gates now taken, the rebels were caught in a trap and fought with the desperation of men without hope of mercy – and, indeed, none was shown. The British exacted a terrible revenge for the atrocities their women and children had suffered. A red mist had descended on the British and all, from private to officer, were blinded by it.

Retreating to the two-storey villa, the fighting became close-quarter and was described by William Mitchell:

'The Pandemonium in the Secunder Bagh was hellish in the extreme: blood-spattered and smoke-stained Europeans and Punjabees trampling over the dead and dying, whose screams and groans mingled with the grunts and curses of those who stabbed and clubbed and cut them down, with the continuous sounds of hacking and bashing and jabbing, and with the constant shrill of the bagpipes ... there was no escape for the desperate masses of the enemy, who were driven and hunted from one place to another – in and out of rooms, up and down stairs – relentlessly pursued and losing their footing on marble steps and floors slippery with their own blood.'

An estimated 2,000 rebels were killed, a figure which contrasted with the comparatively light British casualty list of less than 200.

George Steuart

Born 11 February 1831 in Edinburgh, William George Drummond Steuart was the only son of William Drummond Steuart and Christine Mary.[4] He was brought up on the Steuart family estate at Murthly Castle, Grandtully (pronounced 'Grantly'), Perthshire. Despite being born into one of Scotland's leading families, young George was to have an unsettled childhood. In 1832, the year after George's birth, his uncle, the new laird, and George's father had a violent quarrel, resulting in the latter leaving his wife and son in Scotland and sailing for America.

Reaching St. Louis, which was on the US western frontier, William joined the pack train led by Robert Campbell which was going to the 1833 Rendezvous of Mountain Men on the Green river, Wyoming. Here, Steuart met famed frontier men like Jim Bridger, Tom Fitzpatrick and others. For the next two years, William travelled throughout the Rockies and in 1835 he attended another rendezvous in Wyoming. He took one more trip to the Rockies and on learning that he had succeeded as laird, he returned to Grantully in 1842. He took with him not only his hunting guide and two Native Americans, but also a vast array of artefacts, plants and animals. He planted buffalo grass and released several bison and a bear onto the estate. This caused quite a stir, not least to Queen Victoria, who was startled to see these impressive beasts, noting in her diary that she and her husband had encountered 'those strange hump-backed creatures from America'.

Almost entirely estranged from his father, George attended the Jesuit-run Oscott College near Birmingham, before being appointed ensign by purchase into the 93rd Highland Regiment in 1848. In 1853, while he was stationed at Portsmouth, he had an affair with a girl named Mary, the daughter of a Southampton merchant. She died giving birth to twin boys, who were named George William Drummond and Herbert John. With the outbreak of war with Russia in the spring of 1854, the 93rd were part of the Highland Brigade sent to the Crimea and George left with his regiment. It would appear that his mother, Christine, and his uncle, Archibald Douglas Steuart, took responsibility for his sons. In fact, although he was named as the father, George was not present at the twins' baptism and their certificates were signed by Christine and Archibald.

The 93rd was to gain immortality two months later when just four companies, including Steuart's, stood between the Russians and the British supply port of Balaklava. William Howard Russell, *The Times'* special correspondent, viewed the action from a distant vantage point on the Sapoune Heights. Below him he could see the cavalry camp sited amongst some vineyards at the base of the Causeway Heights. The only infantry he could make out were the 93rd Highlanders, drawn up under the heights above Balaklava and supported by some Royal Marine artillery. Russell arrived just as the Russians overwhelmed Number 1 Redoubt, the furthermost earthwork, and put the Turks to flight. The next two redoubts quickly fell and the plain leading to Balaklava was filled with Turks running for their lives pursued by Russian cavalry. As they came within range, the two ranks of the 93rd, under the command of Sir Colin Campbell, fired a volley. This, together with the Marines' artillery fire, caused the Russians to turn about and return to the Causeway Heights. This was immortalised by Russell who described the ranks of the 93rd as 'The Thin Red Streak tipped with steel', later to be modified as the Thin Red Line.

The 93rd was already at sea and on the way to China when news of the outbreak of mutiny amongst the sepoys of the Bengal Army changed their destination. Arriving at Calcutta in September 1857, the 93rd was in time to join their old commander, Sir Colin Campbell, in his advance to lift the siege of Lucknow.

At the start of the battle for the Secundra Bagh, George Steuart had charged up a long level road, straight towards the fearsome gun muzzles as they were manoeuvred towards him. Narrowly, his company managed to win the race and his exploit was acknowledged many years later by Lord

Roberts in his book, *Forty-one Years in India*. He recalled that this action 'was as serviceable as it was heroic, for it silenced the fire most destructive to the attacking force'.

The nearby large fortified barracks, built in the form of a cross, was then captured and Steuart was later joined by Major Ewart and three companies. They remained there to secure the column's rear until the final evacuation of the Residency two days later. The story that the bodies of the dead rebels were left to rot seems unlikely as Steuart and his comrades were left at the Secundra Bagh to secure the route to the Residency.[5]

In the ballot amongst the officers of the 93rd, George Steuart was selected to receive the Cross, which was gazetted on 24 December 1858.[6] The citation was a masterpiece of brevity: '16 Nov.1857. In leading an attack upon and capturing two guns by which the Mess House was secured. Elected by the officers of the regiment. Steuart was highly thought of by his brother officers and was described by one as an officer of remarkable coolness in action, nothing ever appearing to disturb his equanimity in the very slightest degree.'

Steuart actually received his Cross before the official announcement in London. On 6 December 1858 at a special ceremony at Umbeyla, Major-General Sir Robert Garrett pinned the VC to Steuart's tunic. After nearly four years of continuous hard campaigning, George Steuart returned to the family home, where he was invited by the tenantry of his father's estates to a dinner and presented with a sword of honour. He received this from the hands of his friend and mentor, Lord Panmure, the former Secretary for War. On being promoted to a majority, for which there was no opening in the 93rd, George elected to go on half pay and retired from active service.

There is something of a mystery about George's activities after he left the Army. He did serve for a short time as Assistant Inspector of Volunteers, but the actual dates are unknown. Handwritten notes in the margin of the copy of *History of 93rd Sutherland Highlanders* held by the regimental museum, hint of a man who was a bit of a rake. To quote the notes: 'Drummond had a child by a Miss Wilson, I think, daughter of a fishing tackle maker in Edinburgh. Miss Wilson tried to force a marriage but this failed and the child died and saved complications for the heir.'

The final reference to Steuart's post-service activities happened at Fawley near Southampton. On 18 October 1868, George attempted a trick that he would have seen during his service in India. Amongst the entertainers that frequented the camps or bazaars were snake charmers, magicians and sword swallowers. In an attempt to emulate what he had seen ten years before, it would appear that Steuart thrust a stick down his throat but the trick went horribly, and fatally, wrong.

At the inquest held on 20 October, Robert Harfield, the Deputy Coroner, stated that the cause of death was inflammation of the lungs. The verdict was not recorded as death by misadventure but whilst in an unsound state of mind. This suggests that Steuart committed suicide and that the sword-swallowing story was a cover up. It seems inconceivable that anyone would choose such a painful and lingering form of suicide. On the other hand, the location is significant and one that could have made him despondent. His twin boys were educated at a Catholic boarding school near Southampton, paid for by his uncle, Archibald Steuart. It would appear that a condition was placed on George not to reveal himself to them as their father and they went through their lives never knowing who their father was. It could be that George observed them from afar and, in a fit of depression, deliberately killed himself.

Steuart's body was brought back to Scotland. Three days later it was carried in procession and laid to rest in the same vault as his beloved mother in the church of St Mary, Grandtully.

John Dunlay (Dunlea)

While much is known of George Steuart, very little is known about John Dunlay. He was born in Douglas, Co. Cork, in 1831. His citation, published on 24 December 1858, read: 'For being the first man, now surviving, of the regiment, who on the 16th Nov. 1857, entered one of the breaches in the Secundra Bagh, at Lucknow, with Capt. Burroughs, whom he most gallantly supported against superior numbers. Elected by the private soldiers of the regiment.'

He returned with the 93rd Highlanders and received his Cross from the Queen at Windsor Castle on 4 January 1860. He died on 17 October 1890, aged 58, in South Infirmary, Cork from injuries received in an accident.

Peter Grant

Another Irishman to distinguish himself in the storming of the Secundra Bagh was Peter Grant, who was born in 1824. As the fighting in the villa dwindled, lieutenant-colonel Ewart, who had been prominent throughout the attack, fought two mutineers for their regimental standard, which they were defending. He managed to kill them despite being hacked in his sword arm, and carried off his prize.

Private Grant followed his commander and fought off the rebels as they tried to regain their colour. Grabbing a fallen *tulwar*, Grant slew five sepoys enabling Ewart to present his trophy to Sir Colin Campbell. Much to Ewart's dismay, Campbell severely rebuked him with: 'Damn your colours, sir! It is not your place to be taking colours! Go back to your regiment this instant, sir!'.[7]

Private Grant was elected by his fellow soldiers and received his VC from Major General Robert Garrett at Umbeyla, Peshawar on 6 December 1859.

A notice appeared in the *Dundee Advertiser* stating that: 'On Friday, 27th December, [1867] Private Peter Grant of the 93rd Regiment, was missed from where he lived in Dundee and was not again seen till yesterday morning, when his body was discovered by Constable Bremner floating in the river a little to the east of Craig Harbour. Bremner had the body taken out and conveyed to the deadhouse.'

Grant was stationed with the 93rd in Aberdeen, but had been visiting friends in Dundee. After an evening drinking at a local public house, Grant disappeared, presumably falling into the River Tay. Pinned to his tunic were his medals including his Victoria Cross and Mutiny Medal with Relief of Lucknow and Lucknow clasps.

James Munro

Born on 1 October 1826 at Nigg, Ross-shire, James Munro joined the 93rd on 27 April 1846. By the time he was sent to the Crimea, he was serving as a sergeant, and promoted to colour-sergeant at the start of the Mutiny.

His citation was published on 8 November 1860: 'For devoted gallantry at Secundra Bagh in having promptly rushed to the rescue of Captain Walsh of the same corps, when wounded and in danger of his life, whom he carried to a place of safety, to which place the sergeant was brought in very shortly afterwards badly wounded.'

He received his Cross from the Queen at Windsor Palace on 9 November 1860. Although Captain Walsh recovered from his injuries, Munro's were severe enough for him to be medically discharged. Unlike the other members of the 93rd, Munro's award was not subject to a ballot, which may explain why his was awarded much later, possibly through the recommendation of Captain Walsh.

James Munro died in the Craig Dunain Hospital, Inverness on 5 February 1871 from the wounds he had received during the Mutiny.

David MacKay

David MacKay was born in Caithness on 23 November 1831, the second of thirteen children born to farm labourer Angus MacKay and his wife,

Above: The Revolt at Delhi, June, 1857: a British officer battles his way through a group of mutineers. (Anne S.K. Brown Military Collection, Brown University Library)

Below: Sergeant Richard Wadeson, 75th Regiment of Foot, coming to the rescue of Private R. Farrell, at Delhi on 18 July 1857. (Anne S.K. Brown Military Collection, Brown University Library)

Above: The attack on the Kashmiri Gate (also referred to as the Kashmir Gate or Cashmere Gate) in New Delhi, 14 September 1857. The original caption states: 'The powder having been laid, the advance party slipped down into the Ditch, to allow the firing party under Lieutenant Salkeld, to perform its duty. While endeavouring to fire the charge, Lieutenant Salkeld was shot through the Leg and Arm, and handed over the slow match to Corporal Burgess, who fell mortally wounded, just as he has successfully accompanied the arduous duty.' (Anne S.K. Brown Military Collection, Brown University Library)

Below: British troops charging towards the shattered portal of the Kashmiri Gate (on the right) on 14 September 1857. (Anne S.K. Brown Military Collection, Brown University Library)

Above: The storming and capture of Delhi, in September 1857; a painting by P. Colin.
(Anne S.K. Brown Military Collection, Brown University Library)

Below: Lieutenant Herbert Taylor MacPherson, 78th (Ross-shire) Highlanders, leads his men during an attack in which they 'captured two brass nine-pounders at the point of the bayonet' Lucknow, 25 September, 1857. (Anne S.K. Brown Military Collection, Brown University Library)

Above: The 78th (Ross-shire) Highlanders at the taking of Sucunderabagh, Siege of Lucknow, 1857. A painting by Orlando Norie. (Anne S.K. Brown Military Collection, Brown University Library)

Below: E. Stuart Hardy's depiction of British infantry undertaking a bayonet charge at Lucknow, 1857. (Anne S.K. Brown Military Collection, Brown University Library)

Above: A painting of the relief of Lucknow and the triumphant meeting of Havelock, Outram and Sir Colin Campbell. (Anne S.K. Brown Military Collection, Brown University Library)

Below: The arrival at Cawnpore of the relieved garrison of Lucknow, 28 November 1857. (Anne S.K. Brown Military Collection, Brown University Library)

Above: A painting by Orlando Norie depicting 37-year-old Colour Sergeant William Gardner, 42nd Foot, rescuing Lieutenant Colonel Cameron at Bareilly, 5 May 1858. (Anne S.K. Brown Military Collection, Brown University Library)

Below: The Residency at Lucknow, also known as the British Residency or Residency Complex, still exists, albeit in ruins, and is located in the heart of the city. (Courtesy of Khalid Ahmed)

Above: Artillery pieces in the grounds of the Residency at Lucknow. The cemetery at the nearby ruined church contains the graves of 2,000 men, women and children, including that of Sir Henry Lawrence who died during the siege. (Courtesy of Khalid Ahmed)

Left: Evidence of the bitter battle that raged in the grounds of the Residency at Lucknow can still be seen today. (Jeremy Richards; Shutterstock)

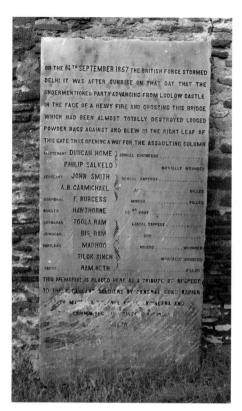

Above: A memorial plaque at the Kashmiri Gate in New Delhi which commemorates the attack on it by British personnel on 14 September 1857. The names of four men awarded the Victoria Cross – Home, Salkeld, Smith and Hawthorne – are inscribed on it. (Courtesy of Fredswd)

Right: The Mutiny Memorial in New Delhi. Situated in front of the Old Telegraph Building near the Kashmiri Gate, the memorial was unveiled in 1863 in memory of all those who had fought in the Delhi Field Force, British and Indian, during the Indian Mutiny. In 1972, the 25th anniversary of India's Independence, the Indian Government renamed the monument 'Ajitgarh' ('Place of the Unvanquished') and erected a plaque stating that the 'enemy' mentioned on it were 'immortal martyrs for Indian freedom'. (Courtesy of Pallav)

Christina. At the age of 19, David enlisted on 23 December 1850 in the 93rd Highlanders and was one of the immortal 'Thin Red Line' at Balaklava.

When the Second China War broke out, the 93rd set sail for the Far East in June 1857. During the sea voyage, MacKay was promoted to corporal. When they reached Simons Bay near Cape Town on 9 August, they learned that they were being diverted to India to help put down the mutiny by the Bengal sepoys.

Advancing through the gardens of the Secundra Bagh, the 93rd raced the 4th Punjabi to be the first through the narrow gap that had been made by the fire of the heavy guns of Captain Peel's Naval Brigade. The first few to enter were all killed or wounded but finally the weight of numbers pushed aside the opposition. It was during this phase of the battle in the grounds that David MacKay performed his act that gained him the Victoria Cross. Spotting an enemy banner of the 2nd Ludhiana Regiment, he attacked and killed the sepoy ensign before carrying the trophy away.

During the next phase of the battle, he was wounded in the lung during the assault of Shah Najaf. Elected by his comrades, he received his Cross from the Queen on 8 June 1858 at Buckingham Palace. Despite his wound, he was retained and promoted to recruiting sergeant in the Aberdeen area before finally discharged as medically unfit. Mackay had various menial jobs until he died on 18 November 1880. He was buried in a pauper's grave at Auchenheath.

Alfred Ffrench

Alfred Kirke Ffrench was born on 25 February 1835 at Meerut, India. The son of the commanding officer of the 53rd (Shropshire) Regiment, it was little surprise that Alfred should follow his father's footsteps into the same colours. After attending Sandhurst, he entered the 53rd by purchase and served in India as a lieutenant.

The 53rd was prominent in the storming of the Secundra Bagh, taking a position on the right flank. Ffrench's citation of 24 December 1858 is typically bland and simply states: 'For conspicuous bravery on 16th November 1857 at the taking of the Secundra Bagh, when in command of the Grenadier Company, being one of the first to enter the buildings. His conduct was highly praised by the whole company.'

He was awarded the VC by ballot from his fellow officers. There is no record of any presentation, so he probably received his Cross by post.

Ffrench was promoted to captain and was garrisoned with the 53rd in Bermuda when he was taken ill. He returned to his home in London, where he died on 28 December 1872, being buried in Brompton Cemetery.

141

James Kenny

Another largely anonymous Irish VC was James Kenny, thought to have been born in Dublin in 1824. Little is known of his service with the 53rd but he was elected by his comrades to receive the Cross. His citation dated 24 December 1858 states: 'For conspicuous bravery on 16th November 1857 at the taking of the Secundra Bagh. And for volunteering to bring up ammunition to his company under a very severe cross-fire.'

When the 53rd was ordered home, Kenny chose to stay in India and transferred into the 6th Bengal European Fusiliers. With the demise of the HEIC, they became the 101st Regiment (Royal Munster Fusiliers). Sadly he did not live for long for he died of disease at Multan on 3rd October 1862 and was buried in an unmarked grave.

Charles Irwin

The other private elected for the Cross was another Irishman, Charles Irwin, who was born at Leitrim in 1824. He was a cutler by trade and joined the 18th (Royal Irish) Regiment at Sligo on 4 September 1842. He served in the Burma War of 1852/3 and throughout the Indian Mutiny. His citation of 24 December 1858 records: 'Although severely wounded through the right shoulder he was one of the forward men of the 53rd Regt. who entered the building under a severe fire.'

At the conclusion of the Mutiny campaign, Irwin and many of his comrades wished to continue service in the East and transferred into the 87th (Royal Irish Fusiliers) which was on its way to Hong Kong. In 1864, at the age of 40, Irwin sought his discharge after twenty-one years of service. Returning to Britain, he was admitted as an out-pensioner of the Royal Hospital, Chelsea. On 8 April 1873, he died in Fermanagh aged 49.

John Smith

John Smith was born in London in July 1822. He joined the 1st Madras European Fusiliers in 1841 and would have taken part in the early events of the Mutiny while under the command of Colonel Neill. His bravery was noted by his fellow soldiers who elected him by ballot for the Victoria Cross, the announcement of which was published on 24 December 1858:

'For being one of the first to try and enter the gateway on the north side of Secundra Bagh. On the gateway being burst open, he was one of the first to enter, and was surrounded by the enemy. He received a sword-cut on the head, a bayonet wound on the left side, and a contusion from the butt-end of a musket on the right shoulder, notwithstanding which he fought his way out, and continued to perform his duties for the rest of the day.' Smith was discharged with a pension in 1861 and stayed on in India, where he died on 6 May 1866 at Tanjore.

SHAH NAJAF, SECOND ENGAGEMENT OF 16 NOVEMBER

The second fight that day came in late afternoon when men, already exhausted by the desperate fighting at Secundra Bagh, came under fire from the nearby walled mosque of Shah Najaf. Set on a small hill by the River Gomti, it was about 600 yards west of the Secundra Bagh and 200 yards to the right of the road leadiing directly to the Residency. The twenty-feet high walls surrounded a massive white-domed tomb of the first King of Oudh, which had been converted into a powder magazine. It was strongly defended and, ironically, one of the holy places that Sir Henry Lawrence had spared.

Now, with daylight fading, Sir Colin Campbell called on his troops for one more final effort to clear the route to the Residency. William Mitchell of the 93rd later described the advance:

'As soon as the terrible fire was opened on us in an effort to bar our advance on the Residency, Sir Colin gave the order for us to man the dragropes of Captain Peel's naval guns for an immediate attack on the Shah Nujjuf [sic]; and the order was obeyed with a cheer ... For more than seven hundred yards, the two 8-inchers and six 24-pounders were dragged along by our men and the sailors in the teeth of a hailstorm of lead and iron from the enemy's batteries; and it was a wonder that any of us survived.' During the attack, four Victoria Crosses were awarded to four members of HMS *Shannon*'s Naval Brigade.

Captain William Peel, who was awarded the VC for gallantry in the trenches above Sebastopol, took command of the newly-built 51-gun steam frigate, *Shannon*. On 17 March 1857, she sailed for China, where the Second China War had begun. When she anchored off Singapore on 11 June, news was received of the outbreak of the Mutiny in India. On 23 June, Lord Elgin and his staff embarked and the *Shannon* and sailed for Hong Kong, which was reached on 2 July. It was while he was en-route that the first Victoria Cross investiture took place in Hyde Park on the 26th. If Peel had been in attendance, he would have been the first man to receive the Cross by virtue of his seniority.

On 16 July, learning that the situation in India was desperate, Lord Elgin re-embarked and the *Shannon* took on board a detachment of Royal Marines and the 90th Regiment before setting sail for Calcutta, which was reached on 6 August. Having been diverted from one theatre of war, Captain Peel offered the Governor-General the services of his crew and guns. This was readily and gratefully accepted.

It took only a week for the main part of the crew, their arms and ammunition to embark on a large barge, called a 'flat', which was towed by a shallow-draught river steamer. Progress up the muddy Ganges was painfully slow and their destination of Allahabad was not reached until mid-September with the remainder of the ship's company not arriving until 20 October. Finally they caught up with Sir Colin Campbell's column and were able to provide the heavier guns required to storm the mutineers' strongpoints at Lucknow.

The brigade had seen plenty of action against the Secundra Bagh and, after ninety minutes' bombardment, a small breach was made through which the infantry poured. For the Naval Brigade, Shah Najaf was a harder nut to crack. With no scaling ladders available, the sailors ran their guns close to the twenty-foot high walls and began to fire but they could make little impression on the thick masonry.

At such an exposed position, the gun crews were being picked off by sepoy sharpshooters firing and throwing grenades from a vantage point on the wall. Captain Peel called for volunteers to climb a tree that overhung the nearer angle of the wall to try and shoot these snipers. Several attempts were made which proved fatal to some. Finally, Lieutenant Nowell Salmon managed to clamber among the branches and managed to pick off several of the sepoys until he was hit in the thigh. Leading Seaman John Harrison then took over and continued the good work.

Nowell Salmon

Born on 20 February 1835 in Swarraton, Hampshire, Nowell was the son of the rector. His maternal grandfather was an admiral and he was destined for the Navy at an early age. Educated at Marlborough, he entered the Royal Navy in May 1847. During the war against Russia, he served in the Baltic Campaign 1854-55.

For his bravery in having witnessed several fatal attempts to climb the tree, Peel recommended him for the Victoria Cross and promotion, both of which he received. His citation was published on 24 December 1858 and he was invested by Queen Victoria at Buckingham Palace on 8 June 1859.

Appointed Captain in 1863, he steadily climbed the promotion ladder and after a long and distinguished career, retired in 1905 after fifty-eight years of service, as Admiral of the Fleet Sir Nowell Salmon. He died on 14 February 1912 at his home in Southsea.

John Harrison

Born on 24 January 1832 at Castleborough, Co. Wexford, Ireland, John Harrison enlisted as Boy Second Class on 2 February 1850 and served on the battleship HMS *Agamemnon* during the Crimean War.

For his part in the Shah Najaf action, he was recommended for a VC and received it from the Queen at Windsor Castle on 4 January 1860. On 27 June 1858, he was made boatswain's mate and petty officer, before being discharged from the Navy on 13 January 1859. Through the efforts of his immediate superior officer, Lieutenant Thomas Young VC, he obtained a post with the Customs and Excise. Suffering from both a wound and bouts of malaria, Harrison's health deteriorated and he died in London on 27 December 1865.

Thomas Young

Lieutenant Thomas Young was HMS *Shannon*'s gunnery officer and it was he that supervised the battering of the walls at the Shah Najaf. With the guns so close to the wall it prompted Sir Colin Campbell to observe that 'Captain Peel behaved very much as if he had been laying the Shannon alongside an enemy frigate'.

The gun crews not only had to contend with enemy sharpshooters, but also masonry splinters that were torn from the wall by the roundshot. Smoke and brick dust covered the attackers who were under constant musketry fire and grenade attack from the defenders. Able-Seaman William Hall, one of the guns crew later said: 'After firing each round we ran the gun forward until finally the crew were in danger of being hit by splinters of brick and stone torn from the wall by the round shot. Lieutenant Young moved from gun to gun, giving calm encouragement.'

Each of the 24-pounders was manned by six men, numbered from one to six, beginning with an officer, usually a lieutenant. Hall was acting as 'No.2' with his gun team. When he saw men shot down at one of the other guns he raced to join the two surviving crew members. The officer in charge of the gun, Lieutenant Thomas Young, shouted, 'Ah, Hall! You're a man!' With the huge loss of gunners, Captain Peel was ordered to withdraw his guns under the cover of rocket fire, but Young and Hall kept sponging, loading and firing and eventually made a breach in the wall.

Several officers and a sergeant of the 93rd peered through the smoke and dust into the compound and saw the sepoys, unnerved by Peel's rockets and fearing they would ignite the powder store, abandoning the temple.

Both Young and Hall were recommended for the VC for their persistence in the face of heavy fire. Their brief citations appeared in *The London Gazette* dated 1 February 1859.

Thomas James Young was born in Chelsea, London, on 21 April 1826. He entered the Royal Navy as a cadet c.1840 and was promoted to mate (midshipman) on 7 December 1848. He took a gunnery course at HMS *Excellent* in 1850 and was promoted to lieutenant on 11 April 1851. During the Crimean War, he was Mentioned in Despatches for his part in the raiding parties that attacked Russian supply bases in the Sea of Azov.

After the relief of Lucknow, Young was with General Wyndham's attack on the large fort at Detea, which was taken and blown up. He was involved in the brutal aftermath when six sepoys were blown away from guns and about twenty village headmen were hung. The following month, Young was again involved in meting out more severe reprisals when 127 rebels were hung from one tree at Mhow.

With Captain Peel's death from smallpox, newly-promoted Thomas Young led the last Naval Brigade detachment back to HMS *Shannon* and returned to Britain. He received his Cross from the Queen on 8 June 1858 at Buckingham Palace. On 28 October 1859, Commander Young was appointed Inspecting Commander of Coastguard at Kingston, Devon. He met and married Louisa Mary Boyes at St James's Church, Paddington on 10 January 1860 and together they produced two daughters. His young brother-in-law, Duncan Boyes, was awarded the Victoria Cross for his gallantry in Japan in 1863,[8] though sadly, on 26 January 1869, the troubled Duncan Boyes committed suicide in New Zealand.

In March 1869, Thomas and Louisa were living in London but for an unknown reason, Thomas travelled to France, where he died on 20 March at Caen. News of both tragic deaths would have reached Louisa at about the same time.[9]

William Hall

William Edward Hall was born on 18 April 1827 at Horton's Bluff, Nova Scotia, becoming, simultaneously, the first VC recipient of Afro-Caribbean origin, as well as the first Canadian-born sailor, and the first Nova Scotian, to be so honoured.

His father, Jacob, had escaped from slavery in Virginia during the War of 1812, fought between Britain and the United States, and made his way to British lines. His mother, Lucinda, had joined the British at the same time as their attack on Washington. Like several hundred other 'negroes', they were evacuated to Nova Scotia at the end of the war and here they were married and began raising a family. Young William was only 12 years when he first went to sea. By the time he was 18, he had developed into a strong and active young man with, for his age, a wealth of seagoing experience.

For about eighteen months he served in the American Navy before returning once more to the merchant marine.

The winter of 1852 found Hall in Liverpool and, on 2 February, he joined the Royal Navy and HMS *Rodney*. In March 1854, *Rodney* was ordered to the Mediterranean, where a fleet was gathered at Malta, and was soon on their way to the Black Sea where, on 22 April, she took part in the bombardment of Odessa.

Notice of William Hall's Victoria Cross was published in *The London Gazette* of 1 February 1859, stating: 'Lieutenant (now Commander) Young, late gunnery officer of Her Majesty's Ship 'Shannon', and Able-Seaman William Hall, Captain of the Foretop of that vessel, were recommended by the late Captain Peel for the Victoria Cross, for their gallant conduct at a 24-pounder gun brought up to the angle of the Shah Nunjiff [*sic*] at Lucknow on the 16 November 1857.'

Hall received his VC, on board HMS *Donegal* on 25 October 1859, from Rear-Admiral Charles Talbot at Queenstown, Ireland. He also received the Indian Mutiny medal with the Relief of Lucknow clasp.

Hall continued to serve in the Royal Navy until 1876, when he was retired while serving as quartermaster and petty officer. He returned to Nova Scotia where he died on 25 August 1904.

John Paton

Born in Stirling, Scotland, on 23 December 1833, to a father who was a soldier, John Paton's choice of career was, perhaps, inevitable. He joined the 93rd Highlanders in 1854 and later told a journalist: 'It was at Balaklava we suffered most hardship, we were badly fed, badly clothed and badly armed. We were given guns in the Crimea which would not punch a hole through a pound of butter at 50 yards. The Russians used to laugh at us.'

The 93rd Regiment was positioned at the south side of the South Valley near Balaclava itself. In the same interview, Paton recalled: 'The Thin Red Line. Well, I was one who helped form that line. Instead of forming a square, as had been usual in facing cavalry charges, the thought suggested itself to Commander Colin Campbell that our fire would be more effective if the men were drawn up in line two deep. You see, with a square only a fourth of our guns would be in action at the one time.'

At the end of the Crimean War, Paton's regiment returned to Scotland but was soon dispatched to China; on their way the Indian Mutiny erupted and they were diverted. Now just 23 years old, he had been promoted to sergeant and, during a day which saw his regiment involved in almost constant fighting, he discovered a way into the Shah Najaf. His citation reads: 'On 16th November 1857, Sergeant Paton went alone around the Shah Nujjiff [sic], at Lucknow, India, under extremely heavy fire and discovered a breach in the opposite side. Later he conducted the Regiment to this breach and by this means, the important position was taken.' His valour under fire won him the admiration of his regiment and the non-commissioned officers nominated him for the VC.

After his regiment was recalled to England, to be stationed in Dover, he had a curious altercation with the spirited teenage Prince of Wales, the future King Edward VII. 'We were in barracks at the time,' he later told a journalist. 'I was busy cleaning my accoutrements in readiness for a review. A young slip of a lad kept interfering, first with this and then with that until I lost patience at the finish and gave him a lick under the ear. "Do you know who that is?" asked an officer standing by. "I don't and I don't care either," I replied. "Well, that is the Prince of Wales and, if he lives, the future King of England". I didn't have time to apologise but learnt afterwards that Queen Victoria, when advised of the incident, said it served the Prince right ... We were expected, not withstanding our experiences in active warfare, to take our places and be drilled amongst raw recruits under officers wealthy enough to buy commissions if not courageous enough to earn them. Many, including myself, rebelled at this and left the army.'

Never one to romanticise war and having won the Victoria Cross, he was not overtly sentimental about it: 'The much vaunted V.C. carries with it a pension of £10 per annum. Now it must be remembered that men who got the V.C. are generally pretty badly broken up in achieving it. I was not, but most of those gaining it have been left minus a leg or an arm, or have been in some way incapacitated. £10 a year seems but a paltry sum to recompense men so badly smashed. My complaint is not a personal one, as I have explained I came through without a scratch.'

An ambitious, capable man who wouldn't accept second class status, he left the military in 1861 and settled in Australia. Finding employment in the colonial penal system he held senior positions at a variety of prisons including Governor of Goulburn and Berrima Jails. In retirement he moved to Summer Hill, New South Wales, in 1896, where he lived with his wife and daughters until his death on 1 April 1914 aged 81.

THE AWARDS FOR 16 NOVEMBER

The next group of five VCs are included in the record number of awards given for the 16 November, even though there is no record of any particular feat of gallantry. They were awarded for the period of eight days during the advance on Lucknow and all received the same citation dated 24 December 1858, which states:

'Elected respectively under the thirteenth clause of the Royal Warrant of the 29th January 1856, by the officers and non-commissioned officers, and the private soldiers of each troop or battery, for conspicuous gallantry at the Relief of Lucknow, from the 14th to the 22nd November 1857.'

Hastings Edward Harington

Born on 9 November 1832 at Hinton Parva, Wiltshire, the son of the local rector, Hastings Harington attended Addiscombe College. In 1852 he entered the HEIC Army as a subaltern in the Bengal Artillery, while his two siblings joined the Indian Civil Service. In 1857, his regiment was in the Punjab when the Meerut mutiny occurred. His received a severe wound in his right foot but recovered in time to join John Nicholson's column in its march to Delhi and the subsequent assault.

Harington was prominent at the battles fought by Greathed's Flying Column before joining Sir Colin Campbell's relief force. He displayed bravery while helping to protect the force left at the Secundra Bagh to keep open the crossing of the River Gomti. His fellow officers elected him to receive the VC.

When he took part in Brigadier Walpole's disastrous assault on Fort Reyah on 15 April 1858 he received a severe wound in his left thigh, which removed him from any further action. He then travelled to Britain for his investiture and to recuperate.

He attended the investiture at Buckingham Palace on 8 June 1859 and received his Cross from the Queen. He returned to India and rejoined his regiment as adjutant in June 1861, but the following month he contracted cholera and died on 29 July aged 29.

Edward Jennings

Rough Rider Edward Jennings was born in Castlebar, Co. Mayo, in 1815. He enlisted in the Bengal Artillery in 1836. He served in the First Afghan War (Ghazni) and the First Sikh War 1845-6. His correct name was Edmond, but a clerical error at the time of his citation shows him as Edward.

During the relief of Lucknow, Jennings performed a daring act that alone was worthy of the VC, but was not officially recorded. While he and two companions were returning from carrying a message to headquarters, he heard the cries of a European. Telling his companions to keep a look-out, he urged his horse to jump a high wall and found himself in a narrow street. At the far end he found a British lieutenant (unnamed) backed against a wall with a small crowd of sword-wielding natives who were attacking him. Galloping forward, he hacked at the assailants until they fled. Jennings dismounted and lifted the badly wounded officer on his horse and took him to the medical tent. A few days later, Jennings received a summons from the hospital and the young officer rewarded his saviour with 1,000 rupees.

He was pensioned in 1859 and returned to England but sadly not in time to receive his Cross from the Queen during a ceremony held at Windsor on 9 October 1860. He moved to the North East and worked as a corporation street labourer in North Shields. He died there on 10 May 1889 and was buried in a pauper's grave. Much more recently, an appeal was launched and, in 1997, an appropriate headstone was erected in Preston Cemetery, North Shields.

Thomas Laughnan

Thomas Laughnan was born at Gort, Co. Galway, in August 1824 and enlisted as a gunner with the Bengal Artillery on 14 July 1844. There is no record of his investiture and he appears to have received his Cross by mail in India in 1859.

When he was pensioned, he returned to his home in Galway, where he died on 23 July 1864.

Hugh McInnes

Hugh McInnes was born in Anderston, Glasgow on 16 January 1816. On enlistment he gave his employment as a cotton spinner. When he was discharged in 1859, he received his VC through the post. Returning to Scotland, he worked as an engineering labourer and died on 7 December 1879 at his home in Cathcart Street, Glasgow. He was buried in an unmarked grave at St Peters RC Cemetery (now Dalbeth Cemetery). A handsome headstone was erected on 26 June 2004.

James Park

Gunner James Park was the youngest of the gun crews to be awarded the Victoria Cross. He was born in Glasgow in 1835 and enlisted in 1855. He would not have known that he was to receive the Cross as he died of cholera in Lucknow on 14 June 1858, six months before his citation was published.

John Guise

John Christopher Guise was born on 27 July 1826 in Highnam, Gloucestershire, the son of Peninsular-veteran, General Sir John Guise. He attended the Military College at Sandhurst and in 1845 was appointed ensign by purchase in the 90th (Perthshire Volunteers) Light Infantry. Promoted captain at the outbreak of the Crimean War, Guise was forced home through ill-health in early 1855. When the Mutiny broke out, he had been promoted to major and he was awarded the VC by ballot by his fellow officers for two acts of gallantry. His citation published on 24 December 1858 states:

'John Christopher Guise, Major (now Brevet Lieut.Colonel), 90th Regt., Perthshire Light Infantry. Dates of Acts of Bravery: 16 and 17 Nov. 1857: For gallant conduct on 16th and 17th at the storming of the Secundra Bagh at Lucknow, in saving the life of Capt. Irby, warding off with his firelock a tulwar-cut made at the head by a sepoy, and in going out under a heavy fire to help two wounded men. Also for gallant conduct throughout the operations for the Relief of the Lucknow garrison.'

Samuel Hill

Sergeant Samuel Hill was born in 1826 at Gelavy, Co. Antrim and enlisted in 1844 into the 67th (Hampshire) Regiment. His citation reads the same as Major Guise's and it more likely that it was he who warded off the *tulwar* blow with his musket rather than his officer.

The *Records of the 90th Regiment (Perthshire Light Infantry) 1795-1880*, indicate the confusion regarding the sequence of events. True, the 90th took a minor part in the storming of both Secundra Bagh and Shah Najaf but it was the following day, the 17th, that Guise and Hill were engaged in the taking of the Mess House and Motee Mahul Palace and performed their life-saving exploits.

Ordered by Sir Colin to capture the Mess House, Captain Garnet Wolseley led the 90th with support from Major Guise and a composite battalion. The opposition soon melted away and Wolseley saw the opportunity to seize the Moti Mohal as well. Despite the heavy fire from the enemy-held Kaiser Bagh, the 90th managed to enter the Moti Mohal and engaged in a series of running battles with the rebels until they were driven out. Instead of heaping praise on Wolseley for his enterprise, Campbell was furious that his orders had not been strictly adhered to but later calmed down and congratulated the future Army Commander-in-Chief for his courage and initiative.

Guise and Hill did receive their Crosses in February 1859 but there is no record of an investiture.

John Guise attained lieutenant-colonel though purchase in 1860 and finally full colonel in 1864. He retired as Lieutenant General Sir John Guise and died on 5 February 1895 at his home at Gorey in Co. Wexford.

Hill transferred to the 90th in 1856 and was elected by his fellow NCOs for the VC. He remained with the regiment in India after the Mutiny but was killed at Meerut on 21 February 1863.[10]

MOST VCS IN A SINGLE DAY: THE FACTS

The record number of Victoria Crosses awarded for a single day, 16 November, is believed to be twenty-four. It is a figure this writer contests is wrong. I think that strictly speaking, the correct number is sixteen and this includes Captain Augustus Anson whose acts of bravery extend from 26 September to 16 November. Major John Guise and Sergeant Sam Hill actually performed their acts of gallantry on the 17th, even though they were present at the Secundra Bagh. The five members of the Bengal Artillery received their Crosses for an accumulation of gallantry over eight days, without the Secundra Bagh or Shah Najaf being mentioned in their citations.

Patrick Graham
The third member of the 90th Regiment elected by his peers was Private Patrick Graham, Dublin-born in 1837. On 17 November, his regiment led the attack on the Mess House and Motee Mahul Palace and Graham was singled out by his fellow privates for the VC. His brief citation of 24 December 1858 read:
'For bringing in a wounded comrade under very heavy fire, on the 17th of November, at Lucknow. Elected by the private soldiers of the Regiment.'
Little more is known of him other than he returned to Dublin, where he died on 3 June 1875.

Charles Pye
Baptised in Forebridge, Staffordshire, on 24 September 1820, Charles Pye embarked on a long and active military career. He enlisted with the 40th (Somersetshire) Regiment and fought at the battle of Maharajpur in 1843. He transferred to the 21st (Royal Scots) Fusiliers and took part in the battles of the First Sikh War. He then transferred again to the 53rd Regiment for the Second Sikh War and campaigns against the warring tribes on the North-West Frontier in the early 1850s. He was serving as sergeant-major during the Relief of Lucknow and was voted by his fellow NCOs for the Victoria Cross: 'For steadiness and fearless conduct under fire at Lucknow on 17th of November 1857, when bringing up ammunition to the Mess House and on every occasion when the Regiment has been engaged.'

He subsequently took part in the Battle of Cawnpore and several other actions. He received his medal by post sometime in 1859. He was also rewarded with a commission to ensign adjutant and promoted to lieutenant in 1861. He then retired and emigrated with his family to New Zealand in 1862. He was commissioned as inspector and captain into the New Zealand Militia and took part in operations during the Maori Wars.

Pye settled at Karaka Hill but died in Australia on 12 July 1876 while visiting his father. He was buried at Tower Hill Cemetery, Koroit, Victoria.

ACTIONS OF 18 NOVEMBER

The relief column was now tantalisingly close to the Residency. News of the British advance and their successes quickly spread throughout the city. The result was an exodus of civilian and sepoy alike. Three key buildings were targeted en route to the Residency, where inside the besieged played their part with constant artillery shelling of the enemy. By the 18th, the three buildings were soon occupied and with relative ease in comparison with the first two encounters.

Although Campbell's concentration was to reach the Residency, he was conscious that the escape route away from the city should be strongly protected. To this end, he had detached the 23rd (Royal Welch) Fusiliers to establish a bridgehead over the River Gomti at the Secundra Bagh. The rebels endeavoured to isolate Campbell's force by taking the crossing and on 18 November, fighting broke out.

During the exchange of fire, a corporal of the 23rd Fusiliers was severely wounded and lay near an intersection of roads, unable to move. Lieutenant Thomas Hackett of the 23rd saw how vulnerable the wounded man was and called for volunteers. He was joined by three artillerymen, Gunners Ford and Williams and Lieutenant Hastings Harington, whose action contributed to him being awarded the VC. The fourth volunteer was 17-year-old Private George Monger, serving as a medical orderly with the 23rd.

Leaving the house in which they had been sheltering, the five men braved the heavy firing from the rebels and rushed to the wounded man. Monger gave some basic medical attention while the others shielded him from being hit. When the sepoys had been driven off, the wounded man was carried back to the British lines. For their life-saving action, Hackett and Monger received the Victoria Cross, as, indeed, did Hastings Harington. There is no record of any decoration for Gunners Ford and Williams.

Thomas Hackett

Thomas Bernard Hackett was born on 15 June 1836 in Co. Tipperary. He was commissioned by purchase in 1854 and served in the Crimea during the siege and fall of Sebastopol. He saw further action after the Lucknow relief and purchased a captaincy in 1858. His citation, dated 11 January 1859, reads:

'For daring gallantry at Secundra Bagh, Lucknow, on the 18th November 1857, in having with others, rescued a Corporal of the 23rd Regiment, who was lying wounded and exposed to very heavy fire. Also, for conspicuous bravery, in having, under a heavy fire, ascended the roof, and cut down the thatch of a Bungalow to prevent its being set on fire. This was a most important service at the time.'

It is not recorded when and where this second part of Hackett's citation took place. He received his Cross from Sir Colin Campbell at Lucknow in May 1860.

Hackett remained with the 23rd and saw further service in the Ashanti War of 1873. He retired as a lieutenant-colonel in 1874 and returned to his estate in Ireland.

On 4 October 1880, while out shooting with a friend, he had tried to push his way through a hedge and his gun discharged, fatally wounding him in the stomach. He was buried at Lockeen Churchyard, Co. Tipperary.

George Monger

One of the youngest VC recipients, George Monger, was born on 3 March 1840 near Basingstoke, Hampshire. He joined the 23rd as a Boy Soldier in 1855 and served throughout the Mutiny. His citation dated 12 April 1859 reads:

'For daring gallantry at Secundra Bagh, Lucknow, on the 18th of November 1857, in having volunteered to accompany Lieutenant Hackett, whom he assisted in bringing in a Corporal of the 23rd Regiment, who was lying wounded in an exposed position.'

Alongside Lieutenant Hackett, George Monger received his Cross from Sir Colin Campbell at Lucknow.

He was discharged in 1868 but found civilian life very hard. He married and had nine children, four of whom died in infancy. He was employed as a plasterer with a Hastings building firm until asthma prevented him working. Slipping further into poverty, he was helped by a local retired soldier, Major General Sherer, who raised funds to help the family. Finally consumption (tuberculosis) took Monger's life on 9 August 1887 and he was buried with military honours in Borough Cemetery, Hastings.

WITHDRAWAL FROM LUCKNOW

After much desperate fighting, Campbell's men reached the Residency, where there was understandable rejoicing. Sadly, this euphoria did not last as everyone was desperately tired and there was much to arrange for a swift withdrawal. Sir Colin was too aware that he was needed back in Cawnpore to deal with the threat from the Gwalior Contingent. He had fully expected the non-combatants to be ready to move out quickly. Instead it took two days to get the slow-moving heavily guarded caravan to the Dilkusha Park. Here they stayed until the 27th before the four-mile column made its slow way to Cawnpore.

General Havelock was in poor health which rapidly worsened. On 24 November, he died of dysentery and was buried in the grounds of the Dilkusha Park. The column met with little opposition on the forty-seven-mile journey, reaching Cawnpore on the 29th. Campbell and much of his force had forced-marched ahead and were relieved to find the bridge was intact, although he saw the entrenchment on the Cawnpore side under attack and much of the town on fire. A few rounds from his artillery were enough for the rebels to pull back and leave the Cawnpore area.

CAWNPORE

When, on 9 November, Sir Colin Campbell had left a holding force at Cawnpore to protect the bridge over the Ganges, he did not expect this small force to be led out to attack the vastly superior Gwalior Contingent. Under the command of Major General Charles Windham, who enjoyed a good reputation for his service during the Crimean War, a defensive line had been formed around the western side of Cawnpore facing the Grand Trunk Road. This was in accordance with his instruction, which was to make as great a show as he could by encamping his 1,700 troops conspicuously outside the city facing the direction the Gwalior Contingent was expected to take.[11] If Windham had to retreat, it would be to the prepared entrenchment by the bridge. He was particularly directed not to move out to attack.

Windham was aware that Tantia Topi's huge force of some 20,000 men was fanned out so that they surrounded Cawnpore to the north and west. In what was a very tense situation, Windham could expect an overwhelming attack at any time and, with no cavalry to gather intelligence, the British were blind to Tantia Topi's intentions.

It was on the morning of 27 November that the rebel artillery opened up on the right flank and in the centre. Out-gunned, the British fell back. Still the rebels did not follow up with an infantry attack and, with the coming of darkness, the British spent an anxious night. The following day, Windham decided to take the fight to the rebels and at least to silence their guns. It was during this phase that the final Victoria Cross of 1857 was awarded to its youngest recipient.

Thomas Flynn

Born in August 1842 at Athlone, Co. Westmeath, Ireland, Thomas was the only son of Corporal William Flynn, a serving soldier in the 64th Regiment. Sadly, Flynn senior died at Cawnpore on 5 October 1857 and thus never knew of his son's brave deeds on the battlefield.

The 15 was made drummer on 17 July 1857 and was part of Sir Colin Campbell's large force formed to relieve the British besieged in the Residency at Lucknow, then found himself a member of Windham's force left behind at Cawnpore.

On 28 November, the rebels opened fire with their forty guns and one particular battery was causing much damage. The 64th was ordered to take and destroy this most troublesome gun battery, which was positioned at a distance of 1,000 yards up a steep ravine with a *nullah* to its front. Led by Major Thomas Stirling, 170 men, including young Thomas Flynn, went forward.[12] Following Lieutenant Standish de Courcey O'Grady, Drummer Flynn raced for the enemy battery and, despite being wounded, engaged two rebel gunners in hand-to-hand combat. The rebels abandoned their guns and retreated. They soon regrouped and counter-attacked in large numbers, forcing the men of the 64th to withdraw back to the entrenchment.

Later that day, Campbell's main force arrived and the rebels pulled back. For his outstanding behaviour, the name of Drummer Flynn was recommended for the Victoria Cross but under the misspelling of 'Flinn'. The award was granted but the spelling error was thought not to be worth changing, so when it was announced in *The London Gazette* of 12 April 1859, it was to Thomas Flinn.

On March 1860, at a Garrison Parade at Karachi, Brigadier-General John Hall presented the VC to Drummer Thomas Flynn. This proved to be the pinnacle of his service career, for his record shows that he later spent fourteen periods in detention totalling 586 days. When he arrived back in England in 1869, he took his discharge and sailed to America. Here he married Mary Ann, a native of Maine. They lived in Johnstown, Pennsylvania, where they produced two sons and two daughters.

Around 1880, Flynn returned to England and was employed as a navvy. He appears in the 1881 census as staying in the Union Workhouse, Halifax,

Yorkshire. By the early 1890s, he had returned to his place of birth in Athlone, living out his life in extreme poverty before dying in the Athlone Workhouse on 10 August 1892 at the age of fifty.[13] He was buried in a common grave in Cornamagh Cemetery, Athlone, where a fine memorial stone was erected in 2008.

Chapter 8

The Tide Turns
October to November 1857

While the priorities for the British were to secure Delhi and Cawnpore and relieve the Lucknow Residency, there were still huge swathes of rebel-held territory to clear. To the south was the Central India Agency made up of six native states – Gwalior, Indore, Dhar, Dewas, Bhopal and Jawra – which was roughly 100 miles south-west of Agra. With the main objectives secured, albeit tenuously, the British could start to turn their attention to Central India. With the monsoon season ended, one of the first Moveable Columns to take to the field was that of Brigadier General Stuart and his Deccan Field Force, renamed the Malwa Field Force, which left Mhow on 19 October 1857.

The mutineers had occupied the town of Dhar and, on 20 October, Stuart's force defeated the rebels outside the town before laying siege. After ten days, the British attacked, but the mutineers quickly abandoned the town.

The Malwa Field Force then advanced to relieve the besieged British garrison of Neemuch (Nimach). This would involve defeating or by-passing an Indian princely army at Mundisore (Mandisur). lieutenant-colonel (later Sir) Henry Marion Durand, the Governor General of India's Agent for Central India, decided that Neemuch was the priority. Once Neemuch was secured, the Field Force then turned its attention on Mundisore and, in a short, sharp action, a Victoria Cross was won.

Harry Prendergast
Indian-born Harry North Dalrymple Prendergast first saw the light of day on 15 October 1834 at Madras. His father was a Collector and Magistrate with the Madras Presidency and there was little surprise when Harry was commissioned into the Madras Army in 1854. Prendergast served in Persia

with 'B' Company Madras Sappers and Miners under Major (later Colonel) Archibald John Maddy Boileau, before returning to India in July.[1]

On 21 November 1857, 300 cavalry accompanied by Lieutenant Prendergast, ADC to Colonel Durand, reconnoitred country in advance of the column. The detachment was under strict orders not to fight but Indian rebel *valaitees* (Afghan mercenaries) opened fire and the small British force counter-attacked. Here Prendergast gained the VC by saving the life of Lieutenant George Meyrick Dew, 14th Light Dragoons. Prendergast was wounded by a matchlock shot fired at such close range that the flash from the discharge burnt his bridle hand. The shot itself bounced off a rib close to the heart and the surgeon who first examined the wound was more alarmed than Prendergast.

To quote Prendergast's description of the incident: 'George Dew was ahead of our party; no accurate formation could be kept, and the regiment was broken up by rocks and streams and trees and hedges in our course, when I observed a fine, tall man step from behind a hedge and cover Dew with his matchlock. Dew passed without seeing him so I shouted to warn my comrade and rode for the stranger; he heard my shout, and prepared to receive me, and waiting till I was so close to him that the superfluous powder and flash from the discharge burnt my bridle hand, fired into my ribs, close to the heart. It was then that Sutherland Orr rode forward and killed the fine fellow who scorning to retire behind the high hedge that was close to him, preferred to remain where he was and fight the regiment.'

The following day, Durand drove rebels, who were holding a nearby village, back into Mundisore. Hearing that reinforcements were arriving, he intercepted them at Goraria and after a heavy artillery bombardment, forced some 200 rebels to surrender. Learning of this defeat, the 2,000 mutineers at Mundisore evacuated the town and scattered. Durand's short campaign had been effective and his force then marched to Indore, where they joined other British forces under the newly-appointed commander, Lieutenant General Sir Hugh Henry Rose.

Various surgeons looked at Prendergast's wounds and recommended different treatments. Eventually an expert military surgeon, William Mackenzie, cut Prendergast's side open from where the bullet entered to its exit point after it bounced off a rib. He did so just in time to stop the onset of gangrene.

At Jhansi in January 1858, Prendergast was again wounded by a sword cut to his left arm which rendered it nearly useless. In a later battle, the British captured the hill fort of Ratghur, during which Prendergast's horse was killed under him and he was shot in the arm. The much-wounded

Harry Prendergast was sent to Britain on sick-leave and, on Wednesday, 4 January 1860, Queen Victoria presented Prendergast and twenty-six other Indian Mutiny VC winners with their decorations at Windsor Castle. They included a major, a captain, five lieutenants, two sergeant majors, two sergeants, a corporal, a bombardier, three lance corporals, six privates, two sailors, a farrier and two civilians. To quote Prendergast: 'It was a foggy, gloomy day and Horse Guards and Foot Guards were drawn up on parade … The recipients had to advance a few steps in line towards her Majesty which we did in a most slovenly style, and then each in succession stepped forward, and Her Most Gracious Majesty attached the decoration to our breasts.'

After the Mutiny, Prendergast was progressively promoted to major and took part in the Ambela Campaign of 1863 and the Abyssinian Campaign of 1868. As a major-general, Prendergast was given command of the Burma Field Force in the war of 1885-6 and in 1892 he retired as a knighted lieutenant general.

He lived in London and sat on the organising committee for the Golden Commemoration of the Indian Mutiny veterans held at the Albert Hall on 23 December 1907. Two hundred and fifty of the surviving 342 officer veterans and 544 out of the 950 surviving NCO and ordinary soldier veterans attended. He played a leading role in raising charitable funding to arrange allowances for Indian Mutiny veterans which enabled eighty-three to leave workhouses and relieved 243 from living on poor law doles.

After catching a chill, Sir Harry Prendergast died at his home in Richmond, Surrey, on 24 July 1913.

THE RAJPUTANA FIELD FORCE

Sir Colin Campbell's plan was for separate columns to be formed by the Madras and Bombay Presidencies. One of these was the Rajputana Field Force commanded by Major-General Sir Henry Roberts, of the North Division of the Bombay Army. Among the regiments he commanded was the 95th (Derbyshire) Regiment which led the assault and capture of the entrenched town of Rowa on 6 January 1858.

Bernard McQuirt
The first VC awarded to a member of the 95th was that to Ulsterman Bernard McQuirt (McCourt) who was born near Lurgan, Co. Armagh, in 1829. Diverted on the voyage to South Africa, the regiment landed at Bombay and formed part of the Rajputana Field Force. During the attack on

Rowa, McQuirt performed his VC act and was recommended for the award on 11 November 1859:

'For gallant conduct on the 6th of January 1858, at the capture of the entrenched town of Rowa, when he was severely and dangerously wounded in a hand to hand fight with three men, of whom he killed one and wounded another. He received five saber cuts and a musket shot in this service.'

Due to the severity of his wounds, McQuirt was returned to the UK and medically discharged. He received his Cross from the Queen at Windsor Castle on 4 January 1860. He returned to Ireland and died in the Shankill area of Belfast on 5 October 1888.

The Rajputana Field Force continued its march and on 30 March 1858, Roberts' men took the fort at Kotah and captured seventy-five guns.

Aylmer Cameron
The son of Colonel William Cameron of the Grenadier Guards (and who was a veteran of the Peninsular War and Waterloo), Aylmer Spicer Cameron was born on 12 August 1833 in Perth. He was commissioned in the 72nd Highlanders in 1852 and served in the Crimean War.

A fellow officer described Lieutenant Cameron's part in the assault on Kotah: 'After occupying the bastions, the troops proceeded to clear the houses. Many a mortal tussle took place. Lieutenant Cameron led a forlorn hope up a narrow entrance to a house, defended by a party of desperate men, two of whom he slew and was himself desperately wounded. He sustained three wounds and lost half his hand from a sword stroke.'

Cameron was recommended for the VC. His citation appeared on 11 November 1859 and he was presented with his Cross on 9 November 1860 by the Queen at Windsor Castle. He was twice Mentioned in Despatches and promoted to captain. In 1871, he transferred to 25th (King's Own Borderers) Regiment as a major and commanded his regiment in 1881. He was appointed Commandant of Royal Military College Sandhurst from 1883 to his retirement in 1888. He died at his home at Alverstoke, Hampshire on 10 June 1909 after a long period of bad health.

GENERAL ROSE TAKES COMMAND

General Sir Hugh Rose assumed command of the Central India Field Force on 16 December 1857. Beset by the usual problems of supplies and organisation, it took him some months before he was ready to put his new force into the field. Finally, on 8 January 1858, the Central India Field Force left Indore. It split into two brigades, marching parallel on separate roads; one was led by Rose and the other by Brigadier General Stuart. The total number of men involved was 4,500, a large proportion of whom were Indians. Rose's instructions were to clear the countryside, relieve beleaguered outposts, like Saugor, and move toward Jhansi. The two brigades were to be joined by that of General Whitlock moving up from Madras.

Delayed by supply and transport problems, as well as debilitating temperatures of 119 degrees in the shade, Rose paused on his advance. On 4 March 1858, he drove the rebels from the town of Madanpur, which effected the abandonment of a strategic pass and several small forts. There was, however, one stronghold that was an obstacle to Rose's advance on Jhansi: Chanderi (Chundairee).

Richard Keatinge

Born in Dublin on 17 June 1825, Richard Harte Keatinge was commissioned and joined the Bombay Artillery on 15 November 1843. In 1851, he was employed in the Political Department as assistant superintendent and then political agent. He was also appointed Commandant of Nimaur Police Corps. In December 1857, he was captain and political agent attached to General Rose's column.

The fort at Chanderi was a large, heavily defended structure. Captain Keatinge was ordered to capture one of the advanced bastions and from there open artillery fire on the main citadel. The fort's walls were so thick that it took days to batter a small breach. Finally, on 17 March, it was wide enough to enable the men of the 86th Regiment to enter and kill all the rebels apart from a few who managed to escape; it was another case of 'avenging the massacres of Cawnpore and Jhansi'. Keatinge was later recommended for the Victoria Cross and his citation, which was not published until 25 February 1862 and one of the last to be accepted by Horse Guards, reads:

'For having rendered most efficient aid in the assault on Chundairee [sic], in voluntarily leading the column through the breach, which was protected by a heavy cross-fire. He was one of the foremost to enter, and was severely wounded in the breach. The column was saved from a serious loss that would have probably resulted, but for Major Keatinge's knowledge of the small path leading across the ditch, which had been examined during the night by himself and a servant, who declined, when required to lead the column without his master. Having cleared the breach he led into the fort, where he was struck down by another dangerous wound. The Commander-in-Chief in India states that the success at

Chundairee was mainly owing to this officer whose gallantry, really brilliant, he considers was equalled by his ability and devotion. Major Keatinge was at the time a political officer with the Second Brigade of the Central India Field Force.'

Richard Keatinge was promoted to major and commanded irregular troops against Seeta Ram Holkar in the Sathpoora Hills and served with Brigadier Parke's in the pursuit of Tantia Topi in November 1858.[2]

He was promoted to lieutenant-colonel in 1866 and Companion of the Star of India. He was appointed Chief Commissioner of Central Provinces in 1870-72 and Assam in 1875. He retired as a lieutenant general in 1887 and died in Horsham, Sussex, on 25 May 1904.

CONFRONTING THE RANI OF JHANSI

The Central India Field Force pressed on towards Jhansi and reached the fortress city on 21 March. The significance of Jhansi was not so much the formidable fortress, but the personality of the Rani of Jhansi, Lakshmibai. She was a strong-willed ruler, more intelligent and influential than most of her fellow rulers who threw in their lot with the uprising. Jhansi became a rallying point due to her political power and charisma. There was also another reason why the British wanted to capture her city and wreak revenge: on 8 June 1857, fifty-five officers, women, children and Eurasian clerks surrendered to the rebels on the assurances that they would be spared. Instead, they were taken to a garden below the fort and massacred.[3]

Jhansi fort stood on a high rock which dominated the city, with walls about twenty feet thick. In order to lay siege, the city had to be cleared of an estimated 11,000 rebels. In a battle lasting five days, the city was finally cleared and Rose's big guns began to bombard the huge walls of the fort.

BETWA

Rose had learned that Tantia Topi and the Gwalior Contingent were approaching following the Rani's appeal to relieve Jhansi and, caught at an apparent disadvantage, he decided to leave a portion of his force to continue the bombardment, while he led just 1,500 men to confront Tantia Topi's force of 20,000. He reached the River Betwa in late afternoon and identified the two fords which the enemy could cross. He then withdrew his men so Tantia Topi would think the crossing would be unopposed. His hidden outposts informed him that the enemy had crossed and were now camped with the river at their back.

During the night, Rose quietly led his men back to the vast plain adjoining the river. As the sun rose, the British attacked, causing panic and mayhem. Accurate musket fire swept the camp and the rebels turned and fled, many drowning in the river. The victory was total. Over 1,500 lay dead, the capture of all the rebel guns and equipment was complete, and the danger to the British evaporated.

James Leith

James Leith was born on 26 May 1826 at Glenkindle, Aberdeenshire to General Sir Alexander Leith. Educated at Blackheath, London, he went up to Trinity College, Cambridge, where he gained a cricket blue. Through his father's connection, Leith joined the 14th Light Dragoons as a cornet on 4 May 1849. He took part in the Persian War and was with the Malwa and Central India Field Forces during all their battles. He was slightly wounded at Mundisore on 22 November 1857.

During the pursuit of the rebels at Betwa, Captain Arthur Need of 14th Light Dragoons had become separated and found himself on difficult and rocky ground. He was soon surrounded by a large number of rebel infantry and mounted men, fighting for his life. Despite putting up a determined defence, his saddle, reins and clothing were slashed to ribbons by the enemy's *tulwars*, and he would certainly have been killed had not Lieutenant James Leith spotted his predicament and charged alone to the rescue.

He was recommended by General Rose for the Victoria Cross, which was published on 24 December 1858. He returned to England and received his Cross at Buckingham Palace from the Queen on 8 June 1859. He was promoted to major and transferred to the 2nd (Royal North British) Dragoons but failing health forced his retirement from the Army in 1864. He died at his home near Hyde Park, London, on 13 May 1869.

Hugh Cochrane

Another Scottish-born VC was Hugh Stewart Cochrane. Born at Fort William on 4 August 1829, he was commissioned without purchase into the 86th Regiment and promoted to lieutenant and adjutant in 1852. His regiment joined Sir Hugh Rose's Field Force and took part in his Central India campaign.

It was at the Battle of Betwa that Hugh Cochrane performed his VC act. His citation dated 24 December 1858 reads:

'On 1 April 1858, near Jhansi, when No.1 company of the regiment was ordered to take a gun, Lieutenant Cochrane dashed forward at a gallop under heavy musketry and artillery fire, drove the enemy from the gun and kept possession of it until the company came up. He also showed conspicuous gallantry in attacking the rear guard of the enemy when he had three horses in succession shot under him.'

He further displayed his bravery during the assault on Jhansi when he planted the colours on top of the palace. On 24 August 1858, he attained the rank of captain and joined the 16th (Bedfordshire) Regiment and, the following year, transferred to the 7th (Royal) Fusiliers. Captain Cochrane received his VC from Major General Sir Willoughby Cotton in a parade at Peshawar.

He continued to serve in India and retired as Colonel of the 43rd (Oxfordshire) Light Infantry in 1882.[4] He died at his home in Southsea on 18 April 1884.

JHANSI FORT

While the Betwa battle was raging, one of the British shells hit a powder store in the fort causing an enormous explosion. News of Tantia Topi's defeat further lowered the morale of the defenders. When Rose returned to the siege lines on 2 April, a breach had been made.

At 3 a.m. on 3 April, the assault went in. The resistance was resolute but finally the British forced their way into the fort and heavy fighting went on until the following day. When it looked as if the British were going to overwhelm the fort and palace, Lakshmibai made her escape, evading the British picquets and riding to Kalpi.

Michael Sleavon

Irishman Michael Sleavon was born in 1826 in Co. Fermanagh. Like many of his compatriots, the Potato Famine in the 1840s forced him to join the British Army. Sleavon enlisted in the Royal Artillery in 1847 but soon his skill as a mason persuaded him to transfer to the Royal Engineers. He served in Bermuda, Mauritius and India, gaining promotion to corporal. He was serving with 21st Company attached to Brigadier Stuart's 1st Brigade when he became involved in the build-up to the assault on the fort.

His commanding officer, Captain John Ballis, wrote a report about Sleavon's coolness under heavy fire: 'I proceeded round to the breach and joined the column of the night attack under Brigadier Stewart [sic], which had forced its way to within a short distance of the Palace. In reaching this position the column suffered very severely from the flank fire of the Fort at a point where it had to cross a small open space at the junction of several streets, upon which the enemy's matchlock men concentrated their fire ... It occurred to me that by running a rough parapet across the opening, a direct communications with breach and a safe removal of the wounded would be secured and the line of buildings thus connected would form an advanced parallel of great importance in the event of the enemy (as would be expected) holding out at the front ...

'I directed Corporal Sleavin, 21st Company Royal Engineers who with one or two others of the company was present with the column to commence the construction of the parapet by piling up doors and bedsteads, boxes and such other materials as were obtainable from the surrounding houses so as to afford the required cover. He commenced at once and the enemy perceiving our intention opened a severe musket fire upon the spot. Scarce a plank was laid without being struck and frequently perforated by bullets and from the great command by the enemy had over us at less than 200 yards distance it was almost impossible to raise the parapet sufficiently to avoid exposure. A Sepoy of the 25th Bombay Native Infantry was shot through the head close to me while pushing forward materials for the sap and several others were wounded and I was compelled to substitute continuous rope to carry forward a constant supply of materials to the sap.

'Corp. Sleavin, however, who was at the head of the sap and consequently much exposed, maintained his position under this heavy fire with a cool and steady determination worthy of the highest praise and he continued his work until the capture of the Palace had placed the greatest part of the town in our possession and open up a safe line of communication with the camp ...

'It may be a means for obtaining for this brave man the due recognition and reward for an act of gallantry unsurpassed, if not unequalled, throughout this campaign.'

Michael Sleavon duly received his Cross in 1860, probably via the mail as no investiture took place. He retired from the Army in 1871 after twenty-four years' service. He returned to Ireland and lived on a farm on the Archdall estate at Dromard near Kesh and died on 15 August 1902.

Henry Jerome

Born on the West Indies island of Antigua on 2 February 1830, Henry Edward Jerome attended Royal Military College Sandhurst and was commissioned into the 86th Regiment on 21 January 1848. He was serving as a captain at the time of the Mutiny and had taken part in most of the Central India Field Force battles. He had an outstanding record of bravery and was recommended on five occasions for the Victoria Cross. Indeed, his Victoria Cross was inscribed with three dates.

During the assault on the Jhansi fort, his gallantry was finally rewarded. His citation dated 11 November 1859 records: 'Henry Edward Jerome, Capt. (now Brevet Major), 86th Regt. (now of 19th Regt.). Date of Acts of Bravery: 3 April and 28 May 1858. For conspicuous gallantry at Jhansi on 3rd April in having with the assistance of Private Byrne, removed under very heavy fire Lieut. Sewell, of the 86th Regt., who was severely wounded, at a very exposed point of the attack upon the Fort; also for gallant conduct at the capture of the fort at Chandairee [sic], the storming of Jhansi, and in action with a superior rebel force on the Jumna on 28th May 1859, when he was severely wounded.'

He received his Cross from the Queen at the investiture of 4 January 1860 at Windsor Castle. He transferred to the 14th Regiment and took part in the Hazara Campaign in 1867. He returned to Britain and served on the Staff for eight years and in 1885 retired with the rank of major general. He died at his home in Bath on 25 February 1901. Although he had been ill for some time, his son said he had died of shock when he learned that his regiment had surrendered to the Boers!

James Byrne
James Byrne, born 1822, was from Newtown, Co. Wicklow. Along with Captain Jerome, he helped carry the wounded Lieutenant Sewell out of the firing line, during which he was wounded by a sword cut.

Byrne received his Cross alongside Captain Jerome on 4 January 1860. He was later promoted to sergeant and returned to Ireland where he died in Dublin on 6 December 1872.

Buried in an unmarked grave, he was honoured with a memorial stone in September 2011.

James Pearson
Fellow 86th comrade James Pearson was born on 2 October 1822 in Rathdowney, Queen's County, Ireland. Pearson was recommended for two acts of gallantry, which were published in his citation printed on 1 May 1860:

'For having gallantly attacked a number of armed rebels, on the occasion of the storming of Jhansi, on the 3rd April, 1858, one of whom he killed, and bayoneted two others. He was himself wounded in the attack.

'Also, for having brought in, at Calpee [Kalpi], under a heavy fire, Private Michael Burns, who afterwards died of his wounds.'

He was invested with his VC in January 1861 by Lieutenant General Sir William Mansfield, General Officer Commanding Bombay. Following his discharge from the Army as a sergeant, Pearson eventually became the governor of Madras Prison. When he died at the age of 77 on 23 January 1900, he was buried in St Thomas's Cemetery, Madras.

Joseph Brennan

Cornishman Joseph Charles Brennan was born in August 1828 in the village of St. Probus. He enlisted in the Royal Artillery on 27 December 1855, giving his occupation as 'Clerk'. His regiment joined Sir Hugh Rose's Central India Field Force at Mhow on 6 January; Brennan was among the men who were detached to fight Tantia Topi at Betwa before returning to join in the bombardment of the Jhansi Fort. He was recommended for the Victoria Cross and his citation was published in *The London Gazette* dated 11 November 1859:

'For marked gallantry at the assault of Jhansi on 3rd April 1858, in bringing up two guns of the Hyderabad Contingent, manned by natives, laying each under a heavy fire from the walls, and directing them accurately as to compel the enemy to abandon his battery.'

He was presented with his Cross at Gwalior on 20 April 1860 and promoted to quartermaster sergeant. In October 1863, while stationed in Delhi with 22nd Brigade Royal Artillery, he was court-martialled for not attending a commanding officer's parade. Found guilty, he was reduced to gunner. He took part in the Bhutan War of 1864-65 before returning to England. He later regained his sergeant rank and married the daughter of a Royal Artillery pensioner in 1870. They had two children born in 1871 and 1872. Tragically, Joseph Brennan died of pneumonia at Shorncliffe Camp, Kent, on 24 September 1872 leaving his widow with two infants.

Frederick Whirlpool

Of all the unusual names to be found amongst the roll of VC winners, none is stranger than that of Frederick Humphrey Whirlpool. He was born c.1829 in Liverpool to Major and Mrs Conker, but at some time the family moved to Ireland, where Frederick received a good education at the Dundalk Institution, now Dundalk Grammar School. Frederick Conker used the surname 'Whirlpool' instead of his hated surname when he enlisted in the Honourable East India Company's 3rd Bombay European Regiment at Glasgow on 23 October 1854.

In the assault on the fort, the 3rd Bombay Europeans made up part of the storming party and at 3 a.m. on 3 April, they charged the heavily defended wall. Using scaling ladders, they managed to force an entry despite musket fire and being pelted with boulders. Predictably, there were many casualties until the rebels were forced to abandon the walls. Before this, Frederick

Whirlpool was seen twice to rescue wounded comrades under heavy fire and carry them to safety.

His citation dated 21 October, contains two separate acts of valour: '3 April and 2 May, 1858. For gallantly volunteering on the 3rd April in the attack on Jhansi, to return and carry away several killed and wounded, which he did twice under heavy fire from the wall; also for devoted bravery in rushing to the rescue of Lieut. Donne of the regiment, who was dangerously wounded. In this service Private Whirlpool received seventeen desperate wounds, one of which nearly severed his head from his body. The gallant example shown by this man is considered to have greatly contributed to the success of the day.'[5]

It is probably apocryphal, but Whirlpool is reported to have said to those who were carrying him to the surgeon, 'Take care, lads! Don't shake my head or else it will come off!' In defiance of the crude medical treatment available, Frederick Whirlpool recovered from his terrible wounds after five months in hospital. He was medically discharged from the army on 2 February 1859.

Without employment, Whirlpool emigrated to Australia, where he changed his name by deed poll to Frederick Humphrey James. He did, however, enlist in the locally-raised Hawthorn and Kew Rifle Volunteers and it was in their uniform that he received his Victoria Cross. On 20 June 1861, the annual review of military forces of the colony of Victoria took place at Albert Park, Melbourne. On parade were 2,072 troops, who formed themselves into three sides of a square. Private Whirlpool's name was called out and he stood before the colony's Governor, Sir Henry Barkly, and his wife. It then fell to Lady Barkly the honour of presenting the first public presentation of the Victoria Cross on Australian soil.

Although Whirlpool had never risen above a private in the Army, he was nevertheless an educated man. He applied to be, and was accepted as, a teacher with the New South Wales Board of National Education and took charge of a new school near Wiseman's Ferry on the Hawkesbury river north of Sydney. Apparently his rather volatile nature caused a serious falling out with the school secretary, who alleged serious impropriety on Whirlpool's part. The parents of his pupils supported Whirlpool but the allegations were accepted and, in 1867, the Board dismissed him. After this black mark, he found it impossible to obtain another teaching post.

With only his £10 annual pension as a VC holder, he withdrew from society and began to live as a recluse in a slab hut near Windsor, NSW. His only contact with the outside world was a Scotsman who befriended him. He died, as he chose to live, alone, and was found on the 26 June 1899, when his weekly groceries were delivered. His VC group is displayed in the Australian War Memorial, Canberra.

KUNCH AND KALPI

With the fort and city in British hands, an orgy of looting and retribution began. The city soon resembled a vast charnel house and the reek of burning bodies was inescapable. British losses in the two battles were comparatively small – 343 killed and wounded, thanks in no small part to General Rose's leadership.

After Jhansi, the next objective was Kalpi (Calpee) on the River Jumna. Before this could be considered, the Field Force needed to rest and recuperate after an exhausting seventeen days of continuous action under a blazing sun. Not least, the commanders had to re-impose discipline after all the killing and looting. After a fortnight's pause, the Field Force continued its advance northwards through rebel-held territory.

In a battle at Kunch, Rose's force outflanked and scattered Tantia Topi's rebels and an outright victory was within his grasp. Once again, the climate intervened with many men struck down with sunstroke. Rose wrote: 'We should have destroyed the enemy had not the dreadful heat paralysed the men. Eleven poor fellows were killed outright by the sun and many more struck down. I was obliged four times to get off my horse by excessive debility … It was 119 degrees in the shade and two hundred men out of less than 400 of the 25th Native Infantry fell out of the ranks, stricken by the sun.'

Although the British could not claim an outright victory, the events at Kunch caused considerable recriminations in Kalpi, with the rebel leaders blaming each other. Many of the rebels left Kalpi, leaving it too weak to resist an onslaught. To add to their discomfort, reinforcements sent by Campbell and commanded by Colonel Maxwell arrived to augment Rose's force.[6] Together they carefully prepared their attack, avoiding the ravines and prepared defences that the rebels anticipated the British would take in their approach.

In the meantime, Kalpi had unexpectedly been joined by 2,000 men of the Nawab of Banda, a relative of Rao Sahib. It may have been them who grew impatient with the seeming inactivity and urged the Rani to go on the offensive.

On 23 May the rebels advanced and made initial gains. The British infantry, still suffering from sunstroke and contending with rifles which were becoming difficult to load because the barrels fouled due to excessive use, were pushed back to their artillery and in danger of being overwhelmed. Fortunately, the arrival of the Camel Corps and the 88th Regiment turned the tide and the rebels were thrown back. With approach of night, Rose decided to break off the action until the next day.

Harry Lyster

Born at Blackrock, Co. Dublin, on 25 December 1830, Harry Hammon Lyster was a young man of action. In 1847, he served as a special constable during the Chartist Riots in London. The following year he was commissioned in the HEIC Army and appointed to the 72nd Bengal Native Infantry, just in time to be present at the Siege of Multan in the Punjab War.

In the Central India Field Force, he served on Sir Hugh Rose's Staff as Interpreter and ADC. During the action at Baroda, Rose ordered him to lead a troop of Hyderabad Cavalry against the retreating rebels. Calling out for the native sowars to follow him, he found that as he clashed with the enemy the only man to join him was a native officer who was soon killed. Lyster charged in among the rebels, killing three and scattering the rest. Spotting the enemy's cavalry he stopped and the rebel commander advanced, brandishing his sword. Lyster took this to be a challenge to single combat and spurred his horse forward. The two men met head-on with Lyster running his opponent through with his sword and sustaining a wounded arm. The rest of the cavalry turned and fled.

On 23 May, as the rebels began to pull back at Kalpi, Lyster performed another act of bravery which resulted in him being awarded the Victoria Cross. His citation, dated 21 October 1859, reads: 'For gallantly charging and breaking singly a skirmishing square of the retreating rebel army from Calpe [sic] and killing two or three sepoys in the conflict.'

This brief and bland citation does little to reflect the sheer guts it took to charge such a formation. Threatened by cavalry, some of the rebels formed themselves into a rallying square. When they were charged, it was not by a squadron, not by a troop, not even by a sergeant's party, but by one horseman. Harry Lyster forced his way in amongst them, broke the square and slew two or three sepoys, before escaping.

In addition to his VC, Lieutenant Lyster was five times Mentioned in Despatches. He received his medal in Calcutta in 1860 and elevated to ADC to the Commander-in-Chief. In the Afghan War of 1878-79, he commanded the 3rd (Queen Alexander's Own) Gurkhas and was prominent at the battle of Ahmed Khal. On his retirement, he had attained the rank of lieutenant general. He died in London on 1 February 1922 at the age of 92.[9]

GWALIOR

The following morning revealed that the rebels had quit Kalpi and made for the fortress city of Gwalior, which they easily captured from its ruler, Maharajah Scindia. Despite siding with the British, most of the Maharajah's army went over to the rebel side. Led by Tantia Topi, Rani Lakshmibai and Rao Sahib, this considerable force wasted much time in celebrating and proclaiming the renewed rebellion.

General Rose had applied for sick leave and was to be succeeded by General Napier. When Rose learned that this new rebel force had occupied Gwalior, he postponed his departure and prepared to march to Gwalior. With the monsoon season approaching, he could not delay. To support him, Sir Colin Campbell sent additional troops under Colonel Riddell, and Brigadier Michael Smith with a brigade from the Rajputna Field Force marched direct to Gwalior.

General Rose made first contact with the rebels on 16 June at Morar to the east of the city, putting the enemy to flight.

George Rogers

George Rogers was a Glaswegian born in January 1829. He joined the 71st Highlanders, later to become the Highland Light Infantry, and went with the regiment to the Crimea. He would have spent months of misery in the trenches before Sebastopol and took part in the Kerch Expedition in Eastern Crimea in 1855. Sent to India, the regiment joined one of the columns involved in the Central India campaign. They arrived with Colonel Riddell's column to join General Rose at Morar and in the brief fight Private George Rogers was recommended for the VC on 11 November 1859.

'For daring conduct at Marer [sic], Gwalior, on 16th June, 1858, in attacking by himself a party of seven rebels, one of whom he killed. This was remarked as a valuable service, the party of rebels being well armed and strongly posted in the line of advance of a detachment of the 71st.' Rogers received his Cross at Gwalior on 11 April 1860.

The 71st remained in India and took part in the Umbeyla Campaign of 1863. The regiment returned to England in 1865 and Rogers took his discharge. In common with many soldiers, he had become addicted to drink, which led to his sad and painful demise. He had returned to Glasgow and, on 9 March 1870, paid a visit to his sister in the hope of obtaining alcohol. She refused and told him to stay in her flat until she returned. Still craving a drink, Rogers searched the flat and found a likely looking bottle in the kitchen. Without checking its contents, he drank it and soon was in agony. His sister returned to find he had consumed a bottle of vitriol (sulphuric acid) and had suffered a wretched death. He was buried in a common grave at the Southern Necropolis in the Gorbals district.

THE REBELS RETREAT

It was General Smith's force that finally swung the balance on 17 June. Arriving at Kotah-ka-Serai, about four miles south-east of Gwalior, Smith's infantry, the 95th (Derbyshire) Regiment and the 10th Native Infantry, forced the rebels to retreat. As they moved forward, the uneven terrain opened onto a plain and Smith was at last able to use his cavalry – a squadron of the 8th Hussars.

Led by Captain Clement Heneage, the 8th Hussars charged into the enemy, laying about them with their swords, capturing two guns and the enemy camp. Sometime during the charge, the inspirational Rani Lakshmibai was shot and wounded before being finally felled by a trooper's sword. With her death, much of the spirit went out of the diminishing number of rebels. Using Clause 13, General Rose awarded the squadron four VCs.

Clement Walker Heneage

Born on 6 March 1831 at Compton Bassett, Wiltshire, Heneage was educated at Eton and Christ Church, Oxford and commissioned into the 8th Hussars as cornet. He was promoted to lieutenant and sent to the Crimea as part of the Light Brigade. He rode in the famous but disastrous Charge at Balaklava.

The regiment returned to Britain but when the Munity broke, it embarked for India and joined the Field Force in Rajputana. The citation for all four men appeared in *The London Gazette* on 26 January 1859 and read:

'Selected for the Victoria Cross by their companions in the gallant charge made by a squadron of the regiment at Gwalior on the 17th June 1858, when supported by a division of Bombay Horse Artillery and H.M. 95th Regt., they routed the enemy who were advancing against Brigadier Smith's position, charged through the rebel camp into two batteries, capturing and bringing into their camp two of the enemy's guns, under a heavy and converging fire from the fort and town.'

Heneage was promoted to brevet major the following month and full major by purchase in 1860. He, along with Ward and Pearson (see following paragraphs), received his Cross at an investiture by the GOC Bombay, Lieutenant General Henry Somerset, on 18 June 1859.

He retired in 20 July 1869 by sale of his commission. He succeeded to his father's estates and devoted himself to the life of a country gentleman and was appointed High Sheriff of Wiltshire in 1887. He died at his home on 9 December 1901.

Joseph Ward

Born at Kinsale, Co. Cork, in 1832, Ward joined the 8th Hussars in the Crimea on 14 July 1855. His promotion through the ranks was swift for he was selected by his fellow NCOs for the VC award for his actions in India. Little is known of him except that he died on 23 November 1872 at Longford, Ireland. His very impressive headstone was erected by the officers and men of his regiment.

George Hollis

George Hollis was born in October 1833 at Chipping Sodbury, Gloucestershire. He joined the 8th Hussars as a farrier on 20 November 1855. After the Mutiny, he left the Army in 1860 and lived in Exeter, where he worked for a wine merchant.[7] He was presented with his VC by the Queen at Windsor Castle on 9 November 1860. He later married and lived in Cowick Street where he died on 16 May 1879. He was buried beneath a handsome headstone erected by his wife.[8]

John Pearson

Born in Leeds on 19 January 1825, John Pearson joined the 8th Regiment of Light Dragoons (Hussars) in 1844. He was a member of the Light Brigade at Balaklava and received his medal with 'Balaklava' and 'Sebastopol' clasps.

After the Gwalior battle, in which he received a sword cut to his shoulder, he was promoted to corporal. Five years later he elected to stay in India and transferred to the newly raised 19th Hussars. He was promoted to sergeant but in 1867 was invalided home to the Royal Hospital at Netley. Medically discharged, he settled in Halifax with his wife, who probably got work locally with a cotton mill, as she was a cotton feeder by profession. In 1880, the family emigrated to Canada and lived on a farm near Lion's Head, Ontario. At the age of 67, John Pearson died on 18 April 1892.

GWALIOR IN BRITISH HANDS

General Rose then joined forces with Smith's column at Kote-ka-Serai and they were reinforced by the rest of 2nd Brigade from Kalpi. Advancing once more on Gwalior, Rose's force routed the rebels and entered the city. On the following day, the formidable fortress was taken.

William Waller

William Francis Frederick Waller was born on 20 August 1839 in Dapoolee near Bombay, the son of a HEIC employee. He entered service as an ensign at the age of eighteen in the 25th Bombay NI and joined General Rose's Central India Field Force in February 1858, taking part in most of the action during the next five months.

On the morning of 20 June, and against orders, newly-promoted Lieutenants Waller and Wellington Rose, a relation of General Rose, were on picquet duty near the main gate of the fort. Hearing gunfire coming from inside, they decided to enter the fortress on their own. In Waller's detailed citation published as late as 25 February 1862, the action was described:

'Lieutenant Rose of the 25th Bombay Native Infantry, who had distinguished himself at the hand-to-hand fighting in the ravines, occupied, with a picquet furnished by his regiment, the Kotwal, or police station, near the main gateway. Lieutenant Waller, a brother officer with a small party of the same corps, held an adjoining post. When Rose heard the firing of the guns and learned that some of the Ghazees were still defending the fort, he went to Waller and suggested that they should attack the stronghold and destroy the desperate fanatics. Taking with them a blacksmith, two picquets, and twenty Pathan police, they crept up the winding road until they reached the main gateway, which they found closed. It was burst open, and surprising the other gates before they could be shut, they reached an archway on which the fanatics had brought a gun to bear. The Ghazees, having taken post on a bastion, flung over the walls all their gold and silver coin, slew the women and the children and swore to die. The gun burst at the third discharge, and the attacking party rushed through the archway and made their way, regardless of the bullets sent down upon them, to the top of the wall. On the bastion, the fanatics withstood them steadfastly, and slaying, were slain. Rose, who was swift to do battle among the foremost, fell mortally wounded.'

Lieutenant Rose was killed by a mutineer, who shot him and then rushed him with a *tulwar*, slashing his wrist and leg. Waller reacted by killing the Ghazi but was too late to save Rose. It was acknowledged that Wellington Rose would have been awarded the VC had he survived.

William Waller received his Cross in 1862 from the GOC Bombay, Lieutenant General Sir William Mansfield. Promotion came slowly for Waller, who was elevated to captain in 1869 and major in 1877. He ultimately attained the rank of colonel in the Bombay Staff Corps and retired to Britain. He died at his home in Bath on 29 January 1885 at the early age of 45.

THE END IN CENTRAL INDIA

With the fall of Gwalior, the campaign in Central India was successfully concluded, despite criticism in some quarters that General Sir Hugh Rose's Central India Field Force achievements were overstated. This is based on the number of casualties his force sustained; 560, out of which 112 were killed.[10]

Given the small size of his force and the hugely superior numbers he was up against, it is to his credit that he avoided sacrificing his men in costly frontal attacks. Instead it was the climate at its harshest and the rough terrain that caused the troops to suffer greatly. Wherever possible, Rose sought to outmanoeuvre his opponents by flanking attacks and keeping the rebels on the move. Hugh Rose could be hailed as the most effective and successful Field Force commander of the war.

With the final defeat at Gwalior, the stuffing had been knocked out of the rebel cause. Tantia Topi and Rao Sahib were now fugitives and Rani Lakshmibai was dead.

Chapter 9

Lucknow Taken
November 1857 to June 1858

On 23 February 1858, Sir Colin Campbell once again crossed the Ganges from Cawnpore and followed his previous route to Lucknow. Instead of a scratch force, he now commanded an army of 31,000 including 104 guns. The downside of such a large force was providing food and forage – not only for the fighting men but for the vast procession of camp followers.

Linking up with Sir James Outram and the 5,000 men left to defend the Alambagh, he again occupied the Dilkusha on 2 March. There were an estimated 100,000 rebels defending Lucknow and expecting Campbell to repeat his previous route. Instead, Outram was sent round the city to attack from the north and link up with Campbell as he began his attack on the Martinière on 9 March.

William Goate
William Goate was born on 12 January 1836 in the Norfolk village of Fritton, to the south of Norwich. His father, a farmer, died when William was only 5 years old, leaving a widow and eleven children to work the farm. On 21 November 1853, William enlisted in the 9th Lancers. In an interview he gave to the *Strand Magazine* in 1891, William Goate recalled his service in India:

'Our fighting began in Delhi. We were at Umballa when the Mutiny broke out, and we were ordered to join in the operations against Delhi. I was present at the siege and capture of that city. I will tell you of a little adventure of my own at this time.

'Before the city was taken, I was on despatch duty at an advanced post with orders to fetch reinforcements when the enemy came out. One day I saw six men trying to steal round by the river into our camp. Believing them to be spies, I asked the officer in charge of the picquet to allow me and two men to go and ascertain what their intentions were. He gave us leave.

'We had a very difficult job to get down to the riverside on account of the rocks and, when we got up to the men, they showed fight. We shot three of them with our pistols – one each. Being on horseback, we then attacked them with the lance. One daring fellow struck at me and I couldn't get at him. He slightly wounded my horse and then made a run for the river. I jumped from my horse and, going into the water after him, ran him through with my lance. Meanwhile, the other two of my companions had settled the two remaining men. All the while, a heavy fire had played on us from the enemy's battery.

'We now had to ride for our lives. On getting back to the camp, the officer in command sent me to the camp with a note to the Colonel of the regiment, who made me lance-corporal then and there.'

'It was on 6 March that I won the Cross in action at Lucknow, having dismounted in the presence of the enemy and taken up the body of Major Percy Smith, 2nd Dragoon Guards, which I attempted to bring off the field, and after being obliged to relinquish it, being surrounded by the enemy's cavalry, going a second time, under a heavy fire, to recover the body, for which I received the Victoria Cross.

'I will try and describe the fight, and what I saw of it. The enemy appeared in great force on the race-course outside Lucknow, and the 9th Lancers, the 2nd Dragoon Guards and two native cavalry regiments were ordered to charge. The brigade swept on in grand style, and clashed into the enemy.

'We had a fierce hand-to-hand fight; but our troops behaved splendidly, and at last we broke them up. Then we were obliged to retire under a heavy fire. As we did so, Major Smith of the Dragoons, was shot through the body, and fell from his horse. Failing to catch him, I sprang to the ground, and, throwing the bridle-rein over my arm, raised the Major on to my shoulder; in this manner, I ran alongside my horse for some hundreds of yards, until I saw the enemy's cavalry close upon me. Clearly I couldn't get away with my burden, so I determined to do what I could for myself.

'Springing into my saddle, I shot the first Sepoy who charged, and with my empty pistol, felled another. This gave me the time to draw my sword, my lance having been left in the field. The Sepoys were now round me, cutting and hacking, but I managed to parry every slash and deliver many a fatal thrust. It was parry and thrust, thrust and parry all through, and I cannot tell you how many saddles I must have emptied. The enemy didn't seem to know how to parry.

'Taking advantage of this, I settled accounts with a jolly lot. I was determined not to be taken alive. At last, some Lancers saw me and came to my rescue. Thinking the Major might still be alive, I went again to rescue him, but it was not until the enemy's forces were driven back that we got his body.

'After the action, General Sir Colin Campbell, General Sir Hope Grant and some of the cavalry officers shook hands with me and complimented me.'

He was gazetted on 24 December 1858 and received his VC on 4 January 1860 from the Queen at Windsor Castle. On 22 November 1864, he was discharged as being medically unfit.

Goate returned to his native Norfolk and lived for a while in Bungay. He married 18-year-old Sarah Ling and had a son, William. Work in rural East Anglia was becoming increasingly difficult as British agriculture declined towards the slump of the 1870s. Goate found work first as a railway porter, then as a warehouseman. Neither of these jobs or his marriage lasted. There was little alternative but to go where there was a demand for labour, which in Goate's case was the shipyards of the North East.

For twenty-two years, William worked for Palmer's, the Jarrow shipbuilder. He also served for many years with the Jarrow Company of Volunteers in the same rank as he held in the cavalry. Age and illness ended his working life and, like many Victorian heroes from the ranks, he fell into deep poverty.

In May 1900, he left Tyneside and took up residence at 22 Leopold Street, Southsea to be close to his son and young family. Within a year, William contracted gastric cancer and died at his home on 26 October 1901.

He was buried in a pauper's grave at the Highland Road Cemetery in Southsea (Plot E, Row 5, Common Grave 20). By a tragic twist of fate, Goate's son, William, died in the Royal Naval Hospital, Haslar and was buried on 29 November 1904 in the same grave as his father.

Thomas Butler
Born on 12 February 1836 in Soberton, Hampshire, Thomas Adair Butler was commissioned into the 1st Bengal European Fusiliers in 1854. His VC action took place on Outram's left flank as they linked up with Campbell's attack on the Martinière. The Bengal Fusiliers were covering Outram's heavy guns as they fired across the River Gomti at the enemy's outer line of works along the canal. It appeared that the works were unmanned and it was necessary to get confirmation to the 79th Highlanders who had just captured the Martinière.

179

Lieutenant Butler and four men volunteered to go the river's edge and were unable to attract the attention of the 79th. Butler then swam across the deep, fast-moving river and entered the enemy position from the rear. He got onto the parapet and, under fire from the rebels, managed to attract the attention of an officer of the 79th. The message was understood, and the position was quickly occupied.

Butler's act was recorded in *The London Gazette* on 6 May 1859 and he received his Cross on 8 June 1859, from the Queen at Buckingham Palace. After the Mutiny, his regiment was transferred to the British Crown and he became a captain with the 101st (Bengal Fusiliers) Regiment. He served in the Umbeyla Expedition and on the North-West Frontier before retiring in 1874 as an honorary major. He died at his home in Camberley on 17 May 1901.

Francis Farquharson

Francis Edward Henry Farquharson was born in Glasgow on 25 March 1837. He was commissioned into the 42nd Highlanders in 1855 and served in the trenches before Sebastopol. On 9 March 1858, the 20-year-old Lieutenant was in the forefront of the attack on the Martinière. Attacking in two lines, the 42nd dashed down the grassy slope in order to minimise their losses. Following Colonel Alexander Cameron, Farquharson stormed a bastion mounting two guns, which he spiked. He then held this position until the following morning but suffered a severe wound.

He was invalided home and his VC citation was published on 21 June 1859. He received his Cross on 4 January 1860 from the Queen at Buckingham Palace. Farquharson was promoted to captain in 1862 and retired with the rank of major. He died at his home in Harberton, Devon on 12 September 1875, aged 38.

William McBean

The son of a ploughman, William McBean was born on 1 January 1818 at Inverness. He joined the 93rd Highlanders and saw service in the Crimea before being sent to India. During the assault on the Begum Bagh on 11 March, Lieutenant McBean took on eleven rebels at the main beach, managing to kill all of them. The last was a *havildar* (commander or sergeant) but when other Highlanders arrived to give assistance, McBean called out for them not to interfere. In the single combat, McBean finally got the better of his opponent and dropped him with a well aimed thrust through the chest.

His bravery was gazetted on 24 December 1858 and he received his VC at a parade on 6 February 1859 from Major General Robert Garrett at Umbeyla.

When McBean first joined the regiment, he declared that one day he would command it. He kept his word and held every rank from private to major-general. He died at the age of 60 in London on 23 June 1878.

The Iron Bridge

Sir James Outram's advance from the north involved crossing the heavily defended Iron Bridge spanning the Gomti river immediately north of the ruined Residency. The 2/60th Rifles was sent forward to skirmish but the approaches to the bridge were through a maze of narrow streets so contact with each other was lost. On approaching the Iron Bridge, Captain Wilmot found himself with only four of his company at the end of a street leading on to the bridge. Occupying the bridge and advancing were dozens of rebels. The VC citation dated 24 December 1858 is the same for each man:

'For conspicuous gallantry on the 11th of March 1858. Captain Wilmot's Company was engaged with a large body of the enemy, near the Iron Bridge. That officer found himself at the end of a street with only four of his men, opposed to a considerable body. One of the four was shot through both legs, and became utterly helpless: the two men lifted him up, and although Private Hawkes was severely wounded, he carried him for a considerable distance, exposed to the fire of the enemy, Captain Wilmot firing with the men's rifles, and covering the retreat of the part.'

Henry Wilmot was born on 3 February 1831 at Chaddesden, Derby, the second son of Sir Henry Wilmot (4th Baronet). He was educated at Rugby School and commissioned by purchase into the 43rd (Monmouth) Regiment in 1849. By 1855, he had purchased a captaincy and transferred to the 60th Rifles. He went to fight in the Second China War before retiring from the Army. He was appointed lieutenant-colonel in the Derbyshire Rifle Volunteers and succeeded to the baronetcy of Wilmot of Chaddesden in 1872. In 1898 he was made KCB and died at his home in Bournemouth on 7 April 1901.

William Nash was born in Newcastle, Co. Limerick, on 23 April 1824. He enlisted as a boy soldier at the age of 14 in 1838. He was serving as a corporal at the time of his VC action. He died on 6 April 1875 in London and was buried in an unmarked grave.

David Hawkes was born in Witham, Essex, in 1822 and was a 35-year-old private at the time of his VC exploit. He instructed that his Cross, in the event of his death, should be sent to his father. His brief moment of glory was short-lived for he was killed in action at Faizabad on 14 August 1858 and his VC was duly forwarded to his father.[1]

Edward Robinson

One of 'Peel's Jacks' was Able Seaman Edward Robinson. Born in Portsea, Hampshire, in 1838 he joined the Royal Navy at the age of 14. During the assault on the Begum Cotee, Peel's guns were protected by whatever material was available. In an interview he gave to the *Strand Magazine* in 1896, Robinson described how he was awarded the Victoria Cross:

'At sunrise the English opened fire once more, the enemy being on their flank as well as in front. Thousands of mutineers swarmed on the other side of the Goomtee River. The fire was briskly returned, and our gallant fellows began to throw up batteries – of a sort.

'These defences consisted of branches of trees, dried grass, straw – anything that would make the dust and sand of the earthworks cohere on either side of the guns.

'The weather was hot; water scarce and difficult to procure. Native carriers, who had manfully stuck by the British, were rapidly being shot down.

'Soon the defensive works became as dry and inflammable as tarred rope. During the night the water-bearers kept pouring the precious fluid on the heaps, but it simply ran through, only to be licked up later on by the fierce morning sun.

'Shell after shell from the sepoy lines came flying into batteries. Suddenly the earthworks blazed up like a furnace, and the guns had to be abandoned.

'A pile of shells were stacked next to the British guns when the sandbags caught fire. If the flames had reached the shells there would have been severe casualties and the guns would have been destroyed. There was no time to move the shells to a safer place – the fire had to be extinguished.'

When Captain Peel called for volunteers to put out the fire, Edward Robinson immediately stepped forward. Behind the batteries were several large tubs of water, together with a number of water bags. Robinson picked up several of the bags and quickly filled them. He then leapt over the small wall which was protecting the Naval Brigade from enemy fire and went back to the burning earthworks. Leaping onto them, in full view of the rebels who were fifty yards away, he began extinguishing the flames. Two engineers, trying to repair the earthworks, were shot down at Robinson's side.

When the water bags were emptied he went back for more water, and succeeded in pouring gallons of water on the burning sandbags. He made five attempts to put out the flames, and threw clear other sandbags.

Robinson was under enemy musket fire every time he went out to the earthworks, but on the fifth occasion he was shot and seriously wounded. A musket ball passed through his shoulder, shattering his collar bone and disabling him for life. He was said also to have been struck in the right arm and the neck before collapsing unconscious into a trench. He was pulled to safety by other members of the Naval Brigade.

He was recommended for the VC which was published on 24 December 1858.

Robinson eventually received his VC on Wednesday, 4 January 1860. That morning, in the Quadrangle of Windsor Castle, the Queen, accompanied by the Prince Consort and other dignitaries, presented VCs to twenty-four officers and men for their heroic deeds in India. The *Windsor & Eton Express* commented: 'Possibly not a man ... thought of the reverses they had endured, and the dangers they had overcome. All was forgotten at that moment, in the flush of honest pride which swelled every heart.'

Robinson left the Navy and, in later years, was employed as gatekeeper at the entrance to Windsor Home Park. He died on 2 October 1896 and was buried in Old Windsor Cemetery.

Robert Newell

Born at Seaham, County Durham, in 1835, Robert Newell was 22-years-old when he was recommended for the Victoria Cross. Sadly, he is another soldier who died before his citation was announced:

'For conspicuous gallantry at Lucknow on 19th March 1858, in going to the assistance of a comrade whose horse had fallen on bad ground, and bringing him away, under a heavy fire of musketry from a large body of the enemy.'

He died of dysentery four months later on 11 July 1858 at Umballa. His medal group is on display in the Lord Ashcroft Gallery at the Imperial War Museum.

David Rushe

David Rushe was born in Woburn on 28 April 1827 and joined the 9th Lancers aged about 18, taking part in the First and Second Sikh Wars. His citation published on 24 December 1858 reads:

'For conspicuous bravery near Lucknow on 19th of March 1858, in having, in company with one other private of the troop, attacked eight of the enemy, who had posted themselves in a nullah, and killed three of them.'

Rushe later achieved the rank of regimental sergeant-major. He received his Cross from the Queen at Windsor Castle on 4 January 1860. Rushe died at Great Marlow on 6 November 1886.

William Bankes

William George Hawtry Bankes was born on 11 September 1836, the fifth child of the Right Honourable George Bankes MP and Georgina Charlotte (née Nugent). The family lived at Kingston Lacy and Corfe Castle, Dorset. Known as 'Willy', a commission was purchased for him in the cavalry, an expensive outlay, and he joined the 7th Hussars as a cornet in the spring of 1857.

On 18 March, it was learned that a strong force of rebels was in the Musabagh, a large palace and grounds about four miles north-west of Lucknow. On the 19th, a force of cavalry and horse artillery, including the 7th Hussars, was sent to prevent these rebels escaping while the main force attacked the palace.

Cornet Bankes was attached to 'H' Troop, which was escorting the artillery. When they halted for a rest and food, a small mud fort or *rezai* in the distance was approached by a vidette. It appeared to be deserted until its occupants opened fire. The Royal Horse Artillery, along with its cavalry escort, was immediately sent to forward to return fire. The effect was to plunge a stick into a hornet's nest.

To the astonishment of the soldiers, about fifty sword-brandishing villagers rushed out and charged the guns. Some reports say that the villagers' ferocious behaviour was fuelled by drugs or they may have been fanatical *ghazis*. The 7th was ordered to charge this mob and was immediately involved in a vicious mêlée. Captain Slade and Lieutenant Wilkin were both severely wounded, leaving young Willy Bankes as the only officer. He charged into the crowd, shooting three rebels. In the swirl of the bitter fighting, a rebel slashed and hamstrung Bankes's horse and Willy was unseated. With his revolver empty, Bankes was powerless to defend himself and he was immediately set upon by the *tulwar*-wielding enemy.

When the rebels were dispersed, Willy Bankes was found barely alive. He had been hacked so badly that he was not expected to live. He was taken to the hospital, where his right arm and leg were amputated and the other wounds treated. He received the best available treatment from the Surgeon General appointed by Sir Colin Campbell. The latter, impressed by the young cornet's bravery, recommended him for the Victoria Cross. Despite the terrible wounds he had received, Bankes appeared to be making a good recovery. He even spoke of going sailing again upon his return home. On 6 April 1858, however, to everyone's sorrow, young Willy Bankes died of blood poisoning due to infected wounds.

THE REBELS SLIP AWAY

Although Lucknow fell, the containment of the rebels had failed as thousands escaped through the great gaps between Campbell's surrounding army. Frederick Roberts wrote:

'Lucknow was practically in our hands on the evening of 14 March, but the rebels escaped with comparatively slight punishment, and the campaign, which should have then come to an end, was protracted for nearly a year by the fugitives spreading themselves over Oudh and occupying forts and other strong positions, from which they were able to offer resistance to our troops until the end of May 1859, thus causing the needless loss of thousands of British soldiers.'[2]

One of the last acts of the HEIC was to vote Campbell a pension of £2,000 a year. He was made colonel of the 93rd Highlanders and the Coldstream Guards and appointed Field Marshal. He died at his London home on 14 August 1863 and is buried at Westminster Abbey.

Chapter 10

Campbell's Oudh Campaign
February to April 1858

On 28 November 1857, Sir Colin Campbell's slow moving column of Residency evacuees reached Cawnpore. He saw what he feared would happen: General Wingham's defeated force manning the entrenchment in their attempt to prevent Tantia Topi's Gwalior Contingent from reaching the bridge. Successfully crossing the Ganges, Campbell's first priority was to evacuate the civilians and sick down river to Allahabad. On 3 December, it was a relieved Sir Colin who saw the back of the non-combatants as they set off to that city. As for his men, there was still much fighting to be done.

Campbell went on the offensive and in a series of operations, the Gwalior Contingent was forced back and finally broken. The saving of Cawnpore and the rout of Tantia Topi and Nana Sahib's army proved to be the turning point of the Mutiny and from then on the mutineers were on the back foot.

Sir Colin could now call on some 20,000 troops deployed in several columns which he used over the next five months to push the rebels northwards towards the border with Nepal. The King of Nepal was close to the British and could be relied to force the rebels back into the arms of the pursuing Allies.

One of the first of the Flying Columns was led by Colonel James Hope Grant, who went in pursuit of the scattered Gwalior Contingent.

Frederick Roberts
Frederick Sleigh Roberts was born in Cawnpore on 30 September 1832, to a serving officer in the HEIC Army. As an infant he lost an eye due to 'brain fever' (meningitis). He was brought to England when he was 2 and his education included three years at Eton. His father tried to dissuade him from joining the Army because of the poor pay but his son wanted nothing

186

else. When he was 16, he left to enter the Royal Military College Sandhurst. His father knew that if his son succeeded in obtaining a commission into the British Army, he would be unable to support himself on the salary alone. He decided that his son should join the Indian Army, where the strain on the pocket was not so severe. Young Frederick therefore attended Addiscombe College and was commissioned as a second lieutenant in the Bengal Artillery, despite having only one eye and standing no taller than 5 feet 3 inches: such were the physical requirements to enter the Army in Victorian times.

During and after the Relief of Lucknow, Roberts was ADC to Colonel Hope Grant and was part of the flying column that left Cawnpore in late December and headed northwards towards Fategarh. As they approached the bridge crossing the Kali Naddi, the column came under fire from the nearby village of Khudaganj. The rebels were in force and inflicted casualties on the British. Roberts later wrote:

'Henry Hamilton Maxwell, a brother officer of mine who had been standing close to me, was very badly wounded in the leg, and both Sir Colin and Sir Hope were hit by spent bullets.

'There was a feeling throughout the Army that Sir Colin was inclined to favour Highlanders unduly; and a rumour that the 93rd were to be allowed the honour of delivering the assault on Kudaganj which was highly resented by the 53rd [Shropshire Light Infantry], and they determined that on this occasion, at any rate, the Highlanders should not have it all their own way …

'We were all waiting by the bridge for the attacking party to form, when suddenly the advance was sounded, then the double, followed by a tremendous cheer, and we saw the 53rd charge the enemy. Sir Colin was very angry, but the 53rd could not be brought back, and there was nothing for it but to support them.'

This was the signal for Roberts to be involved in another charge against the enemy. Fred joined a squadron of the Punjab Cavalry in the five-mile chase. A group of rebels made a stand and fired into the squadron. Roberts saw one of the rebels about to run a *sowar* through with his fixed bayonet. With a back-hand slash, Roberts cut the rebel across the face, killing him instantly.

'The next moment I descried in the distance two sepoys making off with a standard which I determined must be captured, so I rode after the rebels and overtook them, and while wrenching the staff out of the hands of one of them, whom I cut down, the other put his musket close to my body and fired; fortunately for me it missed-fire, and I carried off the standard.'

For these two actions, Fred Roberts was recommended for the Victoria Cross, which appeared in *The London Gazette* dated 24 December 1858.

Returning to Cawnpore, Fred dined with William Peel VC. Tragically, the next morning Peel was struck down with smallpox and died that evening.

Roberts returned home at the end of June and was presented with his Cross by the Queen on 8 June 1859 at Buckingham Palace. He also married and returned to India, where he advanced to become Britain's most celebrated army commander.

At the beginning of the Great War, the 82-year-old field marshal went to France to visit the troops of the Indian contingent. There was something very moving about this old soldier renewing contacts with the army he had last led to victory thirty-four years earlier. On the third day, 14 November, Roberts and his daughter, Aileen, travelled to Cassel.

During this busy day, the cold and damp weather brought on a feverish chill which soon turned to pneumonia. By 8 p.m. Lord Roberts was dead. His body was brought back to London where it lay in state in Westminster Hall, one of only two non-Royals to do so in the twentieth century – the other being Sir Winston Churchill.

He was given a state funeral, with his coffin being conveyed to St Paul's Cathedral on the gun carriage that his son had died trying to save at Colenso.[1]

David Spence

Scotsman David Spence was born in 1818 at Inverkeithing, Fife. He joined the 9th Lancers in 1842 and took part in the First and Second Sikh Wars. At the time of the Mutiny, he was a troop sergeant-major and the deed that won his Victoria Cross occurred on 17 January 1858, recorded thus in his citation dated 24 December 1858:

'For conspicuous gallantry on the 17th of January, 1858, at Shumsabad, in going to the assistance of Private Kidd, who had been wounded, and his horse disabled, and bringing him out from a large number of rebels.'

He was invested with his VC by the Queen on 4 January 1860 at Windsor Castle. He later achieved the rank of regimental sergeant-major before retiring and becoming a Yeoman of the Guard. He died in London on 17 April 1877 aged 58.

James Innes

James John McLeod Innes was born on 5 February 1830 in Bhagalpur, Bengal, the son of a surgeon in the Bengal Army. He entered Addiscombe

College in February 1847 and commissioned into the Bengal Engineers on 8 December 1848. A succession of civil projects occupied him until his promotion to lieutenant in 1854.

When the Mutiny broke out, he was stationed at Lucknow and given the task of blowing up the old fortress of Macchi Bhawan. Innes spent much of the siege employed in mining. Following the evacuation from the Residency, Innes was posted to General Sir Thomas Franks's Field Force during its advance through Oudh.

The Battle of Sultanpore on 23 February 1858 saw General Franks' Field Force with a total of 5,710 men, including only sixty-three cavalry, in action against superior forces. The rebels numbered about 25,000, including 1,100 cavalry, 5,000 sepoys and twenty-five guns. Despite the huge difference in men and guns, the Field Force managed to rout the enemy and capture twenty-one guns. Innes was singled out for mention which led to him being gazetted on 24 December 1858: 'At the action at Sultanpore, Lieutenant Innes, far in advance of the leading skirmishers, was the first to secure a gun which the enemy was abandoning. Retiring from this, they rallied round another gun further back, from which the shot would in another instant have ploughed through our advancing columns, when Lieutenant Innes rode up, unsupported, shot the gunner who was about to apply the match, and remained undaunted at his post, the mark for a hundred matchlock men who were sheltered in some adjoining huts, and kept the artillerymen at bay until assistance reached him.'

On 4 March, Innes was severely wounded at the fort at Dhaurahra near Lucknow. He was promoted to brevet major on 28 August 1858 and received a year's service for the defence of Lucknow. He received his Cross in 1859 from the Viceroy, Lord Canning. Advancing steadily up the promotion ladder, Innes retired as a lieutenant general in 1886. Moving to England, he devoted himself to writing histories of the Indian Mutiny and biographies of Sir Henry Lawrence and Sir James Browne. Innes died after a long illness at his home in Cambridge on 13 December 1907.

Frederick Aikman

The son of a serving officer, Frederick Robertson Aikman was born on 6 February 1828 at Ross, South Lanarkshire. He joined the Bengal Army and was commissioned on 18 January 1845 into the 4th Bengal NI, taking part in the First and Second Sikh Wars. When his regiment mutinied, he raised the volunteer Jalandhar Cavalry, which changed its title to 3rd Sikh Irregular Cavalry. He took part in the Siege of Delhi and capture of Lucknow. He had force-marched from Jalandhar to join General Franks'

Field Force and quickly performed the act that gained him the Victoria Cross at Amethi. His citation, dated 3 September 1858, read:

'This Officer Commanding 3rd Sikh Cavalry on an advanced Picquet, with one hundred of his men, having obtained information, just as the Force marched on the morning of the 1st of March last, of the proximity, three miles off the high road, of a body of 500 Rebel Infantry, 200 horse, and 2 Guns, under Moosahib Ali Chuckbdar, attacked and utterly routed them, cutting up more than 100 men, capturing two guns, and driving the survivors into, and over, the Goomtee. This feat was performed under every disadvantage of broken ground and partially under the flanking fire of an adjoining Fort. Lieutenant Aikman received a severe sabre cut in the face in a personal encounter with several of the enemy.'

Aikman was promoted to captain and in May, due to his injury, returned to England on sick leave. He received his Cross from the Queen at Buckingham Palace on 8 June 1859 and retired from the Army the following year. The Queen appointed him as a member of The Honourable Corps of Gentlemen at Arms, the monarch's official bodyguard, on 13 May 1865.

In 1877, while still a member of the Queen's guard, he was charged with being drunk and disorderly in charge of four horses and a coach. He and a group of friends and servants had been returning from a trip to the Epsom Races when he was arrested for driving recklessly. At the time he was also in command of the Royal East Middlesex Militia and retired as honorary colonel in 1887 and died during a County Ball in Hamilton, Lanarkshire on 5 October the following year. He was buried in a mausoleum in Kensal Green Cemetery, London.

THE FIRST GURKHA VC

Although not attached to any flying column, the following action helped to put more pressure of the rebels. It took place in the bleak Kumaun hills and led to the awarding of the first Gurkha Regiment VC.

John Tytler
John Adam Tytler was born on 29 October 1825 at Monghyr, Bengal, the third son to John (Surgeon, HEIC) and Anne (née Gillies). When he was 5, he was sent home to the care of his mother's sisters until the arrival of his parents in 1835. In 1843, through his father's old friend, Sir Jeremiah Bryant, a Director of the Honourable East India Company, he received a cadetship into the Company's army. He sailed for India in the autumn of that year and receiving his commission as ensign, was posted to the 66th Bengal

Native Infantry in December 1844. The regiment was involved in the Second Sikh War of 1848-9, which was regarded by the sepoys as 'foreign service'.

The 66th mutinied upon the annexation of the Punjab when foreign duty allowance was discontinued. The rebellion was put down and the regiment was marched to Ambala, where it was disbanded by Sir Charles Napier on 27 February 1850. Their colours, arms, stores and so on were handed over to the 1st Nasiri Battalion, which assumed the title 66th Goorkha Regiment of Native Infantry. In 1861 it became the 1st Goorkha Regiment. In 1853, the new regiment was stationed in the hills around Nainital in present day Uttarakhand State, some 200 miles north-east of Delhi.

When the sepoys mutinied at Meerut in May 1857 Lieutenant Tytler and his Gurkha soldiers were at the hill station of Haldwani and were not involved in the terrible events on the plains of Oudh. On 17 September, however, 1,000 rebels attacked Haldwani and Tytler, with just seventy defenders, played a major part in defeating them.

The rebels hid in the bleak Kumaun hills and built up their strength. On 9 February 1858, a force of 500 men of the 66th, commanded by Captain C.C.G. Ross, 200 cavalry and two 6-pounder guns, surprised a rebel force of between 4,000-5,000 infantry, more than 1,000 cavalry and four guns at a small village called Charpura.

The following day, Ross led two companies of the 66th against the rebel right flank in the face of heavy fire of grape from the enemy guns, which staggered the advance. Seeing the men wavering, John Tytler set an example to rally them by spurring his horse forward and dashing on ahead.

Captain Ross later wrote in his report, which was used in the citation: 'Lieutenant Tytler dashed on horseback ahead of all, and alone, up to the enemy's guns, where he remained engaged hand to hand, until they were carried by us; and where he was shot through the left arm, had a spear wound in his chest, and a ball through the right sleeve of his coat.'

For this act of valour, Lieutenant Tytler was recommended for the Victoria Cross. When it at last reached the desk of the Duke of Cambridge, he made the following comments: 'The act of an Officer dashing on horseback ahead of all the Troops and alone up to the Enemy's Guns, though it may be admired for its gallantry can scarcely, in His Highness's opinion, be approved.' Notwithstanding the Duke's stricture, Tytler's VC was approved and announced in *The London Gazette* on 24 August 1858. Like other Indian Mutiny recipients, Tytler appears to have received his Cross through the post for there is no record of an official investiture.

After recuperating from his wounds, Tytler rejoined his regiment for the death throes of the Mutiny. In a six-week period, he was involved in four battles in the Kumaon Hills. As part of Brigadier General Troup's force, the 66th won victories at Pusayan on 17 October and Mittowlee on 9 November, when they re-occupied the fort. Under Brigadier General George Barker, they defeated the last pockets of resistance at Biswah on 18 November and Rasulpore on 25 November.

Tytler went on to take part in the Black Mountain and Lushai Campaigns. At the beginning of the Afghan War in late 1878, newly promoted Brigadier General Tytler took command of the 2nd Infantry Brigade of the Peshawar Valley Field Force under the command of General Sir Sam Browne VC. After a year's hard campaigning, an exhausted John Tytler succumbed to an attack of pneumonia and died on 14 February 1880 aged just 54.

AZAMGARH

After the taking of Lucknow in March, Sir Colin despatched a column led by General Lugard to relieve a small detachment that had been forced into an entrenchment near the town of Azamgarh (Azamgarth). He was beaten to it by Lieutenant-Colonel Lord Mark Kerr of the 13th Somerset Light Infantry who learned of Colonel Milman's plight. Starting from Benares with 450 men of the 13th, some horsemen of the Queen's Bays and two 6-pounder guns, the column completed the fifty miles to the outskirts of Azamgarh on 6 April. Here, they were confronted by up to 4,000 rebels commanded by Koer Singh. The 13th managed to dislodge the rebels to his front but found that a large force had attacked his rear. After fighting off this threat, the small column neared Azamgarh where they were instructed to wait for Lugard's column.

William Napier
Yorkshireman William Napier was born on 20 August 1824 in Keighley. On 10 December 1846, he enlisted in the 13th at Leeds. He served in the Crimean War and was in South Africa when news of the Mutiny was received. Arriving in Calcutta, the regiment was moved up country to relieve Colonel Milman's small force at Azamgarh.

During the fighting, Sergeant Napier saw Private Benjamin Milnes lying severely wounded and went to his rescue. Binding his comrade's wounds, despite being surrounded by the enemy, Napier was hit by a bullet that left a gaping wound over his left eye. Blinded by the blood, Napier continued to fight back and finally picked up Milnes and carried him to safety.

Afterward, Lord Mark Kerr asked Napier whether he would like a commission but the sergeant declined. Instead he was recommended for the VC and promoted to sergeant major. He received his Cross during 1862 and was discharged on 8 December. Two weeks later, he caught a steamer to Melbourne, Australia, where he married and raised a family. He died on 2 June 1908.

Patrick Carlin

Patrick Carlin was born in 1832 in the Belfast Workhouse. He enlisted in the British Army and joined the 13th at the time of the Indian Mutiny. His citation published on 26 October 1858 reads:

'Private Patrick Carlin, No.3611, of the 13th Foot, for rescuing, on the 6th of April 1858, a wounded Naick of the 4th Madras Rifles, in the field of battle, after killing, with the Naick's sword, a mutineer sepoy, who fired at him whilst bearing of his wounded comrade on his shoulders.'

On 29 June 1858, his Cross was pinned to his chest almost on the same spot of his exploit by Sir Colin Campbell. This was almost unprecedented, particularly for the Indian Mutiny, when years could separate the act and the award. Little else is known of Carlin except that he died in the Belfast Union Infirmary on 11 May 1895.

THE AZAMGARH FIELD FORCE

On 29 March the Azimghur (Azamgarh) Field Force under Brigadier General Sir Edward Lugard, was on the march to relieve Colonel Milman's besieged detachment. While the siege of Lucknow was going on, a large rebel force under Koer Singh had crossed the Ganges and moved into the area between Benares and the Himalayas. As a result the small British force, left to defend the district under Colonel Milman, was routed and he withdrew to an entrenchment outside the town of Azmgarh.[2]

Lugard's column met Koer Singh's force at a bridge over the River Tong, which the latter cleverly defended, allowing his main body to retreat. During the subsequent pursuit, two Victoria Crosses were awarded to members of the Military Train.

A Confused Action

There is some dispute over what actually happened when Murphy and Morley attempted to save the life of Lieutenant Hamilton during the charge at the sepoy squares. The recognised account is that of the gazetted citations, which were the official accounts put forward when the claims for

Murphy and Morley's VCs were made. In the case of Michael Murphy, *The London Gazette* dated 27 May 1859 recorded:

'Private Michael Murphy: For daring gallantry on the 15th April 1858, when engaged in the pursuit of Koer Singh's Army from Azimghur, in having rescued Lieutenant Hamilton, Adjutant of the 3rd Sikh Cavalry, who was wounded and surrounded by the enemy. Farrier Murphy cut down several men and, although himself severely wounded, he never left Lieutenant Hamilton's side until support arrived.'

Samuel Morley's citation, which was published nearly eighteen months later, on 7 August 1860, reads:

'Private Samuel Morley: On the evacuation of Azimghur by Koer Singh's Army, on the 15th April 1858, a squadron of the Military Train and a half troop of Horse Artillery were sent in pursuit. Upon overtaking them, and coming into action with their rearguard, a squadron of the 3rd Sikh Cavalry [also detached in pursuit], and one troop of the Military Train were ordered to charge, when Lieutenant Hamilton, who commanded the Sikhs, was unhorsed and immediately surrounded by the enemy who commenced cutting and hacking him whilst on the ground. Private Samuel Morley seeing the predicament Lieutenant Hamilton was in, although his [Morley's] horse had been shot under him, immediately and most gallantly rushed up, on foot, to assistance, and in conjunction with Farrier Murphy, who has already received the Victoria Cross for the same thing, cut down one of the sepoys and fought over Lieutenant Hamilton's body until further assistance came up, and thereby was the means of saving Lieutenant Hamilton from being killed on the spot.'

In the swift-moving chaos of the battle, some eyewitness accounts described a different version.

In Malleson's *History of the Indian Mutiny* there is a different account of the action in that there is no mention of Private Morley and a third hero is introduced, a Captain Middleton of the 29th (Worcestershire) Regiment:[3]

'The loss of the British was considerable. Hamilton of the 3rd Sikhs, a very gallant officer, was wounded and unhorsed when charging the squares. As he lay on the ground, the rebels cutting at him, Middleton of the 29th Foot and Farrier Murphy rushed to his assistance, and succeeded in rescuing his body, which otherwise would have been cut to pieces. The wounds Hamilton received were, however, mortal. A little after the rescue of Hamilton, a body of rebels dashed forward, with talwars drawn, to cut down a wounded and dismounted trooper of the Military Train. Again did Middleton dash forward, drive them back, and, dismounting placed the wounded trooper on his horse.'

194

Murphy received his VC from the Queen in the quadrangle of Windsor Castle on 4 January 1860. When Samuel Morley heard of this, he put in his claim that he too should receive the Cross. A special board considered his application and he, too, received his Cross on 9 November 1860 at Windsor Castle.

Samuel Morley

Samuel Morley is recorded in the Radcliffe-on-Trent, Nottinghamshire, Parish records to have been baptised on 4 June 1829. However, many publications show Morley's date of birth as December 1839. Samuel Morley grew up to become an agricultural labourer in Radcliffe-on-Trent and is shown as such on the 1851 census.

At the age of 25 Samuel Morley travelled to Nottingham to enlist, this happening on 25 January 1855. He joined the 8th Hussars, which was serving in the Crimea, as a 'Battle Casualty Replacement'. After the War, like many ex-cavalrymen, he transferred to the 2nd Battalion Military Train. In 1857, the Corps was sent to Hong Kong, but was diverted to Calcutta to help quell the Mutiny.

In 1862, he transferred to the 16th Lancers but was 'discharged by purchase' in 1864. After four months of civilian life, Morley re-enlisted in the Military Train until it was disbanded in 1870. He died on 16 June 1888 in Nottingham.

Michael Murphy

Michael Murphy was born in Cahir, Co. Tipperary. His recorded date of birth varies quite considerably in documents published, although his death certificate gives his birth date as 1840. However, it is now accepted that he was born in 1837, the son of Michael Murphy, a blacksmith. Michael Murphy enlisted into the 17th Lancers on 27th August 1855 at Cork, but was one of forty-two transfers from the 17th Lancers to the Military Train in October 1856.

After the Mutiny, he was promoted to sergeant and stayed with the Corps until it was disbanded in 1870. He then transferred to the newly-formed Army Service Corps in 1871.

It was only six months after joining the regiment that Sergeant Murphy made the greatest mistake of his life. On 26 January 1872 some oats and hay were being distributed to the sick horses in the 7th Hussars lines. The spare fodder was kept in the boiler room. A civilian by the name of James Green was stopped by a Farrier Major Knott who saw James Green leaving with his donkey and cart. On searching the cart he discovered two sacks, one of six bushels of oats and the other of twelve pounds of hay. Knott then asked the civilian from where he had acquired the goods, to which he replied, 'Farrier Sergeant Murphy'. Sergeant Murphy admitted this and said, 'For Heaven's sake look over this if you possibly can, or I am ruined for life'. Major Knott arrested him. Sergeant Murphy was immediately jailed and this is shown in the pay rolls for the period: in civil prison, 26 January to 13 February; in confinement, 14 February to 1 March; reduced to Private, 2 March. He remained in confinement waiting the convening of the Winchester Assizes on 2 March 1872.

Both Sergeant Murphy and James Green appeared before Baron Martin in a civil court. Murphy was found guilty but not Green. In answer to his Lordship, Murphy said he did not mean to steal the oats, which were surplus ones. All he wanted was for them to be taken down to the forge in order to give them to some of the horses after they had done a hard day's work. Murphy was sentenced to nine months' imprisonment with hard labour.

Just as hard for Murphy, now reduced to private, was the loss of his Victoria Cross. The forfeiture warrant read: 'Warrant directs the erasure of the name of Farrier Sergeant Michael Murphy VC, formally of the late Military Train, from the Victoria Cross Register and the cessation of his pension.'

When Murphy was released from prison, he returned to serve in the 7th Hussars but increasing ill-health finally caused his medical discharge in 1875. He moved to the Northumberland area and worked as a blacksmith. Coincidentally, he moved into a cottage in Blackwell near Darlington, owned by a benefactor, Sir Henry Havelock-Allan VC. Michael Murphy died in Darlington on 4 April 1893 and was buried beneath a gravestone erected by Havelock-Allan.

ASSAULT ON FORT RUHYA

One of the moveable commands sent out from Lucknow was that led by General Robert Walpole, with Brigadier Adrian Hope as infantry commander. The column sent to march through Rohilkhand was a strong one, consisting of veterans from the 42nd, 79th and 93rd, the regiments that formed the Highland Brigade in the Crimea, the 9th Lancers, Punjab infantry and cavalry, and a strong force of cavalry. They were to march on Bareilly and were pleased to leave Lucknow on 7 April with its horrible sights and disgusting smells.

On 15 April as the column was approaching the jungle fort of Ruhya

(Rooyah), a shot rang out. General Walpole ordered an immediate assault on the fort, with disastrous results, because the affair was badly mismanaged and taken without any reconnaissance. General Walpole, who had Campbell's confidence, came in for severe strictures and none more so than from William Forbes-Mitchell, who later wrote:

'The attack on the fort then commenced without any attempt being made to reconnoitre the position, and ended in a most severe loss. Brigadier Hope being among those killed, Lieutenant Willoughby ... Lieutenants Douglas and Bramley of 42nd, with nearly 100 men, Highlanders and Sikhs killed ... After we retired from the fort, the excitement was so great among the men of the 42nd and 93rd, owing to the sacrifice of so many officers and men through sheer mismanagement, that if the officers had given the men the least encouragement, I am convinced they would have turned out in a body and hanged General Walpole. The officers who were killed were all most popular men; but the great loss sustained by the death of Adrian Hope positively excited the men to fury. So heated was the feeling on the night the dead were buried, that if any non-commissioned officer had dared to take the lead, the life of General Walpole would not have been worth half an hour's purchase.'

The sacrifice had all been in vain for there was no attempt to invest the fort and the defenders slipped away during the night to join their fellow rebels at Bareilly. After the fall of Lucknow, many of the rebels had also fled to Bareilly. When Walpole's disgruntled column met with Sir Colin's force, they advanced on Bareilly.

A significant feature of the fighting was the strong presence of Ghazis (Ghazees), fanatical Muslim warriors, who were happy to sacrifice their lives if they could take down an infidel.

On 6 May, the British entered the city and became embroiled in the dangerous work of street fighting. By nightfall, however, Bareilly had been cleared of rebels.

William Café

Born in London on 26 March 1826, William Martin Café entered Addiscombe College and was commissioned in the 56th Bengal NI in 1842. He took part in the Gwalior Campaign of 1843 and the 2nd Sikh War. When the 56th BNI mutinied, he was appointed captain in command of the 4th Punjab Infantry.

During the assault on Fort Ruhya, casualties began to mount in the ditch in front of the fort. Lieutenant Willoughby, for example, of the 4th was mortally wounded in the ditch. Along with Privates Thompson, Crowie,

Spence and Cook, William Café managed to bring away the body.[4] During the rescue, Spence was hit and Café managed to carry him to safety.

Café was recommended for the VC and it was published on 17 February 1860. He received his Cross, probably through the post, in 1860. He was appointed to the Adjutant General's Department in 1860 and spent the rest of his career on the staff, retiring in 1894 and dying in London on 6 August 1906.

Edward Spence
Born on 26 December 1830 at Dumfries, Scotland, Edward Spence joined the 42nd Highlanders and took part in the Crimean War. During the attempt to save Lieutenant Willoughby, Spence was fatally wounded. His citation dated 15 January 1907 states:

'Private Edward Spence, 42nd Regiment would have been recommended to Her Majesty for the decoration of the Victoria Cross had he survived. He and Lance-Corporal Thompson of that Regiment volunteered, at the attack of the Fort at Ruhya, on the 10th April 1858 [*sic*], to assist Captain Café, commanding 4th Punjab Rifles, in bringing in the body of Lieutenant Willoughby from the top of the Glacis. Private Spence dauntlessly placed himself in an exposed position so as to cover the party bearing away the body. He died on the 17th of the same month from the effects of the wound he received on the occasion.'

When it was decided to award the VC posthumously in 1905, the medal itself was sent to the recipient's nearest relative. The exception was Edward Spence and it took six months to trace the closest relative, which proved to be the son of Spence's father's cousin.

Alexander Thompson
Alexander Thompson was born in Edinburgh in 1824. He joined the 42nd in 1842. He served in the Crimea and helped Captain Café bring away Willoughby's body from the glacis. His citation dated 27 May, 1859, is full of errors stating that the battle was on 10 April and that it was a 'Captain Groves' who commanded the 4th Punjab Rifles. Thompson received his Cross at Bareilly from the heartily disliked Brigadier General Sir Robert Walpole at a parade on 7 April 1860. Thompson retired from the Army in 1862 and died in Perth on 29 March 1880.

John Simpson
Edinburgh-born John Simpson was born on 29 January 1826 and was a quartermaster-sergeant at the time of the Mutiny. In the attack on Ruhya, he volunteered to go and collect the wounded Lieutenant Douglas, who

was lying about forty yards from the fort. He then went back with another badly wounded private. He was gazetted on 27 May 1859 and, along with Alexander Thompson, received his Cross on 7 April 1860.

Simpson was later commissioned and in 1883, retired with the honorary rank of major. He died in Perth on 27 October 1884.

James Davis

James Davis Kelly was born in Edinburgh in February 1835. When he enlisted, he dropped the name Kelly. During the 1880s he was interviewed by the *Strand Magazine* and gave an account of his VC action:

'I belonged to the Light Company under the command of Captain (now Sir John) Macleod. We got orders to lie down under some trees for a short time. Two Engineer officers came up and asked for some men to come with them to see where they could make a breach with the artillery. I was one who went. There was a small garden ditch under the walls of the fort, not high enough to cover our heads. After a short time the officers left. I was on the right of the ditch with Lieutenant Alfred Jennings Bramley of Tunbridge Wells, as brave a young officer as ever drew a sword, and saw a large force coming out to cut us off. He said: "Try and shoot the leader. I will run down and tell Macleod." The leader was shot, by whom I don't know. I never took credit for shooting anyone. Before poor Bramley got down he was shot in the temple, but not dead. He died during the night.

'The captain said: "We can't leave him. Who will take him out?" I said: "I will."

'The fort was firing hard all the time. I said: "Eadie, give me a hand. Put him on my back." As he was doing so he was shot in the back of the head, knocking me down, his blood running down my back. A man crawled over and I pulled Eadie off. At the time I thought I was shot. The captain said: "We can't lose anymore lives. Are you wounded? I said: "I don't think I am." He said: "Will you still take him out?" I said, "Yes."

'He was such a brave young fellow that the company loved him. I got him on my back again and told him to take me tight round the neck. I ran across the open space. During the time his watch fell out; I did not like to leave it, so I sat down and picked it up, all the time under a heavy fire. There was a man named Dods, who came and took him off my back. I went back again through the same fire, and helped to take up the man Eadie, Then I returned for my rifle, and firing a volley, we all left. It was a badly managed affair altogether.'

Davis, too, joined his comrades at the VC parade on 7 April 1860 to receive his Cross from the man who had needlessly thrown away so many lives.

William Gardner

William Gardner was born in Nemphlar, Lanarkshire, on 3 March 1821. He joined the 42nd (Black Watch) Regiment and took part in the Crimean War, where he was awarded the Distinguished Conduct Medal. On 5 May 1858, as the British advanced to within five miles of the city, a party of about 360 Ghazis made a furious charge. William Forbes-Mitchell later wrote:

'Sir Colin Campbell was close by and called out, "Close up. Forty-Second! Bayonet them as they come on." But that was not easily done; the Ghazis charged in blind fury, with their round shields on their left arms, their bodies bent low, waiving their tulwars over their heads, throwing themselves under the bayonets, and cutting the men's legs.'

It was then that William Gardner performed his act of gallantry.

'Colonel Cameron was pulled from his horse by a Ghazi, who leaped up and seized him by the collar while he was engaged with another on the opposite side; but his life was saved by Colour-Sergeant Gardner, who seized one of the enemy's tulwars, and rushing to the colonel's assistant cut off the Ghazis head. General Walpole was also pulled off his horse and received two sword cuts, but was rescued by the bayonets of the Forty-Second. The struggle was short, but every one of the Ghazis was killed. None attempted to escape; they had evidently come on to kill or be killed, and 133 lay in none circle right in front of the colours of the 42nd.'

Gardner was recommended for the Victoria Cross which was gazetted on 23 August 1858. The only record of his receipt of the decoration was that it was in India in 1859. He died at Bothwell, Lanarkshire, on 24 October 1897. His VC medal group is on display at the Lord Ashcroft Gallery.

Valentine Bambrick

Valentine Bambrick was born on 13 April 1837 in Cawnpore, India, to a father who was stationed there with the 11th Light Dragoons. Both his father and his uncle, after whom he was named, were troop sergeant majors in the 11th and had seen service from Waterloo to Bhurtpore. His older brother, John, would later join the 11th Hussars, as the 11th Light Dragoons became, and was one of the Gallant Six Hundred who charged down the North Valley at Balaklava.

When Valentine was just 16, he enlisted in the 1/60th Rifles, stationed in India. When the Mutiny broke out in 1857, the regiment was heavily involved at the Siege of Delhi and the hard campaigning that followed as the mutineers were hunted down. It was during the assault on the city of Bareilly, 140 miles east of Delhi, that Bambrick displayed outstanding courage as the British troops charged through the narrow streets and alleyways. A party of Ghazis cornered Bambrick and his company commander, Lieutenant Cromer Ashburnham. Bambrick's citation dated 24 December 1858 is brief and does not convey the desperation of the contest:

'For conspicuous bravery at Bareilly, on the 6th of May 1858, when in a serai, he was attacked by three Ghazees [sic], one of whom he cut down. He was wounded twice on this occasion.'

He received his Cross in 1859 but there is no record of an investiture. When the 60th returned to the UK, Bambrick preferred to stay in India and transferred to the 87th (Royal Irish) Fusiliers. When they returned to Ireland, Bambrick took his discharge at Aldershot on 16 November 1863 and celebrated his introduction to civilian life with a night out on the town. While he was relaxing in an establishment, he heard the cries of a woman from upstairs. Going to her assistance, he found a commissariat sergeant named Russell beating a woman. Bambrick waded in and got the better of the NCO.

Later Russell brought a charge of assault and theft of his medals against Bambrick and was backed up by some of his cronies. Bambrick, at his own expense, paid for the female victim to stay in a hotel until the trial.

When the trial began at Winchester Assizes on 3 December 1863, Bambrick's only defence witness had disappeared. Russell was able to call one of his soldiers as a prosecution witness and his word seems to have been accepted without much of a challenge. Bambrick does not appear to have done his cause much good by verbally abusing the judge, who handed down a guilty verdict and sentenced the prisoner to three years in Pentonville Prison.

This was harsh indeed, but worse was soon to follow. Under the rules of the Royal Warrant dated 4 September 1861, Bambrick was forced to forfeit his Cross – not for going to prison – but for the offence 'Theft of a comrade's medals'. Bambrick could bear the injustice of the prison sentence, but the confiscation of his hard-won Cross was too much to bear and he made this clear in the letter he wrote before he hanged himself in his cell on April Fool's Day 1864. Bambrick's body was buried in the St Pancras & Islington Cemetery, in an unmarked grave.[5]

Once General Colin Campbell had taken Lucknow, the rebels were in retreat. He detached a force under the command of Major General James Hope Grant, which included the 3/Rifle Brigade, which marched out of Lucknow on 11 April with 3,000 men. For eight weeks they moved through hostile country, constantly skirmishing until they were able to face a rebel army of 15,000.

John Shaw

John Shaw was born on an unknown date at Prestonpans, East Lothian. He enlisted into the 1/Rifle Brigade. Promoted to sergeant he went to India. On 13 June 1858, at Nawabgunge, Sergeant Shaw performed his act of bravery:

'In the middle of the fighting, one man, a giant Ghazee, being cut off from his companions seemed determined to make a desperate fight for it. Setting his back to a tree, he stood sword in hand, glaring fiercely on his pursuers, for some officers and men of the 3rd Battalion had followed him into the tope. Some shots were taken at him, which he tried to avoid by dodging round the tree, but was wounded and made him more desperate. At last, a Pioneer of the 3rd Battalion, Sergeant Samuel Shaw[6], rushed at him and closed in single combat. The Ghazee wounded Shaw on the head with his tulwar, but drawing his Pioneer's sword, sawed at him with the serrated edge and killed the Ghazee. Shaw rose from the ground covered in blood, but his opponent lay slain. Many who witnessed it declared that this combat, fought with a fanatic, determined to sell his life to slay his foe, was the greatest instance of cool courage they ever saw.'

General Hope Grant's recommendation for the VC was accepted and published on 28 October 1858. Shaw sailed for the UK in 1859, not yet having received his VC. During the voyage, on 27 December 1859, Shaw jumped overboard to his death. The probable cause was depression induced by the head wound he sustained in his fight with the Ghazi. His VC and the *tulwar* used by Shaw's opponent are held by the Rifles.

Chapter 11

Mopping Up
January 1858 to April 1859

After the capture of Lucknow, there was a spate of officers claiming sick leave and wishing to return to Britain. The feeling was that there were to be no more large-scale battles and that the rebels were now resorting to guerrilla warfare.[1]

Garnet Wolseley, then a captain in the 90th Foot, summed up the prevailing opinion of most of those involved in these mopping up operations: 'Altogether I am thoroughly tired of this life. As long as any honour or glory was attached to it, of course I liked it, but now that the row or whatever it should be called has degenerated down into pursuing small bodies of rebels without cannon and annihilating, not fighting them, I take no interest what ever in the work as I consider it quite derogatory to a soldier's profession.'

There seemed little opportunity to enhance an officer's reputation hence the rush to return to the home country. In fact, there was still plenty of campaigning and fighting to be done, during which time a further sixteen Victoria Crosses were awarded.

Samuel Browne
There seems to be some doubt about where Samuel James Browne was born. His obituary has it as Alnwick, Northumberland; another says it was Dinapur or Barrackpore. He was born on 3 October 1824 to a surgeon in the Bengal Medical Service and entered the HEIC Army at the age of sixteen in 1840. He served with the 46th Bengal NI and took part in the 2nd Sikh War before transferring to the 2nd Punjab Cavalry in 1849. He rose to command the regiment in 1851 and by the time of the Mutiny, was brevet major.

During the operations to clear the last pockets of resistance from

Rohilkhand, Browne commanded a complete Field Force. It was at Seerporah on 31 August 1858, that he performed his VC act:

'For having at Seerporah, in an engagement with the rebel force under Khan Allie Khan, on the 31st August 1858, whilst advancing of the enemy's position, at day-break, pushed on with one orderly Sowar upon a 9-pounder gun that was commanding one of the approached to the enemy's position, and attacked the gunners, thereby preventing them from reloading and firing upon the infantry, who were advancing to the attack. In doing this a personal conflict ensued, in which Captain (now lieutenant-colonel) Samuel James Browne, Commandant of the 2nd Punjab Cavalry, received a severe sword-cut wound, which severed the left arm at the shoulder, not, however, before lieutenant-colonel Browne had succeeded in cutting down one of his assailants. The gun was prevented from being reloaded, and was eventually captured by the infantry, and the gunners slain.'

Sam Browne also suffered a severed sword-cut to his left knee. With these terrible wounds, it was something of a miracle that he survived infection or was not invalided out of the Army. Before the Mutiny, he had experimented with a more efficient way of wearing a sword, which entailed using a belt and a cross belt. It was fortuitous that his design suited his now special needs and very soon the 'Sam Browne System' had been adopted by the Indian and British Armies.[2]

Browne's was one of the late recommendations and his citation was not published until 1 March 1861. He received his Cross from Major-General Sir Sydney Cotton at a parade at Peshawar in December 1862.

He went on to command the Peshawar Valley Field force during the 2nd Afghan War and retired as General Sir Samuel James Browne in 1888. He moved to the Isle of Wight, where he died on 14 March 1901.

James Champion

James Champion was born in Hammersmith, London, in 1834. He joined the 8th Hussars in 1851 and went to the Crimea. Sickness prevented his taking part in the famous Light Brigade charge. He was promoted to troop sergeant and on 8 September, a squadron of 'D' Troop caught up with rebels at Beejapore (Bijapur), south east of Bombay in the southern Indian district of Karnataka.

Of the 850 rebels, no less than 450 bodies were counted dead on the field. When both officers were wounded, Champion, who was himself severely injured, carried on fighting, wounding several rebels, and leading the pursuit. For this action he was recommended for the VC and his citation appeared on 20 January 1860. He was also promoted to regimental sergeant major in October 1858. There is no record of an investiture. He later received the Meritorious Service Medal.

Champion retired in 23 December 1873 and was appointed RSM of the Cheltenham Troop of the Royal Gloucestershire Hussars. He died in Hammersmith on 4 May 1904.

Charles Baker

Charles George Baker was born on 8 December 1830, at Noacolly, Bengal. He led an unusual and adventurous life, beginning with service at sea. He was employed by the P&O Company who conferred on him a testimonial for his part in the rescue of the passengers and crew of the SS *Duro* in 1854, which was wrecked on a shoal off the Paracel Island in the South China Sea. Accompanied by six other volunteers, Baker made a perilous voyage of over 500 miles in an open boat to fetch assistance. Short of water and food, they had to contend with heavy seas and the threat of Chinese pirates until they reached safety.

Charles Baker was commissioned in the Bengal Military Police in 1856 and in 1858 was involved in mopping up operations in West Behar with the irregular horsemen of Rattray's Sikhs. He was recommended for the Victoria Cross, which was published on 25 February 1862. Baker described his action:

'The enemy (at that time supposed to have mustered from 900 to 1,000 strong in infantry, with 50 cavalry) advanced. Without exchanging a shot, I at once retired slowly, followed up steadily by the rebel line for 100 yards clear of the village or jungle, when suddenly wheeling about my divisions into line, with a hearty cheer, we charged straight into and through the centre of the enemy's line; Lieutenant Broughton, with his detachment, immediately followed up the movement, with excellent effect, from his position upon the enemy's left. The rebel right wing, of about 300 men, broke at once, but the centre and left, observing the great labour of the horses in crossing the heavy ground, stood, and receiving the charge with repeated volleys, were cut down or broke only a few yards ahead of the cavalry. From this moment the pursuit was limited to the strongest and best horses of the force, numbering some 60 of all ranks, who, dashing into and swimming a deep, wide nullah, followed the flying enemy through the village of Russowlee and its sugar-cane khets, over two miles of swamp, and 500 yards into the thick jungles near Peroo, when, both men and horses being completely exhausted, I sounded the halt and assembly, and, collecting my wounded, returned to camp at Munjhaen about 6 p.m.'

Sir Colin Campbell described the action as 'having been as gallant as any during the war'.

Promoted to Deputy Inspecting General of Police, Charles Baker received his VC by registered post. He retired in 1863 on health grounds, but in 1877 he joined the Turkish Imperial Ottoman Gendarmerie during the war between Turkey and Russia.

He was captured by the Russians in the Balkans and spent some time in captivity. In 1882, he transferred to the Egyptian police force and retired in 1885 as Chief of Security with the Ministry of the Interior with the rank of major general. He returned to England and died on 19 February 1906 at Southbourne, Hampshire.

George Chicken

Curiously, George Bell Chicken's early career was similar to that of Charles Baker. Born on 2 March 1833 at Wallsend, Northumberland, he was 20 when he became a Master Mariner.[3] Strictly, he was not in the navy but volunteered for the Indian Naval Brigade and was appointed into the service on 31 July 1858.

In the affair at Suhejnee near Peroo (Piru), he charged with Rattray's Sikhs and was soon well ahead of his party. He caught up with a party of about twenty rebels and charged them, killing five until he was knocked off his horse and wounded. Fortunately at that moment the rest of the Sikhs arrived and rescued him. For his determination he was recommended for the Cross, which was gazetted on 27 April 1860. Unfortunately, George Chicken never heard of the award for he was lost during a violent squall in the Bay of Bengal onboard his new command, the schooner *Emily*, along with all of his crew.

Patrick Roddy

Patrick Roddy was born on 17 March 1827 at Elphin, Co. Roscommon and was forced by the failure of the Irish potato crop to seek help in Liverpool. Here he joined the Royal Artillery but soon transferred to the Bengal Artillery, where he could earn twice as much and the prospects of promotion were greater.[4] Roddy was one of those left with Sir James Outram to hold the Alambagh until Sir Colin Campbell's force joined them at Lucknow in March. Sergeant Roddy's conduct was such that he was commissioned to ensign in February 1858. In May, Roddy was attached to the Oudh Military Police Cavalry and joined the column commanded by Major General Sir James Hope Grant. He spent the summer months chasing the rebels in Oudh Province.

In the 12 April 1859 edition of *The London Gazette*, the following citation appeared:

'Patrick Roddy, Ensign, Bengal Army (unattached). Date of Act of Bravery 27 September 1858. Major General Sir James Hope Grant KCB, commanding Oudh Force, bears testimony to the gallant conduct of Lieut. Roddy on several occasions, one instance is particularly mentioned. On the return from Kuthirga of the Kupperthulla Contingent on the 27 Sept.1858, this officer, when engaged with the enemy, charged a rebel (armed with a percussion musket) when the cavalry were afraid to approach, as each time they attempted to do so, the rebel knelt and covered his assailant. This did not deter Lieut .Roddy, who went boldly in, and when within six yards the rebel fired, killing Lieut. Roddy's horse and before he could get disentangled from the horse, the rebel attempted to cut him down. Lieut. Roddy seized the rebel until he could get at his sword, when he ran him through the body. The rebel turned out to be a subadar (captain) of the late 8th Native Infantry – a powerful man and a most determined character.'

Roddy received his VC from the station commander at Ferozepore, Colonel Schopp, at a special parade on 5 September 1861.

He was recommended for a captaincy, which he gained in the following year. In 1868, he took part in General Napier's Abyssinian Campaign and was Mentioned in Despatches and given a brevet majority. He was confirmed major in 1876 and appointed station staff officer at Roorkee.

In 1878, he served in the First Afghan War and was attached to the 20th Punjab Native Infantry, part of General Sir Sam Browne's 1st Division Peshawar Field Force. On 22 November, the 20th PNI were involved in the difficult flanking operations over the precipitous heights in reverse of the Ali Musjid, which forced the Afghans to abandon their mountain-top fort. He again received Mention in Despatches and was brevetted lieutenant-colonel. This was confirmed in 1886 and, on 24 February 1887 Patrick Roddy retired as a full colonel having served in the Bengal Army for 39 years.

He retired to his wife's home on Jersey where he died on 21 November 1895.

Charles Goodfellow

The son and grandson of Bombay Engineers, both of whom became generals, Charles Augustus Goodfellow was born in Poona on 29 November 1836. Passing from Addiscombe College, he joined the Bombay Sappers and Miners in 1857. He served with General Rose's Central India Field Force during early 1858. Although the rising of the Waghers, a fanatical Hindu people living in the isolated area of Kathiawar in western

Gujurat, is not regarded as part of the Mutiny, the single VC it produced is included in the number awarded for the India from 1857 to 1859.[5]

A second expedition against the Wagher's stronghold on the island of Beyt in the Ran of Kutch was led by Colonel Edward Donovan of 33rd (Duke of Wellington's) Regiment, was repulsed with considerable loss; twenty-four officers and men were killed and forty-seven wounded. It was during the assault that Lieutenant Goodfellow rescued a wounded soldier who had been gunned down under the walls of the fort. Dashing forward and ignoring the heavy fire, Goodfellow managed to carry the badly wounded man to safety – though he was found to have died.

That night, the Waghers evacuated the fort and it was blown up by the engineers the following day. Goodfellow's action was recorded in *The London Gazette* on 16 April 1863 and he received his Cross at a parade in Mhow that year.

The rest of Goodfellow's service was uneventful and he retired as lieutenant general in 1889. He moved to Leamington Spa, where he died on 1 September 1917.

Thomas Monaghan and Charles Anderson

Both cavalrymen share the same citation for saving the life of their commanding officer. During the aftermath of a pursuit and defeat of a large band of mutineers at Sundelee near Jamo, Oudh, Major W.H. Seymour of 2nd Dragoon Guards learned that some rebels were hiding in a nearby sugar-cane plantation. Taking about forty men from the Rifles, he rushed into the crops, when, suddenly, the mutineers – standing only a few feet away – opened fire and attacked with *tulwars*. One officer was hacked to death and another badly wounded. Seymour was on the point of being overwhelmed when Trumpeter Thomas Monaghan and Private Charles Anderson arrived to fight off the assailants.

Due to delays, their citations were finally published on 11 November 1862 and they received their Crosses from General Rose at Benares on 5 January 1863. Little is known of their subsequent lives.

Thomas Monaghan was born on 18 October 1833 in Abergavenny, Monmouthshire, and joined the Army in 1847 as a boy soldier. He was discharged in 1873 and died in his home in Woolwich in 1895.

Charles Anderson came from Liverpool and was born about 1827. He joined the 2nd Dragoon Guards in 1845 and left the Army as a corporal in 1870. He moved to the north-east and may have worked as a coal miner. He died at Seaham near Sunderland, when he accidentally fell from a cliff on 19 April 1899.

Hanson Jarrett

Hanson Chambers Taylor Jarrett was born in Vepery, Madras, on 22 March 1837. When he was old enough, he entered the HEIC College at Addiscombe, Surrey and was commissioned on 10 June 1854 as an ensign with the 26th Bengal Native Infantry. The 26th had mutinied on 30 July and fled Lahore before surrendering near Amritsar in the belief that they would receive a fair trial. Instead, 282 sepoys were summarily executed. Hanson Jarrett was promoted to lieutenant and appointed to the Ferozepore Regiment, which later became the 2nd Punjab Infantry. In an action at Baroun near Farrukhabad, Jarrett performed his VC exploit. His citation of 18 June 1859 reads:

'For an act of daring bravery at the village of Baroun, on 14th of October 1858, on an occasion when about 70 Sepoys were defending themselves in a brick building, the only approach to which was up a very narrow street, in having called on the men of his regiment to follow him, when backed by only some four men, he made a dash at the narrow entrance, where, though a shower of balls was poured upon him, he pushed his way up to the wall of the house, and beating up the bayonets of the rebels with his sword, endeavoured to get in.'

Due to the lack of support from the rest of his command, the attempt was unsuccessful and Jarrett and his small party were forced to retreat under heavy fire. Miraculously, he was unscathed. Like many Mutiny recipients, there is no record of an investiture.

Jarrett's post-war career rise was hardly meteoric, despite having the advantage of a Victoria Cross. Like many officers and officials, Jarrett enjoyed the big game hunting that India provided. He sought and obtained civil employment as Deputy Conservator of Forests based at Saugor and was able to indulge his passion for the sport. He retired as a Colonel in 1890 and died the following year aged 53.

Evelyn Wood

The Indian Mutiny saw three famous army commanders gain their first or one of their earliest experiences of campaigning: Frederick Roberts, Garnet Wolseley and Evelyn Wood.

Henry Evelyn Wood was born 9 February, 1838 at Cressing, near Braintree, Essex, into a clerical background. His father, Sir John Page Wood, had been the Chaplain and Private Secretary to Queen Caroline and his maternal grandfather was an admiral. He had four sisters, all of whom led interesting lives – including Kitty, who is remembered as Kitty O'Shea, mistress of the famous Irish nationalist, Charles Stewart Parnell.

Wood attended Marlborough College, which he hated, and, at the age of 14, passed his entrance examination to enter the Royal Navy. He joined HMS *Queen*, commanded by his uncle, Captain Frederick Mitchell. Two years later, he graduated to midshipman. When war with Russia was declared in 1854, HMS *Queen* was part of the fleet that bombarded Sebastopol as the Allies began their year-long siege of the city. Short of heavy artillery with which to shell the Russian defences, the Navy was called upon to send ashore a Naval Brigade to man their 68-pounders in the trenches. Commanding the 21-gun battery was the charismatic Captain William Peel, son of the former Prime Minister, Sir Robert Peel. Peel later recalled that Wood did not miss a day's duty in nine months. It was this sustained exposure to the percussive effects of cannon fire that undoubtedly contributed to Wood's incipient deafness.

The following summer, the Allies attempted a number of abortive attacks on the Russian defences. On 18 June, the British made a suicidal assault on the enemy stronghold, known as 'The Redan', during which they suffered heavy casualties. In the vanguard were the sailors of the Naval Brigade, who carried scaling ladders for the following infantry. Such was the intensity of the defenders' fire that very few managed more than a few yards before being killed or wounded. The 17-year-old Wood carried a scaling ladder and was the only one to reach the Redan, despite being twice wounded by grapeshot. Peel was fulsome in his praise of his young ADC and recommended him for a Victoria Cross. As his friend and rival Edward Daniel had also been recommended for the same action, during which Daniel had bound up Peel's wounded arm, Wood was turned down. Instead, he was awarded the *Legion d'Honneur* and the Order of the Medijidie.

Wood was sent home to recuperate from his wounds and reflected on his future career. When he had recovered, he decided, having tasted the excitement of fighting on land, to resign his commission in the Navy and apply to join the Army. His outstanding service at Sebastopol gained him a cornetcy without purchase in the 13th Light Dragoons. Upon joining this regiment, he was immediately posted back to the Crimea as part of the reinforcements to fill the losses incurred during the Charge of the Light Brigade.

Unfortunately for Wood, he was struck down with both typhoid and pneumonia and was hospitalised at Scutari for five months. This was just the start of his life-long battle against sickness and accidents, for there has rarely been an officer who was as unfortunate with his health. During the next fifty years, Wood was inflicted with malaria, dysentery, sunstroke, neuralgia, deafness, toothache, eye problems and, to crown it all, ingrown toe nails.

Just a year later, in June 1857, Wood exchanged into the 17th Lancers, which was being sent to help quell the Indian Mutiny. A wealthy uncle was persuaded to purchase his nephew promotion to lieutenant and, because he had learned to speak Hindustani, he was appointed interpreter. This led to secondment to the 3rd Bombay Cavalry, with which he saw much action. In one particular action at Sindwaho, he single-handedly attacked and drove off a body of the enemy, for which he was highly praised and Mentioned in Despatches.

Although the Mutiny was effectively at an end, there were still pockets of bandits, who terrorised the more remote areas away from the British military. In the jungles in the Barseah region, an outlaw band kidnapped a local landowner, Chemmum Singh, who had remained loyal to the British during the Mutiny and they made known their intention to hang him.

On learning of the abduction, Wood immediately organised a rescue party comprising just thirteen native troops. With the promise of a pardon, he used a former gang member as guide and set out into the thick jungle. The guide became increasingly nervous and ingested *bhang* (opium) at every halt. Finally, he became too intoxicated to lead, but the bandit's camp fire was spotted in the distance. Leaving three men to tend the horses, Wood advanced with the rest of the party until they reached the edge of the clearing where the seventy-strong gang slept.

Wood later wrote a detailed account of the rescue of the unfortunate Chemmum Singh. 'Between one and two o'clock on the morning of the 29th, I crawled to within ten yards of the hollow in and around which the band was sleeping. I was then perturbed to find that the numbers were greatly in excess of what I had anticipated, and the thought came into my mind to retreat ... after a moment's hesitation I thought of Chemmum Singh's impending fate, and moreover realised my only safety lay in attacking; for although we succeeded in approaching the band unheard, once we attempted to retire we must have been discovered and overwhelmed, so beckoning to the men, they came up silently, and this time so noiselessly as not to attract the attention of the sentry, who with the prisoners and another man were the only persons awake, Chemmum Singh being tied to a tree.

'I stepped forward a little and looked down on the crowd of men lying asleep in the dry pond (nullah). In the depression, the jungle was less thick than outside it, but there were trees in it with branches 3 feet from the ground, against one of which the sentry was leaning, when the click of the men's hammers as they cocked made him look up, and the firelight fell on my white Bedford cords. He asked, without raising his voice, "Who is that?" I replied, "We are the Government," and turning to my men, shouted, "Fire, charge!"

'Having given the word, I ran at the sentry, without perceiving that there were two men sleeping immediately under my feet, in the cummerbund of one of whom my foot caught, and I went headlong into the hollow. The ground was so rough that the cavalry sergeant and private also fell as they ran forward. The rebels jumped up, scuttling away unarmed, the sentry and four or five brave men covering their flight.

'I rose as quickly as I could, with my left hand over my neck to save it from the sentry's sword, and attacked the nearest rebel, a Brahman wearing a sepoy's coat. We cut at each other three times in succession, the boughs intercepting our swords, and as he drew his hand back the fourth time, I going close to him with the point of my sword behind my right foot, cut upwards, wounding him in the fleshy part of the thigh. He staggered to my left, which brought him before Burmadeen Singh, who twice cut in vain at him, his sword catching in the trees, when I shouted, "Point, give the point!"

'Burmadeen Singh now disappeared, and I ran after him, tumbling into a natural drain from the pond, on top of my Sergeant and the rebel Brahman, whom he was killing …

'The Bareli Levy (Police) were still on the edge of the pond where they had stopped to reload … they compensated for their want of activity in charging, by the noise they made, which was perhaps more effective, shouting "Bring up the Horse Artillery, bring up the Cavalry!", until I commanded silence. The private cavalry soldier behaved well, until having wounded a rebel, he saw blood flow, when he became idiotic at the sight, falling on the guide, whom he mistook for one of the enemy. Eventually, to save the guide, I had to knock the soldier down with my fist, by a blow under the jaw.

'I made every man of the party bring away one gun, and having broken the remaining firelocks and swords, we started homewards. The Cavalry soldier was half conscious and the Sergeant dragged him for two miles by his waist-belt, while I took charge of the guide, who was speechless and dreamy from opium.'

This shambles of a rescue should not hide the fact that a relatively inexperienced 20-year-old led a small party of native troops, most of whom were of dubious fighting quality, and routed a hugely superior enemy. The award of the VC was something of an anticlimax as Wood received his by registered post!

Evelyn Wood continued his steady rise up the promotion ladder, despite making some dreadful blunders like his strange conduct during the Battle of Hlobane during the Anglo-Zulu War of 1879.[6]

For a man who suffered ill-health for most of his life, Evelyn Wood lived to the ripe old age of 81, only to die during the influenza pandemic of 1919.

INTO NEPAL

The dwindling bands of rebels were being pushed further to the margins. One area they where they sought refuge was jungles and hills of Nepal. It was also an area heavily patrolled by the British.

Charles Fraser

Born in Dublin on 31 August 1829 to Sir James Fraser, 3rd Baronet of Leadclune and lieutenant-colonel of the 7th Hussars, Charles Crauford Fraser was commissioned by purchase in 1847 into his father's old regiment. During the pursuit of rebels, Captain (Brevet Major) Fraser was wounded in a fight with Ghazi fanatics on 13 June 1858 at Nawab Gunge.

On 31 December 1858, the 7th was positioned on the Nepalese border and received information that Nana Sahib and his army were only twenty-five miles away. They caught up with the rebels attempting to cross a ford on the River Raptee. The river was in full spate and the ford was strewn with tree trunks, quick sands and rocks. When the 7th saw the rebels struggling to cross, they charged and was soon in trouble, with men and horses swept away. The regiment's commander, lieutenant-colonel Sir William Russell, ordered a halt before there were more casualties. It was then noticed that Captain Stisted and three other ranks were stranded on a small sand bank in the middle of the river; none could swim and were under fire from the rebels.

Charles Fraser, despite his wound, volunteered to swim to their rescue. In his Royal Humane Society citation, his gallant action was described:

'Major Charles Crauford Fraser begged to be allowed to go, and he swam out to them under a sharp fire from the enemy, who were on the opposite side, and after great difficulty, owing to rapidity of the stream, he reached them. They were quite exhausted, but he succeeded in saving the lives of Major Stisted and the men with him. It was a most dangerous service, and most gallantly performed by him, when we call to mind that Major Fraser at that time had only partial use of his right hand, owing to a grave wound which he received at the battle of Newab Gunge, and from which he had not nearly recovered.'

Charles Fraser's act of gallantry was published in *The London Gazette* on 8 November 1860 and he received his Cross on the following day from the

Queen at Windsor Castle. The Royal Humane Society awarded Fraser their Silver Medal on 11 January 1860. Fraser was one of only three Victoria Cross recipients to receive both the Cross and the Royal Humane Society Medal for the same act.[7]

Leaving India in March 1859, Charles Fraser purchased his majority and transferred to the 11th Hussars. In 1860, he obtained the rank of lieutenant-colonel through purchase. He served in the Abyssinian Campaign of 1868 and that same year became Colonel of the 8th Hussars. He was promoted to major general in 1870 and appointed Inspector-General of Cavalry in Ireland.

He retired as lieutenant general in 1886 and entered politics. He was Member of Parliament for Lambeth North from 1885 to 1892 and died at his London home on 7 June 1895.

Henry Addison

Born in February 1821 in Bardwell, Suffolk, Henry Addison enlisted in the 43rd (Monmouth) Light Infantry. He and twenty-nine men of the 43rd were part of the 226-strong Saugor Field Force, under the command of Lieutenant-Colonel Gottreux of the Madras Army. In a report, Gottreux wrote that he learned that a band of rebels were in the jungle covered hills near a village called Kurrereah. The small column approached the rebel camp at dawn on 2 January 1859.

'We started at half-past five for the rebel camp and shortly after came in sight of their fires. On our being observed, the enemy opened a sharp fire on us, and commenced their retreat, leaving their baggage ponies in their rear … The main body moved on as fast as nature would allow, for about two miles, many detached small parties of artillery and infantry having hand to hand encounters with similar parties of the enemy, who we found, as we progressed, hiding in the ravines and jungle.

'Lieutenant Willoughby Osbourne, Political Agent of Rewah, was wounded by a sword-cut on the right hand. He was at the time he was attacked, closely followed by three men of the 43rd Light Infantry … Private Henry Addison, of the 43rd Light Infantry, seeing him attacked and on the ground, rushed forward to defend and cover him in a most gallant manner. In doing this, I much regret having to record, that he received two very severe sword-cuts, one on the left leg, which rendered immediate amputation of the limb above the knee necessary, and another causing compound fracture of the left fore-arm.

'The heroism displayed by Private Addison in thus placing himself between Lieutenant Osbourne and his assailant at the critical juncture he did, thereby saving that officer's life, may, I hope, be deemed worthy of the Victoria Cross, for which honour I earnestly beg to recommend him.'

The recommendation went forward and Henry Addison, when he had recovered sufficiently, received his Cross on 9 November 1860, from the Queen at Windsor Castle.

Addison returned to his home town of Bardwell, where he died on 18 June 1887, aged 66.

Duncan Millar and Walter Cook

The 42nd Highlanders were detached from General Walpole's column and sent to guard the crossing points on the River Sarda bordering Oudh and Rohilkand. On the morning of 15 January 1859, it was learned that a strong rebel force had crossed the Sarda at Maylah Ghat. Unable to use his cavalry in the thick jungle, Colonel Smythe sent a detachment of thirty-seven Highlanders to intercept the rebels with the hope that he could reinforce them with men who were on picquet duty. Fixing their bayonets and forming a skirmish line, the Highlanders were soon in the thick of fighting. Soon the two officers were wounded, one mortally, and the sergeant and two corporals were killed which left the privates to do the fighting. Private Robb later related: 'I must confess that any courage I displayed was in great measure the courage of despair ... In the midst of the battle, Duncan Miller tore a medal off his chest requesting that it be sent to his mother if the worst befell him.'

When all seemed lost, the detachment of picquets arrived which the rebels thought were the first of greater reinforcements and they fell back. Sir Colin Campbell praised the discipline of the soldiers: 'Who cut off from their supports, had kept at bay a force of 2,000 rebels for 10 hours in a dense jungle, conduct which was beyond praise.'

Duncan Millar and Walter Cook were singled out and recommended for the Victoria Cross, which was published on 21 June 1859.

Duncan Millar was born on 19 June 1824 in Kilmarnock and served in the 42nd Highlanders during the Crimean War. He received his Cross from General Sir Robert Walpole at Bareilly on 7 April 1860. He died in Glasgow on 7 July 1881.

Londoner, Walter Cook was born on 18 June 1834. He joined the 42nd at the time of the Mutiny but little more is known of him. He died in 1864 and is believed to have drowned in the River Ravi.

Herbert Clogstoun

Born in Port of Spain, Trinidad, on 13 June 1820, Herbert Mackworth Clogstoun was commissioned in the Madras Army on 15 January 1838. He remained with the 19th Madras NI until 1856, when he transferred as second in command of the 2nd Cavalry Hyderabad Contingent. On 15 January 1859, Captain Clogstoun was part of Brigadier Hill's Berar Field Force searching for rebels about thirty-five miles from Hingoli, the HQ of the Hyderabad Contingent. They caught up with a 400-strong rebel band at the village of Chichumbah. Clogstoun was recommended for the Victoria Cross and his citation dated 21 October 1859 read;

'For conspicuous bravery in charging the rebels into Chichumbah with only eight men of his regiment, compelling them to re-enter the town and finally to abandon their plunder. He was severely wounded himself and lost seven out of the eight men who accompanied him.'

Promoted to Major, Clogstoun received his Cross in an investiture held at Madras on 19 January 1860. He took command of his regiment in September 1861 but died six months later on 6 May 1862 in Hingoli.

George Richardson

Born on 1 August 1831 in Co. Cavan, Ireland, George Richardson enlisted in the 34th (Cumberland) Regiment on 4 December 1855. On 27 April 1859, at Bhowaniegunge (Butwa Gonda), near Cawnpore, Richardson performed the last VC action of the Indian Mutiny. After a hard day's march, the rear guard of the column commanded by Colonel Kelly of the 34th was attacked by a large body of rebels.

He was recommended for the VC by his officer, Lieutenant Julius Laurie: 'On 27 April 1859, as we were advancing after a retreating enemy, who by his dress and arms (one of which was a revolver) seemed to be of some importance – post himself behind a tree. He remained there so until we were about 20 yards off when he fired three shots. I saw Pte. Richardson of No.6 Company rush to the front and attack the man with his rifle clubbed (he had previously discharged it without waiting to reload). The man waited until Richardson was about 3 yards off him, when he fired and wounded him in the arm and elbow. Notwithstanding one of his arms being thus rendered powerless, Pte.Richardson closed and held him to the ground until assistance arrived (Lt. Laurie) and the man despatched, when it was ascertained that two chambers of the Colt revolver were still loaded.'

Richardson's citation, published on 11 November 1859, unusually it included additional material:

'Richardson did, despite the fact that his arm was broken by a rifle bullet, and leg slashed by a sabre, rush to the aid of his officer, Lt. Laurie, was attacked by six natives, and that, crippled as he was, succeeded in killing five, and the sixth fled.'

Richardson received his Cross in 1860 and emigrated to Canada in 1862. In 1865, when it was thought that the Irish Fenian movement would invade Canada, he enlisted and served as sergeant in the Prince of Wales Rifles at Sandwich, Ontario. For his military service, he was granted homestead land near Lindsay, Ontario.

In 1916, his house was destroyed by fire and Richardson, who was 85, carried out his wife, who later died of shock. He lost the partial sight in one eye due to burns. His original medals were lost in the fire and replaced by the War Office in 1918.

He was chosen to place Canada's wreath on the tomb of the Unknown Soldier at Arlington Cemetery in Washington in 1921. He died of pneumonia on 28 January 1923, at the age of 92. At the time he was the oldest living recipient of the VC.

Postscript

The death of Rani Lakshmibai, the betrayal and execution of Tantia Topi and the disappearance and probable death of Nana Sahib effectively robbed the uprising of any leaders of note. The Indian Mutiny was effectively finished with the rebels' defeat at Gwalior in June 1858 but it could not be declared over until the last mutineer had been captured or hounded into the thick jungles.

The Royal Proclamation on 1 November 1858 ended the rule of the HEIC and in 1861 the reorganisation of the Indian Army began. The influence of the Bengal army was scaled back and the Brahmin presence reduced. Of the pre-Mutiny seventy-four Bengal Native Infantry regiments, only twleve escaped disbandment. The British increasingly recruited the martial races from the Punjab, the North-West Frontier and Nepal while all Indian artillery, except a few mountain batteries, was replaced by British units. Britain also stationed as many regiments on the sub-Continent as there were Indian.

The awarding of the Mutiny Victoria Crosses was somewhat shambolic due in part to the problem of communication, teething problems and the cavalier attitude of the commander-in-chief, Sir Colin Campbell. Of the 182 VCs awarded, sixty-six were to members of the HEIC, including three civilians and one volunteer. Of the forty-six VCs awarded by ballot, twenty-nine were for the Indian Mutiny.

When the VC recipients came to London, either to receive their Cross from the Queen, or on sick leave or having been discharged from the Army, they were called upon to sit for Louis Desanges, an artist who saw a means of honouring Britain's heroes while at the same time making money. Although an indifferent painter, whose figures appear wooden, he did capture the subject's likeness which has made his output invaluable to

219

historians. He painted at least fifty-six canvases, over half of which were Mutiny subjects and they were displayed for many years at the Crystal Palace and Alexandra Palace. Now the collection has been split up and resides in a labyrinth of museums and military authorities.

Although the high number of VCs awarded would appear over-generous, in most cases they do represent recipients who fought without mercy against a determined or desperate enemy, often at the end of a forced march in a debilitating climate. Many suffered terrible wounds and diseases, from which they died prematurely. While many of the other ranks disappeared into impoverished obscurity, many talented officers rose to become the backbone of the British Army by the end of the century.

References and Notes

Introduction

1. The author has not made an error in counting the absentees. One of the VC recipients was present in London but forbidden to attend as a punishment by Lord Panmure, the Secretary of State for War. Private William Stanlack of the Coldstream Guards had been accused of theft from a comrade and it was felt to be inappropriate for the Queen to invest such a felon. In fact Stanlack was discharged in 1863 as a 'bad' character and was fortunate not to join the ignoble list of men who forfeited their VCs.
2. There is no universally agreed name for the events of this period. In India and Pakistan it has been termed as the 'War of Independence of 1857', 'First War of Indian Independence' or 'Revolt of 1857.' In the UK it is commonly referred to as the 'Indian Mutiny', the 'Sepoy Mutiny', the 'Great Mutiny' and 'Indian Insurrection'.
3. The sepoys of the Bengal Army refused to serve abroad mainly because of the diet they would be expected to eat while on board ship, the unappetising and religiously repugnant salted pork and ship's biscuit.
4. There was a long gap between offence and punishment because it was not safe without the presence of a British battalion. Distance and the scattering of detachments over a wide area meant that it took weeks before the 84th Regiment could reach Barrackpore.
5. The spelling of Pande's name became a contemptuous term used by British soldiers for rebellious sepoys, who were referred to as 'Pandies'.
6. There was one other civilian awarded the Victoria Cross. The Reverend James Adams had a Warrant all to himself. For his bravery during the Second Afghan War, a special Warrant dated 6 August 1881 extended eligibility to the Indian Ecclesiastical Establishments.

Chapter 1: The Siege of Delhi

1. Hugh Gough, who was later awarded the Victoria Cross, had been commissioned into the 3rd Bengal Light Cavalry in 1853.
2. The magazine involved in the action was the expense magazine which contained fifty barrels of powder, not the main Delhi magazine, which held three times as much. This was two miles upstream on the west bank of the Jumna and was later taken by the mutineers.
3. The mounted force was named after Captain R.J. Meade, a former Brigade-Major of the Gwalior Contingent.
4. The rocky Delhi Ridge was about sixty feet high and ran from a point only 1,200 yards east of the city walls to the Jumna (Yamuna) river three miles to the north. A water supply was

provided by a canal that ran through the camp. The building nearest the city was known as Hindu Rao's House. Between the city and the Ridge was a maze of buildings and walled gardens including the suburb of Subzi Mundi.

5. General Barnard succumbed to cholera on 5 July and was succeeded by the indecisive General Archdale Wilson.

6. The early VCs were fitted with a deadly looking prong with which to fix the Cross to the tunic. Jones is one of three known recipients who had to brave Her Majesty's clumsiness at their investiture. The others were Commander Henry Raby, the first VC recipient, and Captain Gerald Graham of Redan fame.

7. Jones was buried close to John Watson VC; a rare thing for two VCs to be buried in such a small community.

8. Thomas Hancock was one of the original eight, six of whom were Crimean veterans.

9. On 15 October 2011, a memorial stone was erected over his grave.

10. CSM Stephen Garvin was the only soldier to receive the VC and the DCM during the Indian Mutiny.

11. Richard Wadeson became the third officer to command a regiment who had obtained his commission from the ranks. The others were John Mackay VC 92nd (Gordons) and William McBean VC of the 93rd (Argyll & Sutherland) Regiment.

12. Ightham has produced two VCs; William Sutton (1857) and Riversdale Colyer-Ferguson (posthumously 1917).

Chapter 2: The Capture of Delhi

1. Figures vary between 15,000 and 30,000.

2. The Gough family hold the unique distinction of not only having brothers who were awarded the VC, but father and son and uncle and nephew.

3. A devout Christian, Nicholson also betrayed a cruel streak. He proposed an Act endorsing a new kind of punishment for those who perpetrated outrages against the British, suggesting flaying alive, impalement or burning. An incident that illustrates his ruthlessness was when he strode into the British mess tent at Jullunda in the Punjab, and said 'I am sorry, gentlemen, to have kept you waiting for your dinner, but I have been hanging your cooks.' He believed the cooks had added poison to the soup and when they refused to taste it, he had them hanged from a nearby tree.

4. It would not have been lost on the officers and men who had served in the Crimea that 14 September was the third anniversary of the landings at Calamita Bay.

5. The wicket gate in the door of the Kashmir Gate was kept open so the defenders could shoot at the attackers crossing the bridge.

6. On 1 January 1858, Sir Colin Campbell, the C-in-C, forwarded General Archdale's General Order in which provisional awards of the VC to Smith and Hawthorne were recommended. The War Office replied that these awards were irregular in not having been submitted through him and that future recommendations should always be received through him. In the event, both Smith and Hawthorne did receive their VCs. This is a further illustration of the difficulties the War Office had to contend with over the Warrant's fine print.

7. As well as Home and Salkeld, three other Mutiny VCs were similarly awarded the VC. It was not until January 1907 that King Edward VII approved the retroactive issue of six Crosses to the relatives of men whose actions were judged to have been particularly worthy of recognition.

8. Even in these harrowing conditions, romance blossomed and one of the officers later married one the Forrests' girls.

9. Another version states that John Smith's VC was sent to his father in Derbyshire and in 1918 was passed to the widow of the only male Smith not to return from the Great War. The family have since lost touch and the whereabouts of the VC is unknown.

10. The men selected by ballot were Lieutenant Alfred Heathcote, Colour-Sergeant George Waller, Bugler William Sutton, Private John Divane and Private James Thompson.

11. Laura May Clifford was the cousin of Hugh Clifford, who was awarded the Victoria Cross for gallantry at the Battle of Inkerman on 5 November 1854.

12. Melvill and Coghill had carried the 24th (Warwickshire) Regiment's colours from the battlefield at Isandlwana on 22 January 1879 at the beginning of the Anglo-Zulu War. *The London Gazette* dated 15 January 1907 announced the following who would have been awarded the VC if they had survived: Edward Spence, Everard Phillipps, Teignmouth Melvill, Nevill Coghill, Frank Baxter and Hector MacLean.

13. An incorrect version has McGuire dying in Lisnaskea Hospital, Enniskillen on the same date as his VC was taken from him. He was said to be buried as Patrick Joseph Donnelly, his wife's maiden name.

14. Even after the heroics of Willoughby, Forrest, Buckley et al, the Delhi Magazine was still standing and operable.

15. Edward Thackeray was first cousin of the novelist William Makepeace Thackeray.

Chapter 3: Other Outbreaks

1. William Olipherts, Bengal Artillery, was later awarded the Victoria Cross for gallantry on 25 September 1857 at Lucknow.

2. Other versions state incorrectly that Peter Gill was born in September 1831, making it highly unlikely that he would have been promoted to Sergeant Major at the age of nineteen.

3. It is something of a coincidence that James Blair performed his VC acts at Neemuch, his birthplace.

4. The other late awards appearing in *The London Gazette* dated 25 February 1862 were those to George Baker, James Blair, John Daunt, Denis Dynon, Richard Keatinge, Arthut Mayo and William Waller.

5. One account has Brown being presented to the Queen at a Levee at St James's Palace on 24 April 1860.

6. Certainly the War Office jealously guarded the awarding of Bars for several VC recipients made claims during the Victorian period. It was not until the First and Second World Wars that three recipients received Bars to their Crosses – Arthur Martin-Leake, Noel Chavasse and Charles Upham.

Chapter 4: Delhi's Flying Columns

1. Robert Blair was a cousin of James Blair, who was awarded his VC at Neemuch – see previous chapter.

2. Now Trumpet-Major, Kells had taken up the offer made to men whose regiments were leaving India to volunteer for another regiment. The 1st Bengal European Light Cavalry was renamed the 19th Hussars in 1861.

3. One source suggests Fitzgerald died at Ghaziabad in North India. His medals are held by Bristol's City Museum and Art Gallery.

4. In 1956, Pakistan became a republic and all titles pertaining to British royalty were dropped. The present 5 Horse, however, continues to be known as Probyn's Horse. There is also a town named Probynabad in Punjab province.

5. The choice of Southsea Common would indicate that Queen Victoria was either going to

or staying at Osborne House on the Isle of Wight.
6. Kensal Green Cemetery is the resting place for fourteen VC holders. It became the most fashionable burial ground in England.

Chapter 5: Against the Odds
1. Colonel Neill's force included 500 men of his own regiment, the Madras Fusiliers, 190 of the 84th Regiment and 150 Sikhs.
2. Major Thomas Stirling was one of five officers of the 64th Regiment, including their commander, who were killed at the Second Battle of Cawnpore on 28 November 1857.
3. An application for Harry Havelock to be awarded a Bar to the VC for this action was wisely turned down.
4. Harry Havelock had a book published abut army reform entitled *Three Main Questions of the Day.*
5. The Alambagh (Garden of the World) was to feature later as a British-held strong-point in the coming battles for the city.
6. In 1867, Assistant Surgeon Campbell Millis Douglas had been the medical officer of the 24th Regiment in charge of the expedition to the Andaman Islands in the Indian Ocean. When the ship *Assam Valley* put into the island of Little Andaman, which was known to be home to native cannibals, a small party of men went ashore and were not seen again. A detachment of the 24th was landed to look for the men. When they were attacked by the natives, they retreated to the beach where they were unable to be rescued due to the heavy surf. Douglas and his crew undertook the dangerous task of rowing in and out of the pounding waves and brought away all of the detachment.
7. Henry Ward's gravestone in Great Malvern Cemetery has recently been cleaned and renovated.

Chapter 6: The Defence of Lucknow
1. A company of the 32nd had been sent to Cawnpore and perished during the siege of Wheeler's Cantonment and Satichura Ghat.
2. He left his widow, Lady Julia Inglis, with six surviving children. Her eldest son, Johnny, had been with her during the siege. He went on to play cricket for Kent and football for Scotland. Her youngest, Rupert, was born just after General Inglis died. Rupert became an England rugby international and was serving as a chaplain when he was killed during the Battle of the Somme in 1916. Lady Julia's eldest brother, Frederic Augustus Thesiger became the Lord Chelmsford who led the British forces during the Zulu War of 1879.
3. The £2,000 Kavanagh received is worth approximately £175,000 in today's money. This was obviously not enough because Kavanagh again went into debt in 1876 and was compulsorily retired from the Indian Civil Service with a pension of £500 (£44,000) per year.

Chapter 7: The Second Relief of Lucknow
1. Eight staff members and sixty-seven boys of La Martinière Boy's College retreated to the Residency and took part in its defence. All the boys received the Indian Mutiny Medal with the Defence of Lucknow Clasp and it is the only school in the world to be awarded a British battle honour.
2. The first major obstacle to overcome was the Secundra Bagh. This palace had been built by a former king as an animal and bird sanctuary and was a formidable looking place, about 130 yards square with double thick walls about twenty feet high.
3. The aperture created in the south-east angle of the wall in a bricked-up doorway was

about three feet square and about three feet off the ground.

4. Captain Steuart took the name George to avoid confusion with his father's name. The family favoured the spelling of their name, which is often spelt 'Stewart'. Also, there is a suggestion within the family that George was born out of wedlock and that his parents married after his birth.

5. The famous photograph by Felice Beato of the interior of Secundra Bagh taken in 1859, which shows the skeletons of the slain sepoys, was staged. It is likely that some remains were dug up to make the photograph more authentic.

6. The 93rd also submitted claims by Captains Burroughs and Cooper for the Victoria Cross. They had both featured prominently in the assault, although not in the same area as Captain Steuart. Their claims were turned down because the ballot rules allowed only one officer to be chosen, even though their claims were quite separate.

7. Sir Colin Campbell later sent for Colonel Ewart and apologised for his rudeness.

8. Midshipman Duncan Gordon Boyes was born in 1846 and was awarded his VC on 6 September 1864 at Shimonoseki, Japan. It was the first time that a VC was awarded to a campaign for which there was no medal issued. Six months after the Queen pinned the Cross to his tunic, he was dismissed from the Royal Navy for what seemed a trivial offence. In all probability it was his increasing alcoholism that contributed to his downfall. He was sent to New Zealand to join his elder brothers on their sheep station but depression and drink drove him to suicide on 26 January 1869.

9. Thomas Young was buried in the Protestant Cemetery, Caen, close to the grave of George 'Beau' Brummell. The Victoria Cross Society erected a new memorial stone on his desecrated grave in March 2010.

10. Samuel Hill's death was described as 'killed in action'. At the time of his death, the 90th had been involved in marching from Meerut to Lahore at the end of some minor engagements against the warring tribes on the North-West Frontier, though not actually involved in any fighting. It may be that he was killed in an accident.

11. The Gwalior Contingent made up the bulk of the force but included many other mutineers picked up along the march.

12. This is the same Major Thomas Stirling who was heavily criticised by Lieutenant Harry Havelock VC. Stirling managed to reach one of the enemy's guns and spike it before being killed.

13. There is an ongoing discussion about the 'true' youngest-ever VC. Andrew Fitzgibbon, who won his VC in the Second China War, was born on 13 August 1842. The margins are so close – if Flynn was born on 14 August he would qualify with an age of 15 years and 99 days against Fitzgibbon's 15 years and 100 days. Much effort to find proof of Flynn's date of birth has so far yielded nothing.

Chapter 8: The Tide Turns

1. Two senior British officers in this war committed suicide. Major General Foster Stalker, a divisional commander, shot himself at Bushire on 14 March 1857. Commodore Richard Ethersey, who commanded the naval units, did the same two days later. The main leadership problems in this war were logistical and medical not tactical and it is believed that the resultant pressures destroyed them.

2. The Sathpoora (Satpura) Hills were south of the River Narbada and about 100 miles south-west of Mhow.

3. It is debatable that the Rani had any hand in this barbarous act.

4. Colonel Cochrane, who succeeded Hugh Rowlands VC, was one of three VCs to command the 43rd in succession.

5. The location at which Whirlpool performed his gallant act on 2 May is not clear, although we know it was one of several skirmishes fought on the route to Kalpi.
6. Colonel Maxwell commanded 200 men of the Camels Corps, two companies of the 88th (Connaught) Rangers and artillery.
7. George Hollis was either retired for medical reasons or bought his discharge as he was in the Army for less than five years.
8. There is an interesting tale regarding a VC found in 1994 in the ground churned up by racehorses at the Curragh in Co. Kildare. It was minus its bar but presumed to have been one of the VCs awarded to the 8th Hussars who were based at the Curragh between 1869 and 1875. Until 1881, soldiers were required to wear all their medals while on duty and it is believed that a member of the Hussars lost his medal while training on horseback on the Curragh. The assumption is that the medal belonged to George Hollis, but as he left the Army in 1860, this is highly unlikely.
9. Harry Lyster was the uncle to another VC recipient, Hamilton Lyster Reed, who attempted to save the guns at Colenso.
10. Agha Humayun Amin, a retired Pakistan Army officer, wrote an analysis on the Defence Journal published in the U.S. in 2000, in which he suggested that Rose's march from Mhow to Gwalior has been projected out of proportion as an outstanding feat of arms.

Chapter 9: Lucknow Taken
1. His VC is housed in the Fitzwilliam Museum, Cambridge, as part of the Lester Watson Medal Collection. Besides David Hawkes' VC, the collection contains another VC, that of Sergeant Edward Mott (27 January 1917) and a rare New Zealand Cross.
2. In May 1858 alone, not less than 1,000 British soldiers died of sunstroke, fatigue and disease, and about 100 were killed in action.

Chapter 10: Campbell's Oudh Campaign

1. Frederick Roberts's son, Freddy, had been mortally wounded trying to save the guns at Colenso during the Boer War. A precedent was made and posthumous Victoria Crosses were awarded thereafter. It took, however, until 29 January 1920 before the Warrant was amended with the words: 'Fourthly: It is ordained that the Cross may be awarded posthumously.'
2. This detachment led by Colonel George Milman of the 5th Fusiliers had confronted a much larger rebel army and been forced to retreat.
3. Captain Middleton was serving as Brigadier General Sir Edward Lugard's Aide-de-Camp whilst he was commanding the 2nd Infantry Division during operations at Lucknow in March 1858. The brigadier was very impressed with the young officer so took him with the field force to Azamgahr. After the Mutiny he wrote of Middleton: 'One of the most gallant and intelligent officers I have ever had under me, he accompanied the troops at every attack.' Such is the process of attaining the Victoria Cross.
4. Lieutenant Willoughby was the brother of Captain Willoughby, one of the nine who blew up the magazine in Delhi.
5. Both governors of Winchester and Pentonville prisons considered Bambrick an innocent man and petitioned for his release.
6. Rifle Brigade historian George Caldwell has made a thorough study of Shaw and is quite certain that he is John Shaw, with a possible nickname of 'Sam'. Somehow the nickname was accepted by the awards board and this was engraved on his VC.

Chapter 11: Mopping Up

1. This was similarly reflected in the Anglo-Boer War. Once the major towns had been captured and there was no longer a standing army, the Boers conducted a very effective guerrilla war which prolonged the conflict for another year.
2. The story that Sam Browne invented his sword-bearing system because of his injury is apocryphal. It is also of note that after the severing of Browne's arm at the shoulder, officers of his regiment sewed lengths of bridle curb chain across their shoulder. This developed into chain mail epaulettes worn throughout the Cavalry and Royal Horse Artillery.
3. There is some controversy about Chicken's place and date of birth. Another version has him being born on 6 March 1838 at Bishopswearmouth, Co. Durham.
4. The HEIC Army paid two shillings a day compared with the British Army of one shilling. The downside was that a recruit had to sign on for twenty-one years with little chance of returning home.
5. No campaign medal was awarded for this short campaign.
6. Although he was in command at Hlobane, he acted more as a spectator as his command disintegrated into shambles. He did, however, make up for this with a resounding victory at Khambula the following day.
7. Apart from Charles Fraser, the other two were Charles Davis Lucas RN in the Baltic in 1854 and Campbell Douglas of the 24th (Warwickshire) Regiment in the Andaman Islands in 1867.

227

Bibliography

Anonymous, *The Register of the Victoria Cross*, 1988.

Anson O.H.S.G., *With H.M. 9th Lancers during the Indian Mutiny – The letters of Brevet-Major O.H.S.G. Anson*, 1896.

Beeton, S.O., *Our Soldiers and the Victoria Cross*, 1923.

Behan, T.L., *Bulletins and Other State Intelligence for the Year 1859*, 1862

Carter, Thomas, *Medals of the British Army and how they were won*, 1861.

Creagh, Sir O'Moore VC and Humphries, E.M., *The Victoria Cross 1856-1920*, 1985.

Crook, M.J. *The Evolution of the Victoria Cross*, 1975.

David, Saul, *The Indian Mutiny 1857*, 2003.

Delavoye Alex M., *The Records of the 90th (Perthshire Light Infantry) with Roll of Officers from 1795 to 1880*, 1880.

Edwardes, Michael, *Battles of the Indian Mutiny*, 1963.

Edwardes, Michael, *A Season in Hell*, 1973.

Elliot Major J.W. and Knolly, Major W.W., *Victoria Cross Heroes and How They Obtained It*.

Fitchett, William, *Retribution: The Story of the Sepoy Mutiny*, 2009.

Forbes-Mitchell, William, *Reminiscences of the Great Mutiny 1857-59*, 1910.

Forrest, George W., *History of the Indian Mutiny, 1857-58*, 1912.

Gough, General Sir Hugh, *Old Memories*, 1887.

Intelligence Branch, Division of the Chief of Staff, Army HQ India, *The Revolt in Central India 1857-59*, 1908.

Ireland, W.W., *History of the Siege of Delhi*, 1861.

Harvey, David, *Monuments to Courage*, 1999.

Harris, John, *The Indian Mutiny*, 1973.

Hibbert, Christopher, *The Great Mutiny – India 1857*, 1978.

Hudson, Roger [Ed.], *William Russell – Special Correspondent*, 1995.

Kempton, Chris, *Valour and Gallantry*, 2001.

Kinsley, D.A., *They Fight Like Devils*, 2001.

MacMunn, Lt.Gen. Sir George, *Armies of India*, 1911.

Malleson, G.B., *The Mutiny of the Bengal Army by One Who Served Under Sir Charles Napier*, 1857.

Malleson, Colonel G.B., *The Indian Mutiny of 1857*, 1890.

Mason, Philip, *A Matter of Honour*, 1974.

Maude, Francis VC, *Memories of the Mutiny*, 1894.

Medley, Captain Julius George, *A Year's Campaigning in India*, 1858.

Napier, Gerald, *The Sapper VCs*, 1998.

BIBLIOGRAPHY

Perkins, Roger, *The Kashmir Gate*, 1983.

Robinson, Jane, *Angels of Albion – Women of the Indian Mutiny*, 1996.

Roy, Kaushik, *The Army in British India: From Colonial Warfare to Total War 1857-1947*, 2012.

Schofield, Victoria, *The Highland Furies: The Black Watch 1739-1899*, 2012.

Spilsbury, Julian, *The Indian Mutiny*, 2007.

Stephens, Henry Morse, *From Allahabad to Lucknow with Havelock 1857*, 1894.

Taylor, William, *Our Crisis, or, Three Months at Patna during the Insurrection of 1857*, 1858.

The Journal of the Victoria Cross Society 2002-2015

Toomey, T.E., *Heroes of the Victoria Cross*, 1895.

Uys, Ian S., *For Valour – The History of Southern Africa's Victoria Cross Heroes*, 1973.

Verney, Edmund Hope, *The Shannon's Brigade in India 1857-58*, 1862.

Wallace, Lt-Gen. Sir Christopher & Cassidy, Major Ron, *Focus on Courage – The 59 VCs of the Royal Green Jackets*, 2006.

Wilkins, Philip A., *The History of the Victoria Cross*, 1904.

Williams, W. Alister, *Heart of a Dragon 1854-1902*, 2006.

Winton, John, *The Victoria Cross at Sea*, 1978

Wolseley, Garnet, *The Story of a Soldier's Life*, 1903.

Index

Addiscombe College, 10, 17, 19, 30, 32, 33, 41, 44, 52, 66, 94, 108, 149, 187, 188, 197, 207, 209

Addison, Private Henry, 214-5

Agra, 5, 7-8, 62-4, 73-5, 129, 133, 158

Aikman, Colonel Frederick, 189-90

Aitken, Lieutenant Robert Hope Moncrieff, 108-10

'Alambagh, 89-90, 125, 129-30, 133, 177, 206

Albert, Prince Consort, 37

Allahabad, 72, 78, 79, 91, 94, 103, 144, 186

Anderson, Captain, 111-2

Anderson, Corporal Charles, 208-9

Azamgarh (Azamgarth or Azimghur), 46, 192-4

Azimghur Field Force, 193

Baker, Major General Charles, 205-6

Bambrick, Rifleman Valentine, 200-1

Bankes, Cornet William George Hawtry, 184-5

Bareilly, 196, 197, 198, 200, 201, 215

Bareilly, Battle of, 74

Barker, Brigadier General George, 35, 126, 192

Barnard, General Sir Henry, 5, 13-4, 19-21

Baroun, 209

Barsatelli, *Signor*, 111

Bashiratguni, 86-7

Beejapore (Bijapur), 204

Benares, 46-9, 79, 94, 192-3, 208

Bengal Artillery, 2, 4, 17, 19, 48, 60, 63, 94, 118-9, 149-50, 152, 187, 206

Bengal Cavalry, 27, 62, 132

Bengal Civil Service, 61, 111-2

Bengal Engineers, 30-3, 45, 189

Bengal European Cavalry, 26

Bengal European Fusiliers, 10-1, 40-1, 66, 142, 179

Bengal European Light Infantry, 72

Bengal European Regiment, 4, 48

Bengal Fusiliers, 20, 28, 40, 65-6, 179-80

Bengal Horse Artillery, 19-20, 44, 52-3, 62, 72-3

Bengal Irregular Cavalry, 12, 19

Bengal Light Cavalry, 25, 27, 75, 129

Bengal Medical Service, 203

Bengal Military Police, 66, 67, 205

Bengal Native Infantry, 7, 19, 39-40, 41, 42, 46-8, 57, 62, 64, 66-7, 171, 189, 190-1, 197, 203, 209, 219

Bengal Sappers and Miners, 29, 34, 45

Bengal Veteran Establishment, 2

Berar Field Force, 216

Bhopal, 12, 50, 51, 52, 158

Bhowaniegunge (Butwa Gonda), 216

Birch, Captain, 111, 117

Blair, Captain Robert, 70-1

Blair, Colonel James, 62-3

Bogle, Lieutenant Andrew, 85

Bombay, 97, 160, 175, 204

Bombay Army, 62, 133

Bombay Artillery, 162

Bombay Cavalry, 62, 211

Bombay Engineers, 207

Bombay European Regiment, 168

Bombay Fusiliers, 133

Bombay Horse Artillery, 173

Bombay Native Infantry, 55, 56, 62, 160, 166, 175

Bombay Sapper and Miners, 207

Bombay Staff Corps, 175

Bradshaw, Assistant Surgeon William, 102-3

231

INDEX

Bramley, Lieutenant Alfred Jennings, 197, 199
Brennan, Sergeant Joseph Charles, 168
British Army,
    2nd (Royal North British) Dragoons, 164
    2nd (Queen's Bays) Dragoon Guards, 71,
        178, 208
    3rd Light Dragoons, 13, 102
    5th Regiment, 60, 88, 90, 103, 119
    6th (Carabineers) Dragoon Guards, 1
    7th Hussars, 70, 132, 184, 195-6, 213
    8th Light Dragoons, 174
    8th (The King's) Regiment, 28, 68, 74, 129
    9th Lancers, 5-7, 12-14, 31, 69, 71-4, 129,
        177-8, 183, 188, 196
    10th Regiment, 46, 49-50, 57, 61, 80, 85, 87
    11th Light Dragoons, 200
13th Light Dragoons, 210
    14th Light Dragoons, 159, 164
    18th Regiment, 84, 142, 153-4
    24th Regiment, 53
    32nd Regiment, 105-8, 111, 113-8, 134
37th Regiment, 10, 57
39th Regiment, 36, 80
43rd Regiment, 214
52nd Regiment, 28, 30, 35
53rd Regiment, 66-7, 129, 135, 141-2, 152, 187
    60th (King's Royal Rifle Corps), 1, 14-5, 20,
        22-3, 29, 36-42, 86, 181, 200-1
    63rd Regiment, 94
    64th Regiment, 15, 79, 80-2, 85, 156
    67th Regiment, 151
    75th Regiment, 9-11, 21-2, 28, 69, 129
    78th Regiment, 79-80, 85, 87, 95-8, 103, 110
    86th Regiment, 80, 162, 164, 166-7
    88th (Connaught Rangers), 9
    93rd Regiment, 134, 137
    Royal Artillery, 9, 72, 91, 95, 97, 118, 165,
        168, 206
    Royal Horse Artillery, 184
Browne, General Sir Samuel James, 192, 203-4,
    207
Buckley, Conductor John, 2-4, 32
Budli-ki-Serai, 5-7, 9, 15, 21, 44
Bulger, Corporal Abraham, 93
Butler, Major Thomas Adair, 179-80
Byrne, Sergeant James, 167

Cadell, Lieutenant Thomas, 10-12
Café, Captain William Martin, 197-8
Calcutta, 6, 19, 46, 49, 60-1, 64, 78-9, 90, 107,
    111, 115, 119-20, 128-9, 137, 143, 171, 192,
    195
Cameron, Colonel Alexander, 180
Cameron, Lieutenant Aylmer, 161
Cambridge, Duke of, 9, 117, 191
Campbell, Colonel George, 28, 30, 31, 36, 100
Campbell, Lieutenant, 87
Campbell, General Sir Colin, 14, 19, 20, 23, 28,
    82, 83, 88, 92, 95, 119, 122, 124, 125, 126,
    128, 129, 130, 133, 134, 135, 136, 137, 140,
    143, 144, 145, 147, 149, 151, 153, 154, 155,
    156, 160, 170, 172, 177, 179, 184-5, 186-202,
    205, 206, 215, 219
Capper, William, 111-2
Carlin, Private Patrick, 193
Carmichael-Smyth, Colonel George, 1
Case, Colonel William, 107
Cashmere Gate, see Kashmir Gate
Cawnpore, 71, 73, 78, 79-80, 83, 84, 87-8, 91,
    103, 105, 106, 114, 119, 122, 128-9, 153, 155,
    156, 158, 162, 177, 186-8, 200, 216
Central India, 6, 158, 176
Central India Agency, 50, 158
Central India Campaign, 56, 164, 172
Central India Field Force, 161, 163, 164, 166,
    168, 171, 175, 176, 207
Central India Horse, 134
Champion, Regimental Sergeant Major
    James, 204-5
Charbagh Bridge, 83, 90-1, 93, 95, 133
Chichumbah, 216
Chicken, George Bell, 206
Chinhat, 106, 107, 108, 111, 114, 119
Chuckbdar, Moosahib Ali, 190
Churchill, Sir Winston, 188
Clogstoun, Major Herbert Mackworth, 215-6
Cochrane, Colonel Hugh, 164-5
Connelly, Gunner William, 52-4
Cook, Private Walter, 215
Cotton, Major General Sir Willoughby, 165
Cotton, Major-General Sir Sydney, 204
Coughlan, Colour-Sergeant Cornelius, 9-10,
    12
Crews, Sergeant, 5
Crimean War, 12, 37, 42, 69, 94, 102, 128, 137,
    140, 145, 146, 151, 154, 155, 161, 171, 172,
    174, 180, 195, 196, 198, 200, 204, 210, 215
Crow, Sub-Conductor William, 2
Crowe, Lieutenant Colonel Joseph, 86-7
Crowie, Private, 197

Cubitt, Lieutenant William George, 19, 107-8

Davis, Private James, 199
Delhi, 1-24, 25-45, 46, 50, 52, 63, 65, 68, 73, 75, 129, 133, 149, 158, 168, 177, 189, 191, 200
Dempsey, Private Denis, 57, 61
Desanges, Louis, 219
Diamond, Sergeant Bernard, 72-3
Distinguished Conduct Medal, 15, 200
Divane, Rifleman John, 22, 36
Donovan, Colonel Edward, 208
Dowling, Corporal William, 112-3, 116
Dunlay, John, 139
Duffy, Thomas, 98-9

East India Company (HEIC), 10, 15-6, 25, 30, 33, 39, 40, 44, 48-50, 52, 56, 63, 72, 89, 107, 142, 149, 168, 171, 175, 186, 190, 203, 209, 219
   HEIC Military Academy, *see Addiscombe College*
Edwards, Sergeant Bryan, 2
Ellice, Colonel Charles, 53

Farquharson, Major Francis, 180
Farrukhabad, 209
Finchampstead, 8
Fitzgerald, Richard, 72-3
Forbes-Mitchell, William, 197, 200
Forrest, Lieutenant George, 2-4, 32
Foster, Captain, 115
Ffrench, Captain Alfred Kirke, 141-2
Flynn, Drummer Thomas, 156-7
Franks, General Sir Thomas, 189
Fraser, Lieutenant General Charles Crauford, 213-4
Freeman, John, 74-5

Ganges river, 32, 34, 46, 56, 84, 86, 88, 129, 144, 155, 177, 186, 193
Gardner, Sergeant Major William, 200
Garvin, Colour Sergeant Stephen, 14-5, 36
Geoffroi, *Monsieur*, 111
Gibraltar, 22, 117, 127
Gill, Sergeant Major Peter, 47-50
Goate, William, 177-9
Goodfellow, Lieutenant General Charles Augustus, 207-8
Goomtee river, 114, 182, 190
Gore-Browne, Captain Henry, 116-7

Gottreux, Lieutenant Colonel, 214
Gough, Lieutenant Hugh, 1, 25-27, 32, 72, 129-32
Gough, Major Charles John Stanley, 26-7
Graham, Private Patrick, 152
Grant, Colonel James Hope, 7, 12-4, 38, 64, 69, 70, 74, 76
Grant, Corporal Robert, 90
Grant, Private Peter, 139-40
Greathed, Colonel Edward Harris, 7, 31, 63, 68-9, 73-4, 129, 133, 149
Green, Colour Sergeant Patrick, 22-3
Guise, Lieutenant Colonel John Christopher, 150-1
Gwalior, 13, 36, 48, 52, 62, 74, 94, 158, 168, 172, 173, 174, 176, 219
Gwalior Campaign, 197
Gwalior Contingent, 62, 63, 73, 129, 155, 163, 186

Hackett, Lieutenant Colonel Thomas Bernard, 153-4
Hall, Commander William Edward, 146-7
Hancock, Private Thomas, 12-4
Harington, Hastings Edward, 149
Harrison, Petty Officer John, 145
Hartigan, Sergeant Henry, 5-6
Havelock, Brigadier General Henry, 78-127, 130, 133, 155, 196
Havelock, Captain Henry Marshman, 79-80
Hawkes, Private David, 181-2
Hawthorne, Bugler Robert, 29-30, 34, 35-6
Heathcote, Lieutenant Alfred Spencer, 23, 37-8
Helstone, Sergeant Henry, 5
Henage, Major Clement Walker, 173-4
Hersey, Lady, 6, 90, 119
Hill, Sergeant Samuel, 151
Hills, Lieutenant General Sir James, 16-7, 19
Hodson's Irregular Horse, 26, 72, 83, 129, 131
Hollis, George, 174
Hollowell, Lance Corporal James, 103-4
Holmes, Private Joel, 91
Home, Lieutenant Duncan, 28-35, 37
Home, Surgeon General Anthony Dickson, 102
Hope, Brigadier Adrian, 196-202
Hutchinson, Major General Sir William, 9
Hyderabad Cavalry, 171
Hyderabad Contingent, 168, 216

Indore, 50, 62, 158-9, 162
Inglis, Lieutenant Colonel John, 12, 107, 110, 111, 114, 115, 118
Inglis, Julia, 114, 115, 117
Innes, Lieutenant General James John McLeod, 188-9
Irwin, Private Charles, 142

Jalandhar, 44, 189
Jalandhar Cavalry, 189
Jarrett, Colonel Hanson Chambers Taylor, 209
Jee, Surgeon Joseph, 95-6
Jerome, Major General Henry Edward, 166-7
Jennings, Edward, 149-50
Jhelum, 52-3
Jones, Lieutenant Colonel Arthur Stowell, 6-8
Jumna river, 1-2, 28, 32, 167, 170

Kabul Gate, 9, 28, 40
Kashmir Gate (Kashmere Gate) (Delhi), 3, 28-29, 31-4, 36-7, 43-4
Kavanagh, Chief Commissioner Thomas Henry, 60, 120-7
Keatinge, Lieutenant General Richard, 162-3
Kells, Trumpet-Major Robert, 71-2
Kelly, Private James Davis, *see Davis, Private James*
Kenny, James, 142
Kerr, Lieutenant William Alexander, 55-6
Kirk, Private John, 47-50
Kirton, Captain, 115
Kolapore, 54-5

Lahore, 120, 209
Lahore Gate (Delhi), 42, 68
Lakshmibai, the Rani of Jhansi, 163, 165, 172, 173, 176, 219
Lal, Kunoujee, 122-6
Lambert, Ensign George, 86
Laughnan, Thomas, 150
Lawrence, Captain Samuel Hill, 113-4, 115, 116
Lawrence, Sir Henry, 78, 105-7, 114, 143, 189
Lawrence, Sir John, 52
Legion d'Honneur, 210
Leith, Major James, 164
Lord Ashcroft Gallery, 40, 61, 90, 183, 200
Lucknow, 48, 60, 61, 70, 73, 75, 78, 83-6, 88-90, 93-6, 99-100, 105-27, 128-57, 158, 177-85, 189, 192, 193, 196, 197, 201, 203, 206

Lucknow Residency, 50, 51, 55, 83, 89, 90, 92, 95, 96-100, 102-3, 105-9, 111, 113-4, 116, 118, 119, 120-2, 125-7, 129, 130, 133, 134, 138, 143, 153, 155, 156, 158, 181, 186, 189
Lugard, General Sir Edward, 9, 12, 192-3
Lyster, Lieutenant General Harry Hammon, 171

Mackay, Sergeant David, 140-1
Macleod, Captain Sir John, 199
MacPherson, Major Herbert Taylor, 95-6
Madras, 158, 162, 168, 209
Madras Army, 158, 214, 215
Madras European Fusiliers, 46, 98, 142
Madras Fusiliers, 46, 85, 89, 92-3, 103, 118
Madras Presidency, 158, 160
Madras Sappers and Miners, 159
Mahoney, Sergeant Patrick, 89
Mangalwar, 86-9
Mangles, Assistant Magistrate Ross, 20, 57-61, 126-7
Mansfield, Lieutenant General Sir William, 167, 175
Maude, Colonel Francis Cornwallis, 91-3
Maxwell, Henry Hamilton, 187
Maxwell, Major General Edward, 117, 170
Maylah Ghat, 215
McBean, Major General William, 180-1
McCabe, Captain, 115-16
McDonell, William, 57-60
McGovern, Corporal John, 15-16
McGuire, Sergeant James, 40-1
McHale, Private Patrick, 119
McInnes, Hugh, 150
McManus, Sergeant Peter, 103
McMaster, Surgeon Valentine, 96-7
McQuirt, Bernard, 160-1
Meade's Horse, 5
Meerut, 1-5, 14-5, 19, 21, 32, 34, 37, 39, 41, 46, 48, 52, 71, 105, 120, 141, 149, 152, 191
Meritorious Service Medal, 205
Metcalfe, Sir Theophilus, 2, 10-1
Mhow, 62, 73, 146, 158, 168, 208
Millar (Miller), Private Duncan, 215
Milman, Colonel George, 192, 193
Milnes, Private Benjamin, 192-3
Monaghan, Trumpeter Thomas, 208
Monger, Private George, 154-5
Morley, Private Samuel, 193-5
Munro, Colour Sergeant James, 140

Murphy, Farrier Sergeant Michael, 193-6
Mylott, Sergeant Patrick, 93-4

Nana Sahib (Dhondu Pant), 79, 84, 186, 213, 219
Napier, Sir Charles, 191
Napier, Colonel, 122-3
Napier, Major General Sir George, 87, 127, 172
Napier, Sergeant William, 192-3
Nash, Corporal William, 181
Nepal, 4, 186, 213, 219
Newell, Private Robert, 183
Nicholson, Brigadier John, 9, 16, 20, 25, 27-8, 52, 68, 149
Norman, Major H.W., 13
North-West Frontier, 14, 36, 52, 76, 84, 94, 95, 152, 180, 219

Olpherts, Captain William, 94-5, 98
Osborn, Lieutenant, 3
Oudh, 38, 46, 48, 85, 105, 117, 129, 143, 185, 186-202, 206, 207, 208, 215
Oudh Irregular Infantry, 105
Oudh Irregular Cavalry, 106
Oudh Police, 110
Oudh Military Police Cavalry, 206
Outram, Major General Sir James, 78, 80, 82, 88, 92, 97-8, 100, 104, 114-5, 117, 119, 122-3, 125-6, 129-30, 177, 179, 181, 206
Oxenham, Corporal William, 111-12, 116

Palmer, Lieutenant Colonel F.R., 38
Palmerston, Lord, 128
Park, Gunner James, 150
Parkes, Doctor Edmund Alexander, 7-8
Paton, Sergeant John, 147-8
Patna, 56-7
Pearson, Sergeant James, 167-8
Pearson, Sergeant John, 174
Peroo (Piru), 205, 206
Peshawar, 52, 140, 165, 204
Peshawar Valley Field Force, 204, 207
Phillipps, Ensign Everard Aloysius Lisle, 38-40
Prendergast, Lieutenant General Harry North Dalrymple, 158-60
Probyn, Captain Daighton Macnaghton, 72, 75-6, 133-4
Punjab Cavalry, 72, 75, 125, 129, 133, 187, 203-4
Punjab Frontier Force, 133

Punjab Infantry, 28, 37, 42, 68-9, 129, 135, 141, 196-8, 207, 209
Punjab Sappers, 31
Purcell, Private John, 12-14
Pye, Lieutenant Charles, 152-3

Rajputana Field Force, 6, 160-1
Ravi river, 52, 215
Raynor, Lieutenant William, 2-4, 32
Reade, Surgeon General Herbert Taylor, 42-3
Rennie, Lieutenant Colonel William, 88-9
Renny, Major General George Alexander, 43-4, 45
Richardson, Sergeant George, 216-7
Roberts, Field Marshal Lord Frederick, 19, 25, 27, 37, 39-40, 52, 68-9, 132-3, 138, 185, 186-8, 209
Roberts, Major General Sir Henry, 160-1
Roberts, Private James Reynolds, 70
Robinson, Able Seaman Edward, 182-3
Roddy, Colonel Patrick, 206-7
Rogers, Private George, 172-3
Rohikhand, 105, 117, 196, 204
Rosamond, Sergeant Major Matthew, 47-50
Rose, General Sir Hugh, 52, 66, 110, 159, 161-4, 165, 168, 170, 171, 172, 173, 174-6, 207, 208
Royal Humane Society, 213, 214
Royal Navy warships,
    Donegal, 147
Excellent, 146
Queen, 210
Punjaub, 64
Rodney, 147
Shannon, 147
Wellesley, 64
Ruhya (Reyah or Rooyah), Fort, 149, 196-202
Rushe, Regimental Sergeant Major David, 183-4
Ryan, Drummer Miles, 40-1

Sahib, Nana, see Nana Sahib
Salkeld, Lieutenant Philip, 28-30, 32-5, 41
Salmon, Admiral of the Fleet Sir Nowell, 144-5
Sam Browne System, 204
Sarda river, 215
Saugor Field Force, 214
Scott, Major, 12
Scully, Conductor, 2-3
Secundra Bagh, 134, 137-49, 151-4
Seymour, Major W.H., 208

Shah Najaf, 143-5, 147, 151-2
Shaw, Conductor William, 2
Shaw, Sergeant John, 202
Shaw, Sergeant Samuel, 202
Shebbeare, Lieutenant Robert, 41-2
Simla, 10, 14, 110-11
Simpson, Major John, 198-9
Singh, Burmadeen, 212
Singh, Chemmum, 211
Singh, Koer (Koor), 58, 192, 193-4
Sinnott, Private John, 119-20
Sitwell, Captain, 123
Sleavon, Corporal Michael, 165-6
Smith, Brigadier M.W., 6
Smith, Lieutenant Colonel Richard Baird, 28-9
Smith, John, 142-3
Smith, Sergeant John, 28-30, 33-5
Somerset, Lieutenant General Henry, 173
Spence, Private Edward, 197, 198
Spence, Regimental Sergeant Major David, 188
Strand Magazine, 177, 182, 199
Steuart, William George Drummond, 136-9
Stewart, Sergeant Peter, 2
Suhejnee, 206
Sultanpor, 106, 189
Sundelee, 208
Sutton, Rifleman William, 23-4

Thackeray, Lieutenant Edward, 44-5
Thomas, Quartermaster-Sergeant, Jacob, 118
Thompson, Lance Corporal Alexander, 198
Thompson, Rifleman James, 20-1, 36
Tombs, Major Henry, 16-19
Tong river, 193
Topi, Tantia, 56, 129, 132, 155, 163, 165, 168, 170, 172, 176, 186, 219
Travers, General James, VC, 12, 51-2
Turner, Major Frank, 72
Turner, Private Samuel, 12, 14
Tytler, Brigadier General John Adam, 190-2

Umballa, 2, 5, 10, 21, 41, 177, 183

Victoria, Queen of the United Kingdom, 4, 9, 13, 15, 16, 20, 21, 22, 24, 27, 30, 36, 39, 40, 41, 43, 49, 50, 60, 61, 70, 71, 74, 75, 76, 77, 83, 91, 93, 94, 96, 102-3, 108, 112, 113, 116, 118, 120, 126, 127, 136, 139-41, 144, 145, 146, 148, 149-60, 161, 164, 167, 174, 179, 180, 183, 184, 188, 190, 192, 195, 215, 219

Wadeson, Lieutenant Colonel Richard, 21-2
Waller, George, 36
Waller, Colonel William Francis Frederick, 175
Walpole, General Sir Robert, 196-7, 198, 200, 215
Ward, Joseph, 174
Ward, Quartermaster-Sergeant Henry, 97-8
Watson, General Sir John, 8, 133-4
Wheeler, Major-General Sir Hugh, 78-9, 105
Whirlpool, Private Frederick Humphrey, 168-70
Willoughby, Lieutenant George, 2-4, 197-8, 241
Wilmot, Lieutenant Colonel Henry, 181
Wilson, Major, 116
Wilson, Major General Archdale, 25, 27-30, 32-4, 36
Wilton, Captain F.R., 21
Windham, Major General Charles, 129, 155, 156
Windsor Castle, 15, 21, 22, 24, 27, 36, 41, 44, 60, 61, 71, 75, 86, 92, 94, 96, 108, 112, 113, 116, 118, 120, 127, 139, 145, 160, 161, 167, 174, 179, 183, 184, 188, 195, 214, 215
Wood, Field Marshal Sir Henry Evelyn, 209-13
Wolseley, Captain Garnet, 69, 70, 83, 94, 151, 203

Young, Lieutenant Thomas James, 145

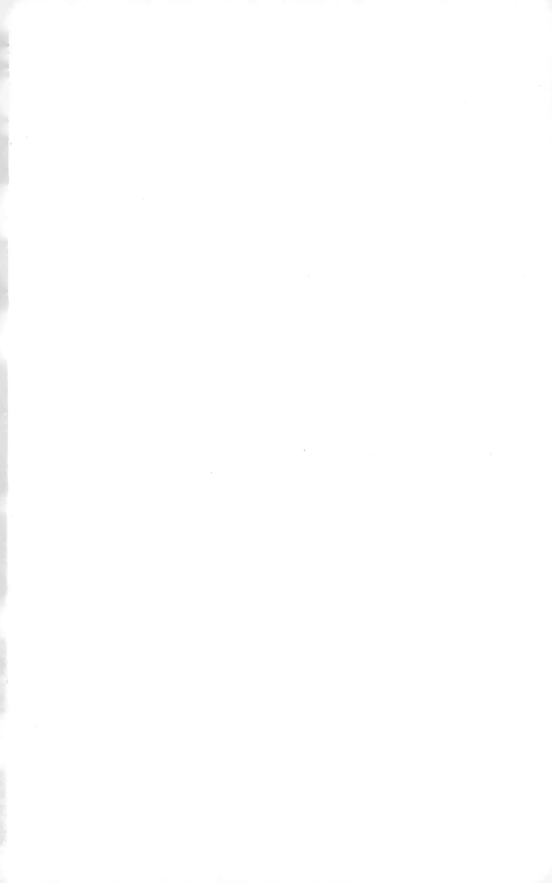